Creating a Human World

Creating a Human World

A New
Psychological and Religious Anthropology
In Dialogue with Freud, Heidegger, and
Kierkegaard

Ernest Daniel Carrere

Scranton: University of Scranton Press

Library of Congress Cataloging-in-Publication Data

Carrere, Ernest A.
  Creating a Human World / Ernest A. Carrere
    p. cm.
ISBN 1-58966-116-8 – ISBN 1-58966-122-2(pbk.)
  1. Life. 2. Quality of life. 3. Conduct of life. 4. Human beings.
  I. Title.
BD431.C294 2006
128–dc22   2006042099

Distribution:

The University of Scranton Press
Chicago Distribution Center
11030 S. Langley
Chicago, IL 60628

Remembering our brother Donnie
Edward Donelson Carrère
1955–1970

&

for E. E. M.
who would be surprised to discover
that she had been part of this project

If . . . we could ever see clearly and be moved by the value of each unique person in the world. . . .

—Martha Nussbaum, *Fragility of Goodness*

There are certain risks . . . that we cannot close off without a loss in human value, suspended as we are between beast and god, with a kind of beauty available to neither.

—Martha Nussbaum, *Fragility of Goodness*

The life span of man running toward death would inevitably carry everything human to ruin and destruction if it were not for the faculty of interrupting it and beginning something new, . . . an ever-present reminder that men, though they must die, are not born in order to die but in order to begin.

—Hannah Arendt, *The Human Condition*

Contents

Acknowledgments

This work remembers, and is inspired by, my brother Donnie. Donnie was a delightful, endearing person who touched all who came into contact with him, so it was devastating to discover, following a collapse one Thanksgiving, that he would not be able to live beyond his eighteenth year. At the age of seven he had undergone a successful operation to correct a congenital defect of the heart. Now we learned that an extraneous circulatory system in his head could not be corrected and would prove fatal as he grew taller, distancing his head and heart. The verdict was absolute. Then eleven, Donnie died one month and five days after his fifteenth birthday.

His last years were a poignant inspiration to us all, and as his plight grew worse and worse with each of a succession of increasingly severe seizures, I saw what it was to embrace the poverty of one's humanity as Donnie cheerfully accepted the onerous limits of a situation that was his very self.

The concluding years were happy ones, and the last was especially so. Recognizing that Donnie was incapable of moving to high school, his teachers were kind enough to suggest that he repeat the eighth grade with them. Donnie's new classmates were carefully prepared for his return and debilitated condition. The response of these intelligent but rough-and-ready young adolescents to an increasingly handicapped peer was heroically generous and sensitive. We shall be forever grateful. "Oh, Momma," Donnie once protested in a celebration of gratitude when Mother proposed gifts for a few who "officially" assisted him, "we can't give to just some—*everybody's* so good to me." It's hard to believe those wonderful youngsters are now turning fifty.

Donnie was notably happy on the night before his last at a prenuptial celebration our parents gave at home for one of our neighbors. The following morning, July 17, he apparently suffered a cerebral hemorrhage, although the pain quickly passed and he did not lose consciousness. He rested comfortably, but by evening it was clear that he could not possibly live. As he lay in the hospital's maternity ward, for no other space was available, I looked into his eyes and into the span of his short life, and they told me that there was no tragedy in dying but only in living, that we would die as we had lived, and that the quality of our life would be the quality of our death.

No longer could he speak. I wasn't certain how reliable the communication of our eyes could be but, in any case, that alone would not be enough. I took his right hand. For two years his left motor abilities had increasingly atrophied, and precisely because of his many falls, or his generally successful attempts to prevent them, his right hand had developed a grip surpassed by none. It had not lost its strength; I was relieved. Many times had we shaken. Now we renewed our covenant definitively. It seemed essential to be nakedly truthful in this moment, so I restrained the automatic impulse to say, "You'll be OK," or "Everything'll be all right." It also seemed imperative not to contribute to his alarm and to offer, if possible, a measure of support for the ultimate situation in which he now found himself, since I did not begin to question that Donnie knew he was dying. His body told him so. "I'll see you, Buddy." And he could not answer, as he might otherwise with a twinkle in his eyes, "OK, Ernestine!" It was time to go. I was only a brother, and our parents deserved his final moments, whatever they would be.

Around 2 a.m. the phone rang. Dad and I picked it up simultaneously, and I heard Mother calmly tell him, "Ernie, they can't get a pulse."

Donnie had died peacefully in his sleep. Perhaps with Donnie's death, and even more with his life, was this work conceived.

Dick Colton, George Gensler, and Octave Livaudais, great and lifelong friends, each contributed in disparate ways to the endeavor. To Octave, George, and Dick, and to our extraordinary friend Phil Farnsworth, I owe very much.

John Fenton, now sadly and prematurely deceased, provided a great encouragement at the threshold of writing that continued to be a support throughout the enterprise.

In varying ways Sherry Faubion, Jim Champion, Brigitte Manteuffel, and Richard Rawls each encouraged publication, while interest and collegial support from Mike Ellis over the years greatly helped to sustain the project. Joe Hendricks was good enough to provide an affirming ear throughout our ongoing dialogue as some of the book's themes were explored. Peggy Walker, Interlibrary Loan Officer at our Nelson County Public Library, graciously and tirelessly secured whatever works I needed, especially as writing neared completion and I wished to take account of this or that or sought to check one thing or another. I can't thank her enough. Nor Jill Santucci, who prodded me to bring odds and ends to completion. Above all, Anna Kieburtz and Hal Kieburtz merit the greatest appreciation for their considerable wherewithal.

Chapter epigraphs from the 1960 Nobel laureate come from the *Collected Poems* of St.-John Perse, published by Princeton University Press.

Fore-Sight

Quintessentials

Mankind has always known that it possesses spirit; I had to show it that there are also instincts.[1]

[T]he life of the Spirit is not the life that shirks from death . . . but rather the life that endures it and maintains itself in it.[2]

[T]he death cry is indeed the shriek over being born.[3]

We can never be born enough. We are human beings; for whom birth is a supremely welcome mystery, the mystery of growing. . . .[4]

What we cannot reach flying we must reach limping. . . . The Book tells us it is no sin to limp.[5]

Prologue

This essay addresses the conundrum of how a person or group moves from a closed, defensive existence to a life that is open and sharing, not only tolerating otherness but celebrating others. In essence, it explores the crisis of being human: Is the securing of our tenuous position amid the vicissitudes and ambiguities of life inimical to the position of others? Does one's success in the enterprise of living signal an hegemony that inadvertently, or necessarily, jeopardizes all or any others? What makes possible a shared world?

In a terribly radical way, Sartre has underscored Heidegger's perception that *Dasein*—human being—is the being whose Being is in issue. The "passion of man," Sartre has written, "is the reverse of that of Christ, for man loses himself as man in order that God may be born. . . . Man is a useless passion."[1] The ignominy of the human and the burden of the finite somehow drive us from our very selves.

Does Sartre's apodictic and disquieting utterance give insight into the human drama? Are we but a useless passion, losing our humanity that an illusion might come to be? Is this passion, which Sartre claims we are, simply and solely an attempt to evade the powerlessness of temporal being, vainly seeking to transpose our ultimate situation into an impervious absolute of Olympian security?

It is, if Freud is correct and our species is driven exclusively by Eros. Instead of "being there" in vulnerable contingency, humanity gropes for—or flees toward—an impregnable apotheosis that would secure it from the insults of finitude. It appears that Freud's Eros would abolish the tension of existence by assimilating everything to itself or by growing beyond the arena of misfortune. Striving to make the organism ever greater and omnipotently beyond challenge, the Erotic being is voracious in its self-aggrandizing avarice. Perceiving all as subservient to its own relentless need, others are reduced to object status by Erotic possessiveness. At its most benign the issue of Eros is that it is without issue, sterile and totally self-absorbed, insulated and isolated from living relationship. In its more avaricious dimension, promising to swallow everything by its insatiate, infinite consumption, Eros fosters conflict as it facilitates the autonomous character of its own organism. The effect is to create competing centers of aggrandizement, inimical to the integrity of other beings.

We can understand that such a mode of living easily turns to aggression when anything or anyone proves recalcitrant to its endeavor or threatens in any way the desperate project it proves to be. At the level of individual psychology that is ominous enough, but at the corporate, collective, or cultural level it is all the more foreboding. Not only is personal and particular identity jeopardized by absorption in the mass, the clash of cultures and worldviews is virtually assured.

Incongruent with a shared world, such a collective would be an illusion—or delusion—insofar as it would or could attribute reality only to that which was homologous with itself as an exclusive center. Implicitly, therefore, such a social and cultural environment would be a closed one, a world where the ego-syntonic or self-same is regnant and therefore opposed to whatever may differ from it. Under the aegis of Eros, the options are ominous. To ask the question anew: Does our presence jeopardize the presence of others? Is there no room or space for an other, however alien that otherness might seemingly be? What makes possible a shared and human world?

The desperate urgency for some mode of being that can not only accept disparity and tension as well as stand before the alien and new without hostility or fear, but discover also the disarming openness that is good ground for a fruitful, invigorated, and shared life is clearer everyday in both domestic realms and international regions. Such a transformation would go to the root tension, allowing one to exist in a way that is nonoppositional and nonacquisitive. It would allow the human organism to be open to others and to reality as is, without defense or evasion.

In a re-cognition of the earth of our humanity, the very humanity that Heidegger maintains we flee and Freud has shown we repress, these explorations will propose that it is paradoxically but precisely the finite world, the embraced world of finite being, that is a shared world and the abdication of an avaricious, aggressive one. The clash of titans or Olympian deities need no longer resound. We are fulfilled *as* finite being and not through a vain struggle for Promethean divinity.

Thus, proposing *kenosis*, or self-emptying, as a psychological category for a deepened understanding of the dynamism (and pathology) of being human, this essay brings Freud, Heidegger, and Kierkegaard into dialogue, evoking the conclusion that the key and core of being genuinely human is the ultimate exodus of kenotic incarnation.

Kenosis and incarnation are constituent aspects of a single dynamism. Kenosis is a relinquishing, emptying, or "dying to" the fraudulent apotheosis of omnipotently structured defenses that subject one to a less than fully human existence in a resistance to contingent, vulnerable human being. Incarnation is the coincident embrace of finitude and one's concrete, embodied existence. As an integral dynamism, kenosis and incarnation is at once individuating and social, clearing space for relationships grounded in reality, beyond self-distorting illusions.

This exploratory anthropology, integrally philosophical, psychological, and religious, opens with an investigation of *Beyond the Pleasure Principle* that unites with an examination of *Inhibitions, Symptoms, and Anxiety* to recognize that humanity eschews its embodied finitude through repression and defensive flight. Securing the evasion, Eros aggressively impels the organism to become ever greater and fortified against the vicissitudes and vexations of human contingency, creating competitive hegemonies that prove antithetical to living relationship.

If Freud's intuition of dual instincts is correct, we might suspect that death, the opposing or counterdrive of Eros, might offer a clue to the dynamism of being human. Certainly a movement from the security of a proposed omnipotence or infinity, however illusory or fraudulent it might be, would entail a passage of reversal and diminishment somehow akin to death. At least it would demand a movement—or voiding—from the riches of an imperious existence to the relative poverty of ordinary living. That, too, can be experienced as a terrible and deadly ordeal. Such a transition would appear to be, in its movement toward finitude, the opposite of that delineated by Sartre.

Alarmingly, however, one notes that the death instinct, as commonly apprehended in *Civilization and Its Discontents*, is an aggressive instinct indeed. A similarity between this instinct and Eros is manifest. Where Eros eliminates the other by assimilation, the death instinct eliminates the other by violence. The eradication of others is precisely what the death instinct entails in such works following *Beyond* as *Civilization and Its Discontents*. Clearly, death is not a real counterforce to Eros—both are protecting the self, or the organism, from what Hamlet would call the "slings and arrows of outrageous fortune." Were a real opposite to Eros and its usurpation possible, it would undoubtedly be the antithesis of such hegemonic aggression. Instead, it would allow the (human) organism to be open. The life of oppositional tension between others—not the self or the other—would be abolished.

In contrast to this aggressive character, a close scrutiny of *Beyond the Pleasure Principle* reveals that the death instinct of this earlier work can be distinguished by the fact that it is neither directed at another nor aggressive. Instead, as first articulated in *Beyond*, the death instinct bears the character of discharge or release. Already the peculiar character of Eros as it appears in *Beyond the Pleasure Principle* has been noted. It is precisely the terrible cost and tension of such a besieged and defensive life that death, or *Beyond's* death instinct, seeks to escape. The death instinct of *Beyond* is a dynamic *on behalf of the self,* seeking *release* for the self. In *Beyond,* the death instinct seeks to discharge the bizarre burdens of conflicted existence.

This suggests that it is not mistaken to suspect that Freud's dual-instinct theory, and notably the death instinct, provides a clue for moving beyond the fraudulent and divinizing tendency of an avaricious Erotic being toward a more authentic and finite human being.

Thus, a first resolution to the crisis of being human is offered in the thesis of Heidegger's *Being and Time* that the transition from inauthentic and collective being to authentic and finite being is contingent upon an encounter with death. In the anthropological language of Victor Turner, facing death is the "liminal" or threshold experience that discharges one from the structure and grasp of collective deceptions.[2] A scrutiny and reinterpretation of Freud's earliest cases cautions, however, that an encounter with death can precipitate a more profound and pathological evasion.

Nevertheless, the heuristic potential of Kierkegaard's transformation into maturity through an ongoing "dying away" from illusions is highlighted by these considerations. Kierkegaard speaks of "dying away from immediacy" as the path from a self-absorbed and more or less symbiotic bonding with the environment to a truly constituted self. This path is the end—or death—of one kind of being, relationship to reality, and self in the birth of another. Not unlike Margaret Mahler's separation-individuation process,[3] it is nevertheless an ongoing dynamic. In further contrast to Mahler, Kierkegaard's notion is concerned, not with an initial psychological individuation, but with individuation of a more advanced and profound degree. This promising dynamic is tested and amplified through select works of Heidegger's later authorship.

Bearing resemblance to both *Beyond's* death instinct and Kierkegaard's "leap" of transformation, a dynamism is revealed in Heidegger's later work that would provide a true reversal of the Erotic tendency. This dynamic would release one into, or free one for, an authentic self open to others. We are called to forever transcend our immediate present into a "presencing" beyond our possession and self-identity. Briefly stated, Heidegger's mature writings culminate in a disclosure of the self-effacing Event that grants space to all in a celebration of the new autochthony of a shared world.

Through contributions from Kierkegaard, the bare bones of the movement Heidegger has elucidated receive personal embodiment in the self-emptying kenosis that embraces the earth of our humanity, transcending narcissistic defenses and illusions of hegemony. This voiding that we ourselves are, or may be, is an ongoing openness or dis-closing that calls us into relationship with others, beyond a myopic self-interest. The paradox is that we are uniquely human to the measure we are empty and open, with room for the other. The work concludes with a cross cultural corroboration of its principal themes.

1

To Be or Not to Be

Ego, Eros, and the Pleasure Principle

... carrying letters of marque from no masters but ourselves.
—St.-John Perse, *Chronicle*

Beyond the Pleasure Principle (1920) is a terribly convoluted work. So torturous is its path that Freud himself threw up his hands in abandonment, effectively inviting anyone to assist in casting a ray of light on the theory of instincts.[1] More than a decade after this summons, and just seven years before his death, Freud would say of libido and the instincts: "This is a region in which we are struggling laboriously to find our bearings and make discoveries . . . yet we are never sure that we are seeing them clearly."[2]

This exploration, then, is a collegial response to Freud's invitation.[3] While the engagement could be called a Derridean reading[4] of *Beyond the Pleasure Principle*, exploring the fissures and faults of the text into the possibility of a new understanding, it is actually no more, and no less, than an acceptance of the very methodology and spirit that animated Freud. Throughout *Beyond the Pleasure Principle*

Freud, ever the pioneer, never hesitated to change directions, explore new possibilities, admit impasses, contradict cherished findings. The probing is incessant. For this very reason *Beyond* is a tribute par excellence to Freud's characteristic genius.

The potential for reconnoitering and revision was constantly underscored by the father of psychoanalysis. "It must not be supposed," Freud averred in a classic statement, "that these very general ideas are presuppositions upon which the work of psycho-analysis depends. On the contrary, they are its latest conclusions and are 'open to revision'. Psycho-analysis is founded securely upon the observation of the facts of mental life; and for that very reason its theoretical superstructure is still incomplete and subject to constant alteration."[5]

Some few years earlier he had insisted, "Psycho-analysis is not, like philosophies, a system starting out from a few sharply defined basic concepts, seeking to grasp the whole universe with the help of these, . . . having no room for fresh discoveries or better understanding. On the contrary, it . . . is always incomplete and always ready to correct or modify its theories."[6]

While generally stressing the empirical and nonspeculative character of his work, Freud was always aware of the hypothetical nature of psychoanalytic assumptions, even the figurative, fictional, and mythological dimensions of his constructions,[7] and quite frankly entered into the boldest speculation in *Beyond,* "diverging widely from empirical observation."[8] While this as much as its agonistic convolutions has issued in the book's general neglect, it cannot be forgotten that hypothesis is not antithetical to science but the cornerstone of its methodology. If hypothesis is speculation before the fact, speculation is hypothesis after the fact.[9] If, in *Beyond,* Freud allowed himself to follow a line of thought "wherever it leads out of simple scientific curiosity," he was reflecting, nevertheless, on the same clinical data that contributed to the very possibility of analytic thought.[10]

As the central focus of *Beyond's* theorizing, the death instinct may play no little part in the book's obscurity. This major development in Freud's thinking is generally lamented in psychoanalytic circles.

While the possibility of an aggressive instinct is admitted to orthodox consideration, apart from the work of Melanie Klein, an equiprimordial death instinct is more frequently acknowledged by an obligatory reference or an embarrassed silence, if not repudiated altogether.[11] On occasion it is the subject of vigorous renunciation.[12]

In some sense, *Beyond's* novelty undermines—or threatens to undermine—the whole Freudian project. In another sense, it is the basis for the two decades of fruitful work that follow. Without an appreciation of *Beyond*, it is impossible to recognize the significance, nuances, or problematics of the subsequent work. Without a knowledge of *Beyond*, it is impossible to evaluate the aggressive instinct or the interplay of forces that Freud, under the rubric of a dual and conflictual instinct model, championed throughout his authorship. *The Ego and the Id* (1923) and *Civilization and Its Discontents* (1930), perhaps the most widely read books in Freud's corpus, are deprived of foundations without it.

There is no doubt that *Beyond* occupies a pivotal position. Not only does the instinct theory undergo a profound if unsettling metamorphosis, but something of importance enters the Freudian arena. Following *Beyond*, new directions emerge; ego psychology is broached in the structural model, and larger issues of social and cultural psychology occupy Freud for the remainder of his life. Psychoanalytic theory is forever altered. The neat, well-confined categories and organization of Freud's science become undomesticated.[13] A certain unwieldiness and confusion now adhere to his expositions as though a vast, not fully channeled force is released. With this vitality, Freud faces the expansive currents of cultural issues, although the full promise and potential of *Beyond* is never realized, even ignored, or in some measure abandoned as the ghosts of former theory incessantly arise to cloak and constrain the not yet mature insights.

It is worthwhile, thus, to return to *Beyond*, not only to accept Freud's invitation, but, especially, to enter its vigorous and unrestrained exploration in order to be charged with vitality and insight. If Freud's conclusions and formulations were tentative and not wholly to his satisfaction—or to others'—*Beyond* nevertheless promises a heuristically rich investigation. At the very least, it may provide a clarified, simpler, perhaps more nuanced understanding of Freud's psychology or of the dynamism of being human. At the very most, we might discover what Jacques Derrida has called "a grace beyond the work, [something] owing to the work but without it, a gift given there, but above all given there without meriting any responsibility for it. . . ."[14] It would be, perhaps, a pearl of some price, latent in the manifest record bequeathed by Freud.

"Our views have from the very first been *dualistic,* and to-day," Freud insists in the sixth of *Beyond's* seven chapters, "they are even more definitely dualistic than before—now that we describe the opposition as being, not between ego-instincts and sexual instincts but between life instincts and death instincts."[15]

In the context of Freud's reflection, the significance of this invigorated assertion is transparent. The long-standing model of dual and conflicting drives[16] that Freud regarded as the very foundation of his new psychoanalytic science was in jeopardy. Three years later, in *The Ego and the Id,* he would confess that "the distinction between the two classes of instincts does not seem sufficiently assured and . . . facts of clinical analysis may be found which will do away with its pretension."[17] Already in *Beyond,* however, it is clear that Freud realized he was facing a possible emasculation of the prized dualism he had so faithfully championed. This impasse, and Freud's urgent denial, climaxed a survey of the path his instinct theory had traveled.[18]

The second phase, following a first that had opposed object-directed libidinal or sexual instincts to ego instincts of self-preservation, now emphasized the libidinal character of self-preservative instincts, highlighting what Freud called narcissistic libido. The ego had "found its position among sexual objects."[19] In facing the consequences of this reorientation and the obvious issue of whether or not all instincts were of a libidinal nature, Freud conjectured that instincts in addition to the sexual ones probably were present in the ego, but he was forced to admit that "[a]t all events there are none other visible."[20]

This crisis of the "pan-libidinal" threatening a forced agreement "with the critics who suspected from the first that psycho-analysis explains *everything* by sexuality"[21] was exacerbated by the new and third phase of instinct theory revealed in *Beyond*.[22] Uniting the sexual and self-preservative instincts under the name of Eros, "the preserver of all things," Freud derived the ego's narcissistic libido "from the stores of libido by means of which the cells of the soma are attached to one another."[23] It was at this point that Freud faced the terrible question, "are there perhaps no other instincts whatever but the libidinal ones?"[24] Although Freud suspected "that instincts other than those of self-preservation operate in the ego, and it ought to be possible for us to point to them," he forthrightly acknowledged: "Unfortunately, however, the analysis of the ego has made so little headway that it is very difficult to do so."[25]

Confronted by this impending reversal, a new and ominous specter menaced. Apparent and portentous agreement with the "monistic" views of Carl Jung demanded, with greatest urgency, that the dualistic perspective not be abandoned.[26] In the face of strong counterindications, Freud's rebuttal is a recalcitrant one that offers, for an empirical scientist, a painfully insubstantial warrant for the conflictual character of the psyche: "The difficulty remains that psycho-analysis has not enabled us hitherto to point to any instincts other than the libidinal ones. That, however, is no reason for our falling in with the conclusion that no others in fact exist."[27] It is not surprising that such jeopardy for a life's work would occasion its restatement, with the endangered model reinforced by opposing a death instinct to the agglutinated Erotic ones, yet later in the same essay Freud is drawn to aver more honestly: "But we still feel our line of thought appreciably hampered," admitting in the process that the very foundations of his death instinct seemed in issue.[28]

The journey toward the death instinct opens where *Beyond* begins. Though its progress is often like a pilgrim's regress, *Beyond's* twists and lapses and leaps frequently conceal a rich, if not fully explicit, psychological wisdom. From a more analytic perspective it could be said that *Beyond* is like—or *is*—a massive free association or dream, the dream work camouflaging latent issues in the Freudian psyche.[29]

Beyond sets out with Freud's concern about the pleasure principle. No principle of hedonism, this basic psychoanalytic assumption (the word is Freud's) simply avers that the pleasure principle *automatically* regulates as well as dominates mental processes. Triggered by unpleasurable tension, the mental apparatus functions in such a way that it reveals a tendency to reduce the excitation. "Pleasure" simply indicates a *diminution* or, if possible, an avoidance of stimuli, while "unpleasure" denotes an increased quantity of excitation.[30]

Inexplicably, and not expressly until the conclusion of chapter 2, Freud embarks upon a quest for some "primary event" or tendency that is *beyond,* or more primitive than, the pleasure principle and that, as an independent force, might counter or override its domination.[31]

The search for this independent operation has no sense of urgency except for the "inefficient and highly dangerous" valence the pleasure principle betrays in the organism's environmental context—that is, the external world and its conundrums.[32] It is the reality principle[33] that faces these challenges and, temporarily enduring tension or the unpleasure of increased excitation, displaces the pleasure principle. In fact, Freud fails to note, this is only a modification of the pleasure principle since the reality principle "does not abandon the intention of ultimately obtaining pleasure" but effects "the postponement of satisfaction . . . as a step on the long, indirect road to pleasure."[34] Nevertheless, the pleasure principle often overcomes the reality principle "to the detriment of the organism as a whole."[35]

It is the clinical transference that finally gives Freud the key he seeks, for here he discovers a recurring episode of unpleasure.[36] This episode is simply the repetition of the early oedipal crisis within the analytic setting. Marked as it is with the terrible loss of exclusive love through the infidelity of one's first love object, its reoccurrence, Freud is certain, must always and only manifest the greatest unpleasure.[37] He is astounded at the terrible and infantile tactics patients will resort to in order not to recognize and accept the earlier tragedy.[38] Instead, memory is replaced by (unconscious) repetition. This compulsion to repeat an earlier state of affairs becomes a second criterion, conjoined with unpleasure, for considerations that follow in Freud's investigation.

A strong instinctual character to this compulsion is recognized by Freud, and this leads him to a stunning reversal: from the instinctual valence of the compulsion to repeat, he now estimates that the compulsion to repeat is a universal characteristic of all instincts and of organic life in general.[39] If this is so, the question naturally arises as to what the prior or initial state might be that is sought by instincts in their compulsion. The answer seems clear enough to Freud. The living organism must seek the quiescence of its initial inorganic, inanimate condition. This is simply a manifestation of the inertia of matter and the assumption that the evocation of life was produced by external forces disturbing, then diverting, the organism from this absolute and profound restfulness to which it naturally seeks and desires return. "If we are to take it as a truth that knows no exception that everything living dies for *internal* reasons—becomes inorganic once again—then we shall be compelled to say that *'the aim of all life is death'*. . . ."[40]

The alert reader quickly discerns that the argument has taken a cruel and curious twist on its master. Originally, a function that could inhibit and supersede the pleasure principle was the grail of contention. The toleration of unpleasure by the reality principle, inter alia, contributed "unpleasure" as the hallmark criteria. The unpleasure of the transference led to the search for a compulsion to repeat an earlier state of unpleasure that, in turn, led Freud to search for the initial state intended by instincts, with the criteria of "unpleasure" slipping from view. The ultimate prize turned out to be the inorganic or inanimate and nonliving state of death, a realm in which the issues of pleasure and unpleasure (or tension) fall upon deaf ears with utterly no relevance whatsoever.

Initially, Freud portrayed a living organism threatened by possible destruction from the external world's excessive stimuli, with the organism's need to be shielded from such disaster. Now, stimuli still endanger and must be warded off, but instead of threatening extinction, they threaten life and the unpleasure of existence. In other ways the twist turns out to be a restoration of the very starting point, for the inanimate state of death does not manifest unpleasure but the ultimate condition of pleasure, the nirvana of absolute tensionlessness.

Death serves the pleasure principle! The inspiration for these peregrinations is frustrated with the anticipated telos unattained. In fact, one more twist remains since, at the book's conclusion, Freud announces that it is not death that serves the pleasure principle but the latter that serves the former, although this appears to be a distinction without a difference. His efforts, inaugurated in the face of the transference, were directed toward securing the acceptance of unpleasure in the service of reality. Now we discover that reality is not to be faced; rather, it is to be avoided or fled wholly and at all costs.

Those familiar with *Civilization and Its Discontents* will notice immediately that the death instinct portrayed in that well-read work is strikingly different from the death instinct presented in *Beyond*. In *Beyond,* the death instinct is a drive *on behalf* of the organism. In function of the pleasure principle, it seeks to protect the individual from the tensions and burdens of existence. Thanatos, the death instinct of *Civilization and Its Discontents,* on the other hand, is an aggressive and violent drive, indeed. No longer a self-oriented internal function seeking absolute respite from the excitation of life and the vexation of external forces, it is, in the later work, directed *against* objects in a purely hostile way. There is an important similarity, however, that reveals the two death instincts are not incongruous but work in tandem. In the face of environmental onus, the death instinct of *Beyond* seeks the oblivion of death as a haven, while that of *Civilization and Its Discontents* seeks the annihilation of the burden or danger itself. In either case the instinct is a drive toward the pleasure of an existence that is entirely free from the harsh realities, tensions, and oppositions that might impinge upon the organism. Each serves the pleasure principle in disparate but complementary ways, with the organism enjoying primacy and remaining utterly secured. One dynamism flees in the face of reality's real or imagined threats; the other attempts to destroy them. Each serves the pleasure of a facile, largely unconscious existence. What both inclinations have in common is a relationship to the external world. Rather, it is a nonrelationship—the inability to face reality apart from an undisturbed, impregnable position or to deal with it on any terms other than one's own.

This defensive posture of fight or flight is adumbrated in the reactive quality Freud attributes to the incipient organism, which appears as a fragile, defensive entity in an inhospitable milieu. The fourth chapter considers living matter in its most elemental form, confronted by "an external world charged with the most powerful energies." "[I]t would be killed by the stimulation emanating from these," Freud continues, "if it were not provided with a protective shield against stimuli."[41] Reception of stimuli occurs under guarded conditions with the organism prepared always to exclude unsuitable amounts or kinds of excitation or to retreat whenever necessary. Excitations from the external world that are powerful enough to penetrate the protective shield are experienced as traumatic and set in motion "every possible defensive measure."[42]

These primitive and defensive traits amid hostile circumstances foreshadow as well the narcissism of the human organism. The narcissistic hypercathexis that Freud considered a necessary reaction to physical injury is all the more urgently required to guard the psychological vulnerability of one besieged. Analogous to the defensive shield of elementary life, narcissism serves as the ultimate protective barrier in a threatening world, both censoring and blocking out dangers through unconscious self-absorption. The violent and aggressive tactics of Thanatos might prove the reaction to dangers impinging too gravely, but midway between fighting and fleeing, the narcissistic organism can simply refuse to see incompatible phenomena until, too massive or immediate, they threaten to disturb the primacy of its slumber.

Evidence of such narcissistic denial appears in the clinical transference, as Freud has already noted, where the ego refuses to acknowledge realities uncovered in successful therapy precisely because they disclose what Freud has called a permanent injury to one's self-regard.[43] At the very moment the patient appears to be at last in the most favorable position to recognize its true situation, "the phenomena of transference are obviously exploited by the resistance which the ego maintains in its pertinacious insistence upon repression."[44] Clinging as it does to the pleasure principle, the ego is not inclined to recognize or peel away the narcissistic scab or to wake from its redeeming illusion.[45]

If *Beyond* contributes decisive insights with regard to the self-invested organism, Freud first broaches this important development in psychoanalytic thought in his 1914 essay, "On Narcissism: An Introduction." Let us trace its salient features.

The opposition between sexual instincts and ego instincts, Freud recognized in this metapsychological[46] essay, was not as absolute as he had previously imagined. What emerges in the paper is a theory that comprehends the ego as a "unity" that necessarily must evolve: "it is impossible to suppose that a unity comparable to the ego can exist in the individual from the very start; the ego has to be developed."[47] Freud elucidated this development as a movement from primary narcissism to a secondary one—which is nothing other than "a vigorous attempt" to recover the original.[48] Defining narcissism as "the libidinal complement to the egoism of the instinct of self-preservation," Freud described secondary narcissism as the withdrawal, to the ego's advantage, of libidinal cathexes from the objects of the "external world."[49] Moreover, the "original libidinal cathexis of the ego," or primary narcissism, is preceded by primordial autoerotic instincts that function in the service of self-preservation.[50] The priority of the autoerotic epoch compels Freud to conjecture that "there must be something added to auto-erotism—some new operation in the mind—in order that narcissism may come into being.[51] Freud does not speculate what this unknown might be, but with the transition to primary narcissism, the ego has begun its emergence toward that configuration Freud has characterized as a "unity" or, in the language of *The Ego and the Id*, a "coherent organization."[52]

Part of the ego's original narcissistic cathexis is eventually yielded up to objects, states "On Narcissism," "when the cathexis . . . exceeds a certain amount" and "our mental life pass[es] beyond the limits of narcissism."[53] This "transcendence," however, is never fully realized or truly achieved. The transition from autoerotic self-preservation through primary narcissism to object-oriented cathexis, that is, relationship to the outer world, is short-circuited at the threshold of the ego's emergence as a fully relational organization. Primary narcissism is never truly abandoned; it is only transposed. At the very moment object-cathexis becomes a possibility, the immature ego is threatened by alien realities that relentlessly assail its "immortality" and "omnipotence."[54] Coincidently, in an effort to maintain the megalomania of infantile narcissism, an ego ideal is established that deems itself the possessor of all perfections; to it is conveyed the omnipotence of childhood.[55]

In consequence of this bipolar convergence of external threat and internal ideal, a repression is exerted to protect the security of the narcissisticly immortal organization, withdrawing cathexes from objects for the maintenance—and bolstering—of the ego-unity and its self-regard.[56] Only those relationships (libidinal cathexes) are permitted that are "ego-syntonic," or in accordance with the ego's tendencies. This is simply to say that these relations are motivated by narcissism in the service of an infantile and illusory perfection that seeks to remain exempt from the insults of vulnerability. Any relations that are not in the ego's service, or might be directed toward a too terribly alien reality, are repressed.[57] The sexual (relational[58]) instincts, "at the outset supported upon the ego-instincts," are never fully emancipated, however independent they may theoretically become. "[W]e have an indication of that original attachment in the fact that the persons who are concerned with a child's feeding, care, and protection become his earliest sexual objects. . . ."[59] In other words, the distinction between anaclitic and narcissistic love is a distinction without significance: both "relations" are in the service of a fragile and endangered ego.[60] Love is not object-directed but self-oriented: "love is assessed like any other activity of the ego."[61]

Thus, primary and original narcissism is abandoned only for the secondary configuration of an omnipotent and immortal ego ideal that, unwilling to forgo the gratifications of childhood perfection and rejecting all that may be incompatible with itself, voraciously arrogates libidinal cathexes in its own insatiable direction, releasing (outward) only those cathexes that further enhance its illusory self-regard.[62] Whatever remains of the ego's potential for maturing beyond a state of narcissism to reality-oriented object-cathexes, or relationship toward the external world, is short-circuited through repression.[63]

"On Narcissism" was reluctant to fully acknowledge the implications of its developments, with Freud painfully denying that the now recognized libidinal nature of the narcissistic ego, or of ego-cathexis, necessitated the abolition of "the hypothesis we first adopted of an antithesis between ego-instincts and sexual instincts."[64] Nevertheless, as previously noted, *Beyond* wedded the pair as Eros, with the interconnection between Eros and narcissism clearly evident.

Deriving the ego's narcissistic libido "from the stores of libido by means of which the cells of the soma are attached to one another," *Beyond* attributes this power of attachment to the binding or bonding of Eros, defined as a vector of coalescence, "which holds all living things together."[65] If, however, narcissism has the Erotic character of preserving its own self-invested, coherent, and inclusive organization, Eros manifests a no less narcissistic quality, with the bonded cells "requir[ing] their libido, the activity of their life instincts, for *themselves*." "Combin[ing] organic substances into ever larger unities," Eros succeeds at best in creating a symbiotic merger or "vital association" for prolongation and survival that retains libido and "pays none of it out in object-cathexes." Hoarding all for itself, it "behave[s] in a completely narcissistic fashion."[66] Subsequent "momentous constructive activity" can only be Erotically syntonic, that is, congruent with the ever greater self-adhering organism. "The clamour of life"[67] is solely on behalf of the reinforced organization, and no authentic communication issuing toward independent objects in the larger world appears. There is virtually no movement or cathexis beyond the conserving or "centripetal" boundary of the self-absorbed organism.[68] The relational and external realm of object orientation that began to recede in "On Narcissism" has effectively disappeared in *Beyond*. As in the former essay, *Beyond* allows for only a closed system, isolated from (with an implicit denial of) other and independent realities, cathecting objects solely for its own enhancement and survival.

Eros, then, is the driving force of the narcissistic orientation. Significantly—and paradoxically—in *Beyond's* new conception of Eros, "the preserver of all things," the ego instincts do not become integrated into, or endowed with, the object-cathecting relational powers of libido. Instead, the life instinct is characterized by, and defined in terms of, the insatiable, arrogating tendency of the ego's self-preservative instincts that Freud correlates to hunger.[69] Eros thus proves to be a vector of aggrandizement in a movement to secure the fragile organism's tenuous position in an ambivalent and apparently alien world. All is reduced to whatever sustenance it contributes to the Erotic being's entrenchment as it seeks to become ever greater. The narcissistic organism, as an exclusive center enhanced by higher faculties from the ego, attempts to manipulate everything, ever threatened anew by whatever is not or cannot be reduced to its centripetal and consuming unity.

However infinite its ingestive or introjecting capacity might be, this is an extremely narrow, restricted, and impoverished organization, indeed a closed entity. Paradoxically, however, the organism—although recognizing no difference or other but itself alone—is symbiotically fused with the environment at large to the extent, but only to the extent, it provides a pleasurable fund of ego-enhancing replenishment for a consumptive identity that resists change and the pain of (psychological and personal) growth.[70] With narcissism's omnipotent self-regard, parity is impossible.

At its most benign, Eros creates a nonrelational world; in its sinister aspect, a competitive, hostile universe is produced as each organism perceives all as subservient to its own voracious but unconscious need.

Freud's essay "Instincts and Their Vicissitudes" (1915) first previewed this malign aspect of the narcissistic dynamism. There Freud warned that the entity's first response to the external world was one of hate because the world represents all that is non-ego and alien.[71] A function of the instincts of self-preservation, hate "derives from the narcissistic ego's primordial repudiation of the external world."[72] Since love is defined as "the relation of the ego to its sources of pleasure," and the ego identifies itself only with what is pleasurable, anything that is not ego-syntonic and "introjected," or taken by the ego into itself, is subjected to a hate that "can afterwards be intensified to the point of an aggressive inclination towards the object—an intention to destroy it."[73] While "pleasure-giving objects" can be found throughout the environment—and this environment is pleasing, and therefore safe, to the measure it affirms the narcissistic project—anything that fails to affirm and remains extraneous to the organism's narcissism is identified by the ego as unpleasurable and experienced with repulsion.[74]

Clearly, in a dual-instinct model, an aggressive drive is not the counterforce to a "life" instinct such as this. Virulent enough with its usurping tendencies, Eros is sufficient rationale for an aggressive world, incorporating as it does the destructive tendencies of the self-preserving instincts.[75] What is needed, instead, is a trajectory that would liberate one from the imperialism of Eros and its conflicting hegemonies that produce nothing but a coercive, explosive world.[76] What is needed is a force that could de-fuse symbiotic narcissism, which captivates and eclipses everything in its self-absorbed blindness, and defuse the violence of an Erotic world.

This trajectory would be a movement *outward*, a movement toward objects and what Freud calls "the external world." This would be a dynamism *beyond* as well, a force that takes the entity beyond itself, transcending the limited, restrictive organization that is essentially insulated from and closed to the larger relational environment. Undoubtedly, the ego, as a conscious entity impelled to transcend the safe but moribund "unity" of a closed system, would perceive and experience this action as a "death," a painful "dying" (to its encapsulated psyche) in opening to a universe beyond its control. Overcoming the inertia of the pleasure principle, this dynamic ("destroying" the consuming hunger of ego-Erotic narcissism) would be a death, moreover, insofar as the tacit infinity of exclusive and omnipotent self-concern is relinquished for the finitude of parity and exposure to a real world. Perhaps obviously, this dynamism, itself, would be resisted. We might wonder, consequently, if it is libido, *qua* libido, that is repressed by the ego or, instead, this trajectory that shatters the protective illusions of a private domain. Suspending this conjecture, it appears, nevertheless, that such a dynamic would fulfill or complete the Freudian intuition, for we can see that such a trajectory would effect authentic cathexes in lieu of the self-aggrandizing ego-syntonic ones. The potential that remained stillborn via repression or narcissistic arrogation would at last be realized through genuine cathexes establishing *relations*—that is, other-relatedness and reality-relatedness (not merely narcissistic links)—with the world beyond.[77] Objects, heretofore impoverished (as had the true character of libidinal energy) through servitude to the voracious Erotic project, would be discharged from our driven needs to receive their full existential import as realities of independent existence having integrity and value in their own right, quite apart from narcissistic assimilation. Losing their merely functional, appendage role to the inflated ego-ideal, objects would assume, especially in the instance of personal objects, the quality or character of "other," disclosing themselves as appropriate subjects for dialogical engagement.

The ego-unity, now authentically "in touch" with other realities, would experience something of its own transformation, a "realizing" of the ego in lieu of narcissistic pseudo-identity, through the influence and interaction of this encounter. No longer would the organism be a closed system, but an open one entering into relation with objects and other conscious beings. Neither assimilation, nor arrogation, nor isolation, but relationship and interrelatedness would be an actuality, a genuine interaction with the world beyond. Thus, we could speak of a real or "fulfilled" reality principle, not merely one serving the pleasure principle as it exerts the apparatus to alter "the real circumstances in the outer world" for the sake of "mental equilibrium" and the satisfaction of inner needs.[78] Perhaps most significantly, the ego would be capable of genuine development rather than the truncated pseudo-development of secondary narcissistic prescription.

In a recapitulating glance, we see that the conflict between the ego-organization and the libidinal powers of the organism, which issues in an aborting of all relational cathexes (except those in harmony with the narcissistic regard of the ego-ideal) and in resultant self-enclosure, tacitly demands and, indeed, indicates the possibility of a trajectory beyond the immediate self-absorption of narcissism. Without such a dynamism, the organism remains a closed system, hostile to any reality but its own, immersed in the illusion of its own dream. Beyond the death of Erotic isolation and avaricious, hegemonic self-concern, this would be a trajectory into the risk of openness and growth vis-à-vis new and independent existences and re-newed, more vulnerable unities: a dying into reality, beyond the pleasure principle.

The pleasure principle, however, is a dominant not easily overthrown. Not surprisingly, therefore, Freud's manifest intent to move beyond the pleasure principle proves to be a dream, and like a dream coming full circle, *Beyond* ends with a return to its beginnings. Although a concluding chapter of "secondary revision"[79] closes the work, argument breaks off in chapter 6 with a myth that Freud believes is a corroborating warrant for the compulsion to repeat. "[I]t fulfils precisely the one condition whose fulfilment we desire. For it traces the origin of an instinct to a *need to restore an earlier state of things*."[80] The myth about primeval humanity is presented by Aristophanes in Plato's *Symposium*: Our original ancestors were doubled, having four arms and legs and dual heads. "Eventually Zeus decided to cut these men in two. . . . After the division had been made, 'the two parts of man, each desiring his other half, came together, and threw their arms about one another eager to grow into one'."[81]

The desire within the myth, emblematic of the human psyche in general, fulfills Freud's desire: In spite of assertions about reality and unpleasure, the earlier state that is secretly sought and at last retrieved is an affirmation of original fusion. A self-envelopment that abolishes any reality but its own, this restoration of the primordial One, refusing the demands of individuated existence, denies a world of difference and multiplicity in an absolute assertion of the pleasure principle.

Not mythology alone, this dynamism has already been reflected in the crisis of clinical transference. Fighting to maintain unconscious bliss, the ego resists memory and recognition of its authentic situation in a world that has relativized its once absolute universe. What appeared to Freud as the repetition of unpleasure in the transference neurosis was actually a struggle to get behind the trauma to a state that preceded the shattering of preoedipal unity.[82] Locked in oneself, immersed anew and definitively one in the pleasure of self-satisfaction, the return to Aristophanes' primal merger would eradicate the onus of differentiation and consciousness in a wish-fulfilling triumph of the therapeutic evasion.

Nevertheless, these dynamics are not restricted to a special moment in the peculiar setting of psychoanalytic therapy. To the contrary, Freud observes that such "transference . . . is a universal phenomena of the human mind . . . and in fact dominates the whole of each person's relations to his human environment."[83] In other words, a narcissistic symbiosis, evaporating the dire otherness of a dreadfully real world, submerges the species—proximally and for the most part, as Heidegger would say—in an unconscious evasion with potentially ominous consequences, as noted heretofore.

Is there any liberation, the question begs to be asked, from the bonding and bondage of Erotic forces that drive us inexorably into the nirvana of narcissistic supremacy? Is there exemption from this oblivion, any way out of its omnipotent, though illusory, universe wherein we carry "letters of marque from no masters but ourselves,"[84] hostile to any challenge? Can we, and if so how might we, be open authentically to others, discharging them from our objectifying utility? Might we share, instead of hoard, valuing the difference and differentiation of life as, coincidently, we are freed from the sterility of our own confinement? What dynamic might lead us beyond the satisfaction of self-serving Eros and into a human world?

2

Symbiosis and Seduction

Kierkegaard, Freud, and das Man

> ... humanity is in question, in its human presence. ...
> —St.-John Perse, *Winds*

Kierkegaard's "Diary of a Seducer," presented by pseudonymous Victor Eremita in the first volume of *Either/Or,* gives flesh to this narcissistic-Erotic dynamism in its portrayal of Johannes, a seducer, through journal entries and a sample of letters to Cordelia, the object of his desires. The seducer is incapable of perceiving others apart from their function or utility in his self-arrogating universe. Devoid of value and significance in their own right, others are means to the insatiable end of self-aggrandizement.

In a dual sense, Cordelia is the object of seductive designs. Despite articulations about seeing and viewing, it is clear that Johannes never truly beholds Cordelia; she is apprehended only in the light of his contrivances. More offensively, she—as any other—is not regarded as a peer in the enterprise of living. Instead, the poor girl is a plaything, manipulated to assuage abysmal needs.

This exploitation is not diminished by romantic jargon but is revealed, in fact, by discourse about "being mine" and "belonging to me." To speak in such fashion betrays an avaricious Eros striving to be ever greater and more secure. Mere possession is not sufficient for the seducer, however; the goal is a capitulation of the "most absolute self-surrender," deceptively evoked as Cordelia is drawn toward and ultimately "ensnared in my web."[1]

This vector of aggressive self-orientation is not without subtlety, which is clearly ingredient to the general cast of woven deception. The seducer is no bungler but "an aesthete, an eroticist" with ultimate confidence in his captivating arts, an elaborate dissembling that camouflages contempt.[2]

This double eclipse—his inability to see and value another and the obscuring of Cordelia's own vision by his designs—underscores an important aspect of Erotic being, which perceives itself as an exclusive center and is blind to, unable to comprehend, any other apart from reference to its own centrality. The bottom line of the eroticist's perspective and agenda is simple as well as preemptory: "She must belong to me."[3]

This possessiveness reveals a second and consumptive aspect of the Erotic-narcissistic impulse. Preyed upon by self-serving manipulation and reduced to an item, commodity, or abstraction as one is drawn into the ego-syntonic world, the other feeds the seducer's egotism. When exploitation is complete and the commodity is irrevocably the eroticist's own as an ingredient of self-reference, the eclipse of the other is total in the hegemony of the self.

This eponymous function of our consumer society is highlighted by Freud's insight that hunger is the principle analogue of the self-preserving inclination. This analogy—of a self sating itself for fulfillment and preservation—complements the dynamics of eclipse noted above: Once a hunger is satisfied, having had one's fill of the desired object, the commodity no longer stimulates the satiated self. The seducer's philosophy, thus, is consistent with the fluctuations of Erotic appetite: "Every erotic relationship should cease as soon as one has had the ultimate enjoyment," and his habit of casting off individuals as he cast off Cordelia becomes understandable.[4]

Highlighted by Robert Coles, Walker Percy has expressed this same dynamic in his own delightfully insightful way:

> New things are grabbed and devoured; goods are endlessly consumed. We crave a piece of furniture or a painting not because we really need it, not even because we are interested in it or curious about how it will "work" in our house, but in order to have and, ultimately, in order to prove that we *are*: If I can lay my hands on that painting, then things will change—in Percy's words, "my life will be different, my nothingness will be informed by the having of it." . . . But, alas, once possessed, once in "the zone of my nought," the object loses its allure, its promise, and becomes of no consequence whatever; it "only participates in my nothingness." So it is that a week later, days go by and I ignore what once I lusted after, couldn't take my eyes off.[5]

The gradual but total eclipse of another (as mine) Emmanuel Levinas has called "neutralization," the reduction of the other as object to "the same."[6] "Possession is preeminently the form in which the other becomes the same, by becoming mine."[7] Underscoring the essential violence of this act, Levinas says that the inner and ultimate logic of the neutralization or obliteration of the other is—to use his startling metaphor—murderous.[8] Cordelia, herself, recognizes the violent character of her ordeal when, anticipating Levinas by little over a century, she accuses Johannes: "my murderer, the cause of my unhappiness, the grave of my joy, the abyss of my destruction."[9]

The violence exercised by the narcissistic self that was detailed in "Instincts and Their Vicissitudes" is extended in the erotic engagement highlighted by Kierkegaard's seducer. In Freud's essay, hostility, with possible eradication, was directed at a feared or hated other. In the "Diary of a Seducer" violence is suffered by others who are objects of a want or desire that seeks only itself and defines itself in terms of what it possesses.

Although at first glance there appears to be a generous sample of altruistic concern for Cordelia's genuine blossoming, Johannes himself alerts the reader that all may not be as it appears: "It may indeed look as if it were she whom I would make my confidante . . . , but this is only by glimpses."[10] *Stages on Life's Way* cautions further that in the matter of love "it is utterly impossible to determine whether it is a knight or a seducer who is speaking. . . ."[11] Thus, noble sentiments that "she must be strong in herself," that "she must be developed inwardly . . . so that everything there is in her, the whole divinely rich nature, may come to its unfolding," and that "she must owe me nothing; for she must be free, love exists only in freedom . . . [and] only thus will I love her"[12] can only be understood in the context of the seducer's peculiar mentality and motivation.

A closer scrutiny uncovers an alarming egocentrism in the apparent regard for Cordelia's enrichment. "*I* set her free. . . . She must never suspect that she owes this freedom to *me* . . . ; yet *I* am striving to bring it about . . . before *I* let her take rest in *me*."[13] Johannes anticipates the moment "when *I* have brought her to the point where she has learned what it is to love" and exults in the vanity that "*I* am one of the few who can do this."[14] He speaks of "*my* operation in the domain of her soul," and if there is any doubt that he is a manipulator, one is disabused of the misperception by his confidence that "one can so arrange it that a girl's only desire is to give herself freely."[15] He calculates that one must "know how to compass a girl about so that she loses sight of everything which he does not wish her to see . . . [and must also know] how to poetize himself into a girl's feelings so that it is from her that everything issues *as he wishes it.* . . ."[16]

The horribly deceptive quality of this manipulation is transparent: "It takes something more than honesty to love such a girl. That more I have—it is duplicity."[17] Baldly asserting that "if a man does not understand how to put himself in rapport with a girl, he should never attempt to deceive," Johannes will brag that "I have known how to drug her aesthetically."[18] He is able "to weave her into my plan" only because "she is not on guard against me; instead she regards me as a trustworthy man. . . "[19] While he gains "some amusement out of watching the artificiality of these artistic performances" created by his deceptions, he laments that the method is a tedious one, while acknowledging that it can "advantageously be used against an individual."[20]

The essential violence of his method, operation, and plan is betrayed by the martial imagery he employs. He speaks of "beginning my assault," of a more direct attack, and of a two-stage war.[21] He wishes to "encompass her" as "my possession."[22] In spite of ethereal discourse about Cordelia's freedom consisting "in being mine, as mine [consists] in being yours," his hypocrisy is revealed in the polarity that "she is free; but she shall yet be *mine*."[23] Only two breaths later he declares, shattering any illusion of mutuality: "the second war is just beginning, and in this second war I shall be the victor. . . ."[24]

With no parity in the seducer's conception of love, it is not surprising to discover on one occasion—unquestionably emblematic of this operation as a whole—that he "was with her today, quite carried away by an idea that has always engaged my thought. I had neither eyes nor ears for her."[25] A modicum of reflection permits one to recognize that this idea was nothing other than a consideration of himself. If Cordelia is blind to the truth, since "she almost worships me as her ideal,"[26] others are not, and the seducer is forced to dissimulate in the face of their accusations: "People say that I am in love with myself. . . . I *am* in love with myself, why? Because I am in love with you; . . . and so I love myself because this myself belongs to you. . . ."[27] Beautifully spoken, but Johannes acknowledges his true character even as he counters the assertions: "What is, then, in the profane eyes of the world an expression of the greatest egotism . . . [and] the most prosaic self-preservation is in your sacred sight an expression for the most enthusiastic self-annihilation."[28]

Those not ensnared by seduction have perceived aright, for Johannes's designs involve a love that is defined solely in reference to himself. "The highest conceivable enjoyment," the seducer tells himself, "lies in being loved; to be loved is higher than anything else in the world."[29] If true enjoyment is first known in the submission of a girl whose "only desire is to give herself freely . . . [and] almost begs to make this free submission"[30] (however manipulated or arranged that inspiration might be), nevertheless, there can be no enjoyment, the seducer believes, "if there is not the most absolute self-surrender, at least on one side."[31]

It is this total surrender that is the telos of the seducer's machinations, for he is engaged in conquest: "The first war . . . was only a game; the second is a war of conquest, it is for life and death."[32]

The stakes are clear; his own life is in issue, and it is for this that he struggles; hers is expendable. In spite of his rhapsodies to Cordelia, the only annihilation he has contemplated is her own, for "she must be quite . . . ensnared in my web."[33] Replenished, feasted, and filled with her strength, freedom, and spirit—revealed, now, to have been cultivated for his own consumption—what remains of the prize is simply expelled as valueless refuse of no significance to him. "[I]ndividuals," Victor Eremita commented in a less vicious metaphor, "were merely a stimulus to him; he cast them off as a tree sheds its leaves—he burgeons again, the leaves wither."[34]

Relationships should cease when the conquest is won, the seducer believed, rationalizing that the essence or "very concept of woman" (representing all that attracts his desire or promises to assuage his needs) "requires that she be vanquished."[35] "With every movement of mine she becomes stronger and stronger," he had boasted, "love is awakening in her soul."[36] Sadly, it is now recognized that, for the seducer, love signifies only self-oriented sustenance. When he admits, at the conclusion of his diary, "I would change her into a man," it is recognized that the man he intends is himself, energized by her passion and power and abundant strength, the great spoils of victory.[37]

In his peculiar reasoning, the ultimate possession and conquest occur only with Cordelia breaking their engagement. He thus maintains the "everlasting delight" of an ego affirmed and self-regard enhanced, while exempting himself from any encumbrances. No burdens, obligations, or limitations of a concrete and lasting relationship will be his: "Although she must belong to me, it must not be in the unlovely sense of . . . a burden."[38] It is precisely the broken engagement that assures him "of a more beautiful and significant relationship to Cordelia. . . . When . . . the engagement breaks like an imperfect mold, . . . she belongs to me,"—an absolute conquest for his narcissism, without the vexing inconveniences of an imperfect human being. "Others, he adds, "become engaged, and have a good prospect of a boring marriage for all eternity. Well, let others have it."[39] Johannes insists that Cordelia be manipulated into breaking the relationship because he refuses responsibility for this act of emancipation that definitively crowns the conquest he craves: "To poetize oneself into a young girl is an art, to poetize oneself out of her [life] is a masterpiece."[40]

According to the seducer, love fears limitations; what it desires and loves is infinitude and enclosure—undoubtedly signifying protection from the insecurity and vicissitudes of the finite, for this paradise of Erotic narcissism should be a haven where "everything finite and temporal is forgotten, only the eternal remains, the power of love, its longing, its happiness."[41] This love has proven to be the vicious self-absorption of *Beyond's* Eros, with Johannes also appealing to the primal myth from Aristophanes' discourse in the *Symposium*.

"When we keep together," Johannes urges Cordelia toward the very end of his project and in an idiom that reflects the bonding of Eros, "then are we strong, stronger than the world. . . ."[42] His desperation reveals the fragile organism, jeopardized by the world at large, that focused Freud's concern in *Beyond*. "You know," the seducer writes Cordelia,

> there once lived a race of people on the earth who were . . . each self-sufficient. . . . Yet they were mighty, so mighty that they could storm heaven. Jupiter feared them, and divided them so that from one came two, a man and a woman. Now, if it sometimes happens that what had once been united is united again in love, then is such a union stronger than Jupiter. They are not only as strong as the [primal] individuals were, but even stronger. . . .[43]

His concern, like that of Prometheus, is for an infinite, omnipotent self-sufficiency; his desire is to be mightier than the immortal deities. Love is understood only in terms of power, but—defined by conquest—this is a power for him*self* alone. Indeed, this is power to be exercised and extracted at the expense of another (and unquestionably many others, as Victor Eremita informs us) in the process of filling the black hole of his elusive, unconscious needs. He plunders where he may.

In this desperation for the infinite, for immortality and omnipotence, we recognize the narcissistic psyche that, as Freud has emphasized, labors to reinstate and maintain the lost perfections of a former and unperturbed epoch. In Johannes's struggle to coerce ego strength and enhance self-regard, we recognize, in addition, Freud's analysand, indelibly scarred by injured self-esteem. His wistful longing for the paradise of preoedipal unity echoes as well in the seducer's cry that the greatest and only enjoyment is being loved. Thus, the seducer connives to break the relationship not only to secure the ideal trophy of enduring, unalterable conquest but, and perhaps especially, to assert control like Freud's clinical, if adult, child, lest he be devastated anew by another failure in love.

What most characterizes this state of the aesthetic, Erotic mentality of which the seducer boasts is what Kierkegaard calls "immediacy." This is a condition of childlike merger with one's environment, a condition that prevails, in general, the whole of one's life. There is a profound lack of self-awareness or consciousness of being a self, in spite of the fact that one is profoundly self-oriented. This selfishness or self-seeking might be called narcissism, and the predilection is ratified by the discovery that Kierkegaard identifies this state as one emblematic of the "me" of a child.[44] One remains "just about on the same level as the young child"; "fundamentally, most people virtually never advance beyond what they were in childhood and youth." "The child wants to have everything it sees, and youth is not much better, wants everything to conform to it, and the whole world to indulge its wishes. . . ."[45]

It is a dreaming state,[46] Kierkegaard says, wherein one is unable to distinguish oneself from the environment at large or others in particular. There is no differentiation because one is bound up in a nonrelationship of "immediate connection with 'the other' . . . in desiring, craving, enjoying, etc., yet passively."[47] Lumped together with everyone else, one is engrossed in the throng and "merges in some abstract universality."[48]

If there is no sense of other, there is no genuine sense of self:[49] "The appearance of such words as 'the self' and 'despair' in the language of immediacy is due, if you will, to an innocent abuse of language, a playing with words, like the children's game of playing soldier. . . . Immediacy actually has no self, . . . and therefore generally ends in fantasy."[50] Even the life of a genius, omnipotent champion of aesthetic immediacy, "is always like a fairy tale. . . . In the deepest sense, the genius does not become significant to himself."[51]

Kierkegaard elsewhere laments, as if responding to the seducer, "What wretchedness that we are engrossed in or encourage the human throng, . . . deceived instead of being split apart so that each individual may gain the highest, the only thing worth living for. . . ."[52]

Perception of another as an other is initiated only with the onset of a separation from symbiotic merger that is akin to an awakening "whereby the self becomes aware of itself as essentially different from the environment and external events and from their influence upon it."[53] "Awake, the difference between myself and my other is posited; sleeping [unconsciousness] . . . is suspended."[54]

Nevertheless, few ever realize the transition. Immediacy may be susceptible to degrees insofar as it ranges from a pure immediacy, without any measure of awareness or reflection, to an immediacy with some quantitative reflection,[55] but Kierkegaard proposes that this "little dash of reflection" or inwardness is forgotten and abandoned when immediacy escalates as a matter of course.[56] Even with an initial breach, relapsing into immediacy is so frequent that immediacy is rarely overcome for long, and once again life is embraced in terms of trivialities.[57] One feels secured, but in fact, one is devoid of spirit—that is, not yet constituted as a human self.[58] Thus, the possibility of separation and differentiation remains stillborn: "There are very few persons who live even approximately within the qualification of spirit [the basis of consciousness and selfhood]; there are not many who even try this life, and most of those who do soon back out of it."[59] One remains superficial, "in a life that is so immersed in triviality and silly aping of 'the others'."[60]

Two paradoxes are apparent. The first might be called the bank-ruptcy of the self: in spite of narcissistic preoccupation, one is, in fact, devoid of a self. "However vain and conceited [people] may be," Kierkegaard says with a twinkle in his eye, "they usually have a very meager conception of themselves, . . . but vain and conceited they are. . . ."[61]

The second paradox could be called the seduction of the self. Although preoccupied with oneself, one is, nevertheless, absent and alienated from oneself. Lacking depth or inwardness, one is utterly dependent upon the extraneous for self-understanding. "The man of immediacy does not know himself, he quite literally identifies himself only by the clothes he wears, he identifies having a self by externali-ties."[62] A life qualified only by immediacy cannot find itself. "[L]ay hold of itself, it cannot, as long as it has itself outside of itself."[63]

Kierkegaard unites these two paradoxes, acknowledging that one engrossed in immediacy may possess exceptional abilities and com-petence, indeed: "They use their capacities, amass money, carry on secular enterprises, calculate shrewdly, etc., perhaps make a name in history, but themselves they are not; spiritually speaking, they have no self, . . . however self-seeking they are otherwise."[64]

This life of infantile—or narcissistic—merger is rooted, not sur-prisingly, in a wish to have power to do everything and in the confi-dence that such a power is possessed.[65] For the immediate psyche the categories of perception and understanding are the pleasant and the unpleasant[66] or fortune and misfortune,[67] remarkably resem-bling Freud's pleasure and unpleasure. While offering an opportu-nity to grow beyond immediacy, any breach with fortune or the pleasant, Kierkegaard notes, is usually survived, met by the artifice of lying perfectly still, as if dead.[68]

This brings Freud to mind. In Freud's conceptions, the locus of this radical environmental merger, or symbiosis, is precisely the latency period when libido, the energy of life, was believed to be dormant—asleep or effectively dead.

Scarred by the narcissistic wound of oedipal failure, the alienated child unconsciously determines never again to suffer such a blow. "Compliance brings immediate rewards," Winnicott has remarked, commenting on the submissive child, "and adults only too easily mistake compliance for growth. The maturational processes can be by-passed by a series of identifications, so that what shows clinically is a false, acting self, a copy of someone perhaps; and what could be called a true or essential self becomes hidden, . . . deprived of living experience."[69]

Vulnerable and insecure, uncertainty and self-doubt compounded by exposure in a vast and unknown "outer world," the precarious latency child unconsciously transfers the identification and symbiosis that had originally been manifest in dyadic bond with the maternal environment to the environmental matrix of the greater culture. Cut off from the preoedipal haven, the child takes refuge in the only direction possible, embedding itself in the womb of culture and short-circuiting the ideal separation-individuation opportunity initiated in the oedipal crisis.

Abandoned to this foreign realm following the perceived oedipal rejection, the child's entire energy focuses upon an exhaustive, urgently defensive, ego-syntonic compliance and assimilation. Freud called this period of enculturation the latency period because he assumed that the libido, thwarted in the primary maternal bond, lay dormant until adolescence. In fact, this ongoing cultural initiation is an intense endeavor. Freud failed to reevaluate the concept of latency in light of his theoretical shift toward narcissism. Had he done so, he might have realized that the latency period is a highly libidinous period, in many ways the most libidinous, in its diffuse and universal narcissistic embrace of the world beyond the familial threshold. In this capitulation to authorities of the cultural imperative in the hope of warding off further impingement upon a fragile sense of self and worth, objects and environment are dutifully encountered, but exclusively and defensively for the sake of the (oedipally) jeopardized self.

Thus, and however unconsciously, the ego-syntonic structure of the transposed symbiosis produces the peculiar illusion Kierkegaard noted. One imagines oneself the center of one's world, with others as the elements of an elaborately enclosed security, even as one capitulates to cultural demands and "societal seduction."[70]

In truth, this is exactly the work of the latency period: to assimilate everything possible and, thus, to become as typical and ideal a constituent of the environment as may be practicable, obscuring boundaries between oneself and others, camouflaged in a haven of anonymity, lest one be exposed and wounded anew. The task of conformity is never ending for the youth, virtually infinite in its progression. Nevertheless, the more dedicated one is to the endeavor, the greater the confirmation that seems to be acquired, including the ultimate reward of becoming a "good child." By compliance with "environmental demands," the latency youth "builds up a false set of relationships [and] . . . even attains a show of being real," Winnicott writes.[71] Typically, one is—or should be—seen and not heard. With no voice of one's own, one cannot speak in his or her own name but tacitly reflects the conventional milieu. A unique identity is effectively denied; emergence as a person in one's own (vulnerable) right is eclipsed.

The enculturation of latency would be described by Kierkegaard as a process of "leveling"[72] since it reduces all to the common denominator of generic humanity. Leveling stifles and impedes as everything, robbed of its own power, sinks into stagnant anonymity. No room exists for the specific and unique. Annihilating the "relative concretions of individuality,"[73] each is alienated from oneself in this victory of abstraction over the individual and personal. Inwardness, or the intensity of self-deepening, is obliterated, with a resulting impoverishment of the interpersonal. "[L]eveling is a principle that forms no personal, intimate relation to any particular individual," fostering only "the same for all."[74] What remains are insubstantial phantoms who are never genuinely united and never can be, for leveling is "the negative unity of the negative mutual reciprocity of individuals."[75] The power behind this process is the public, mass, or crowd, a "monstrous nonentity" that is both all and nothing.[76] Outnumbering the totality of a population, the public is a body composed "of individuals in the moments when they are nobodies."[77]

Leveling is the "severe taskmaster" that educates one for subordination in the quantitative or "mathematical equality" of this monstrous abstraction and "negative community."[78] Exceptional or superior abilities are thwarted, aggressively if need be. The most successful in the school of leveling is without distinction, while the greatest achiever, Kierkegaard says, becomes a "nonhuman nonentity" who shirks all personal responsibility.[79] No one belongs to oneself; each functions as a serf to the estate of this "most dangerous of all powers."[80]

Nevertheless, more and more aspire to become nobodies, seeking comfort in the public aggregate, enticed by its mirage.[81] Arrogating this mammoth and its illusions to themselves, everyone is absorbed by "the broad vista of abstract infinity," with its alluring distractions from the paltry "concretions of actuality."[82] Fancying "themselves greater than kings,"[83] the indolent crowd enjoys the delusive contentment of an infantile narcissism that, as Freud has shown, is so reluctantly abandoned.

Enmeshed in such conceits, all are lumped together and carried along with the crowd in myopic immediacy, seduced by status, self-importance, and effervescent pleasure, adopting the same opinion as a public that can rarely account for its judgment, alternating opinion from day to day.[84] A superior force that no individual can control, the leveled mass is a deceptive consolation of evasion and dissipation that vitiates even as it binds together.[85] Swept into the trivial, frivolous, superficial, uniform, and boring, many lives are squandered in the vacuum of this "prodigious something" that understands nothing of itself, even as everyone egotistically thinks they know exactly what they are about.[86]

With converging insights, psychoanalyst Harold Searles has stressed that our species tends to merge not only with the human environment, but with the nonhuman environment as well. One "comes to discover how pervasive, at largely unconscious levels of ego functioning, is symbiotic relatedness not only with one's fellow human beings but also with the totality of the 'outside' world, including the vastly preponderant nonhuman realm of that world. . . ."[87] Although Searles is speaking of patients, he emphasizes in numerous contexts that what differentiates the pathological from the ostensibly normal person is not qualitative but quantitative variations; that is, the pathological is a matter of degrees, with phenomena that appear in neurotics—and psychotics—present in the healthy as well.[88]

This underscores that symbiosis and individuation are not stage-specific or once-and-for-all events of infancy and early childhood.[89] On the contrary, to focus on the healthier side of the spectrum, "symbiotic relatedness . . . forms, at largely though not entirely unconscious levels, the dynamic substrate of adult living."[90] "It may well be that the predominance of personality functioning, even in healthy adult persons," Searles proposes,

> is subjectively undifferentiated, at an unconscious level at least, from the great inanimate realm of the environment—that only in comparatively minor part do we function as subjectively animate beings; that we function in even smaller degree as animate *human* beings; and that we function to a still lesser degree . . . as predominantly *uniquely* living human beings. Probably, in waking life we function all the time on all levels simultaneously, in varying degrees. . . .[91]

Although human maturity is defined as achieving "a full emergence, a full realization and acceptance of [one's] status as a human being," in symbiotic processes self and object are not clearly demarcated, and there remains "the subtle persistence of nondifferentiation between ego and outer world."[92] Thus, no one is so individuated, mature, or secure in humanness that identity formation is ever definitively concluded; instead, it is a lifetime task.[93] In some measure, then, every individual shares or suffers the condition of the autistic (Searles's term for the narcissistic) personality, of which he notes: "Many patients who seem to be leading lives filled with relatively active and well-differentiated interpersonal relationships prove, on closer scrutiny, to be living predominantly autistically."[94] Such people, Searles concludes, cannot be said to have yet established a basically human identity. While this latter observation embraces the most seriously ill of his client population, Searles reminds us anew that in much lower intensities and in less detectable forms, "pathological process[es are] . . . taking place . . . on a broad scale among the 'normal' members of our culture."[95] It must be insisted, therefore, that "adult living involves an unceasing struggle to maintain, and ever more deeply realize and develop, one's humanity vis-à-vis the surrounding nonhuman world."[96]

If the normal or healthy adult is engaged in phases of symbiosis and reindividuation, the hallmark of "any human being's identity struggle . . . consists in [one's] efforts to demarcate [one]self as a single, living, human entity over against an outer world, which is, in by far its vastest part, objectively nonhuman. . . ."[97] The goal, Searles stresses, is to be "warmly human," not in polarity with the greater world, but in harmony with it. Differentiated, separate, integral, integrated, or individual identity is not opposed to mature relationship but is, instead, the very foundation and possibility of authentic relatedness. The antithesis of relationship is unconscious, symbiotic merger with the totality of one's environment. Free of this "infantile-omnipotent" disposition, a sense of "intimate kinship" with the greater world becomes possible.[98] With differentiation, "the person does feel a sense of real and close kinship, but does not lose . . . awareness of [one's] own individuality; that awareness is, instead, deepened."[99] One is "at once uniquely individual and indissolubly part of the universe."[100] Identity comprehends both the individuated self and the world.[101]

If this emergence is vital with regard to the nonhuman world, it is all the more urgent and significant with regard to the human environment. With a sense of paradox equal to Kierkegaard's, Searles realizes that, once freed from unconscious embeddedness, the emerging individual has greater access to the primal mother-infant symbiosis that serves as bedrock for personal identity and subsequent maturation; one's life is enriched with energies and capacities for creative relatedness.[102] To become an individual, the emerging child must acknowledge, identify with, and accept the "mother-as-individual" precisely in her *unpossessable* individuality.[103] Control as well as symbiosis must be relinquished. We tend to resist an individual identity, Searles says, because we perceive that it will terminate the "world-embracing oneness" initially shared with the mother.[104] If this emergence fails to be fully realized, one may or may not become pathological, but one's "status as a human being" remains in doubt, however matters might otherwise appear to be.

These perspectives from Kierkegaard and Searles, in conjunction with Freud's concept of the latency period, lend something of a context for understanding Heidegger's concept of *das Man*. Proximally, Heidegger says, one is a constituent of the collectivity[105] *das Man:* the "they."[106] For the most part, one remains ever so. "[I]t is not 'I', in the sense of my own Self, that 'am', but rather the Others, whose way is that of the 'they.'"[107]

The phenomenological evidence Heidegger marshals for this conclusion is the "constant care" that preoccupies one about how he or she differs or is distanced from the Others, whether the difference is to be evened out or the distance overcome, as one endeavors to "catch up in relationship to them."[108] In common parlance we know this as keeping up with the notorious Joneses and, if at all possible, surpassing them to enhance our status or self-esteem.

This tendency can be called unconscious insofar as Heidegger speaks of it as hidden. Analogous to the dynamics of psychoanalytic repression, the more inconspicuous this everyday life is, "all the more stubbornly and primordially does it work itself out."[109] Specifically, what is hidden or masked is the fact that not only does one think, feel, fear, and enjoy as the "they," but "they"—not surprisingly in view of latency's enculturation—determine all modes and standards of everyday interpretation and evaluation.[110] "They" ordain what is granted success or denied it, as well as what may or may not be ventured. All possibilities of Being are leveled to the homogeneity of averageness, insensitive to every difference. Anything exceptional, different, or genuine is suppressed into, and covered over by, mere publicness.[111]

"What is decisive," says Heidegger, "is just that inconspicuous [or unconscious] domination by Others which has already been taken over unawares. . . ."[112] In spite of—and because of—this tyranny of the "they," the Others are nothing definite; any one can represent another; every Other is like the next. As distinguishable or explicit, the Others evaporate more and more. Not only the

Others are undifferentiated; since one's everyday self is the they-self, each is dispersed into the undifferentiated concernful absorption of the "they's" averageness.[113] "In this inconspicuousness and unascertainability, the real dictatorship of the they is unfolded" as identities dissolve in the symbiotic mass, enhancing "their" power.[114]

Needless to say, the Other here is not a person in his or her unique otherness. Rather, the Others are "those from whom, for the most part, one does *not* distinguish oneself."[115] Simply, the Others represent the alienated non-self of inauthenticity, the self-*other-than-its-self* that constitutes the "they." "Everyone is the other, and no one is himself."[116] While this "not-Being-its-self" is the mode of living or Being that is closest or most proximal to oneself, it is distinguished by Heidegger from the authentic Self—and not surprisingly, for the "who" of the everyday they-self is no self at all but "the *'nobody'* to whom every[one] has already surrendered."[117]

This nobody is precisely the agency of the "they," the "no one" that dominates without accountability, dictating the (inauthentic) kind of Being of everydayness.[118] The authentic self, on the other hand, is defined by the emancipated capacity to decide and to choose (with regard to one's existence) from one's most vital self, according to one's ownmost (or unique) possibilities and potentiality-for-Being.[119]

While the crux of authenticity is a life rooted in decisions growing out of one's own Being, the "they"—while making no decisions and evading choice—preempts such responsibility by claiming all judgment and decision as its own.[120] More significantly, ways of Being[121] have already been determined by the "they," preventing each from existing in his or her creatively unique way. Tacitly relieved of choice, one is carried along by the nobody, ensnared more and more by inauthenticity. Everyday possibilities of Being are for the Others to dispose of as they please. "One belongs to the Others oneself"; one's Being has been usurped by the "they."[122]

Nevertheless, this disburdening of one's Being provides a seductive incentive—or temptation—to fall more profoundly into the self-dispersal of the inauthentic but accommodating "they," consolidating "its stubborn dominion."[123] Not surprisingly, "fall-ing"—the basic kind of Being that belongs to everydayness—has the dominant characteristic of Being-lost in publicness.[124] Public-ness will be recognized under the constituents of distantiality (care about how one differs from others), leveling, and averageness.[125]

Falling, as the downward plunge of one's unique Being into aver-age everydayness, is not only tempting; it is tranquilizing as well. Bolstered by its all-consuming mass, self-certainty, and "decided-ness," the "they" complacently supposes that one is leading the full-est and most genuine life possible, with all "in the best of order."[126] Ingredient to this tranquility is the presupposition that the "they" is in possession of everything that matters or that everything, other-wise, is easily within reach.

Liberated from the more substantial issue of Being authentically oneself—and Heidegger says our very Being is in issue for us—this tranquilized state does not bring rest but, instead, a driven "self-dis-section" that aggravates the foundational alienation of falling, inau-thentic Being. Uninhibitedly comparing oneself to everything, one drifts toward a profounder estrangement wherein one's most genu-ine possibilities and potentials become obscured and closed off. The narcissistic foundation of this self-absorbed scrutiny is underscored in the paradoxical fact that falling ultimately proceeds by its own inner dynamism to a self-entanglement that only hides one from oneself.[127]

Each, as self-dispersed, lost, and hidden in the "they," must first find oneself. If this is to occur, Heidegger says, it will be realized as a "clearing-away of concealments and obscurities, as a breaking up of the disguises" with which one has barred one's own way.[128]

This self-discovery may be a matter of some urgency. Searles has underscored several of the hazards and horrors of the collective mentality that drive one to the absolute and irrevocable conclusion of falling, a radical and complete self-annihilation. Pathological pro-cesses that have been fostered by contemporary culture, Searles believes, continue to hinder us from becoming differentiated from the environment and emerging from symbiotic embeddedness.[129]

Through various identifications, elements of the nonhuman environment have invaded our personalities.[130]

At deep levels, there is an unconscious desire to actually become inanimate in order to escape failure, imperfection, and death.[131] Wondrously powerful although dead and inanimate, technology, with a "seemingly omnipotent dominion over nature, provides us with an increasingly alluring object upon which to project our 'nonhuman' unconscious strivings for omnipotence."[132] Identifying with a seemingly infinite and immortal technology not only shields one from the insignificance, deprivation, and loss of mundane life, which pledges only the inevitability of growing old and dying,[133] but also promises to return one to the invincible hegemony and perfection of infancy. Narcissistic yearnings are immediately fulfilled as "we identify unconsciously with this technology which, being inanimate, cannot die."[134]

Ominously, these unconscious processes work themselves out in more hazardous directions. On the one hand, an ecologically deteriorating world, perhaps the gravest impingement humanity has yet faced, threatens the extinction of ourselves and our globe as pollution increasingly strangles the environment. In the meantime, while dreading the potential of atomic holocaust, we readily identify with the fascinating technological arsenals of destruction. Excited by these nearly infallible—save for human error—wonders of annihilation, it is "alluring to give oneself over to secret fantasies of omnipotent destructiveness."[135]

On the other hand, frustrated by the impoverishment of our human lives and the knowledge that we are merely mortal, we find secret assurance in the expectation that nuclear power or some more magical energy will propel us beyond the earth into infinite interstellar realms, far beyond the circumscription of our world.

These dreams of "[b]reaking the chains that have always bound our race to this planet,"[136] as well as suicidal pollution, nuclear jeopardy, and regional conflicts that annihilate populations while ravaging the earth, all signify a negative regard, if not hostile contempt, for the terra firma of mundane, finite existence. In the fantasies of our narcissism, Searles notes, "mother earth is equivalent to all of reality, which is a drag and hindrance to our yearnings for unfettered omnipotence, *and we want to be rid of it.*"[137]

All is in issue and at risk as we, shirking burden and responsibility, unconsciously defend ourselves, Searles writes, "against the experience of becoming an individual human self."[138]

3

Individual Integrity

Heidegger's Dasein

> ... the simple thing, the simple thing of here, the simple
> thing of being here as day drains away ...
> —St.-John Perse, *Exile*

It is death alone, Martin Heidegger proposes in *Being and Time*, that is capable of shattering the tenacity of collective merger, restoring one to oneself. Death, itself, is this potential—"the possibility of no-longer being-able-to-be-there"—that puts in issue one's very Being.[1] In light of this crisis, with the individual claim levied by death, one's lostness in the undifferentiated "they" is disclosed, along with the realization that any and all others will fail one absolutely in the face of this "uttermost" phenomenon.

Forced to confront and embrace death's "non-relational character" alone, for no other can assume one's place, other possibilities open, including the possibility of Being oneself. Heretofore, a genuine understanding of self had been suppressed, with refuge taken in substitutes and in the tranquilizing diversion and endless multiplicity of the collective; now, "for the first time," authentic understanding and choice are liberated to be taken up from oneself, of one's own accord, in one's own way, without support.

"Anticipation" is Heidegger's term for the individual act of "comporting" or "projecting" oneself toward—or existing in—this "ownmost potentiality-for-Being."[2] Anticipation—Being-toward-death—radically individualizes one "down to" one's very self and out of conventional publicness: "[I]n this distinctive possibility of its own self, [one] has been wrenched away from the 'they'."[3]

In the face of possible annihilation, one's own existence is perceived as the incomparable value it is. Freed through anticipation to accept one's death, one is freed as well for one's unique existence, recognized as finite in light of death's finality. Released from the tyranny and illusions of the "they," one is emancipated, as "an impassioned freedom toward death,"[4] from the fantasies of immortal omnipotence that plague, as Searles has reported with alarm, the unconscious aspirations of the collective mentality.

However, anticipating the "indefinite certainty" of death opens one to the "constant *threat* arising out of its own 'there'." The only way such authentic openness can be maintained to its uttermost possibility is through anxiety. Here one is "*face to face* with the 'nothing' of the possible impossibility of its existence. . . . Being-toward-death is essentially anxiety."[5]

Heidegger's cure for inauthenticity marshals a sympathetic defense for the intransigence of *das Man*. Quite apart from the vital risk of succumbing to this ontological remedy, however "ownmost" the ultimate possibility may be, it is easy to wonder if one is liberated simply to flounder, perplexed and unguided, on one's own.

Death may wean from the "they," but might not this experience be disorienting, at least initially, without the certitudes of collective prescription? Unsupported, is one helpless to discover the way to proceed? How is the potentially authentic self to be guided in its authentic ways. What or whom provides direction? All this suggests that matters are more ramified than at first may appear, and, thus, Being-toward-death must be qualified and placed in context.

Throughout the whole of his authorship, Heidegger was concerned with Being. His foundational contention is that Being is not a thing; it is not an entity, a being among beings, one being among others and, thus, something self-evident to be taken for granted. Being is not a concept so general and universal, or an idea so abstract, that it is indefinable, superfluous, or devoid of significance and can be, or should be, forgotten.[6]

This precisely is his lament: somewhere not long after Heraclitus and Parmenides and following—or with—Plato and Aristotle,[7] the Western philosophical world forgot Being. Be-ing,[8] open, disclosive,[9] emerging, and dynamic in its original apprehension, was eclipsed. The question of the meaning of Being suffered complete neglect. Metaphysics exclusively preoccupied itself with entities, with beings, rather than with the Being of beings.[10] Heidegger's whole enterprise is an attempt to retrieve the sense or meaning of Being.

In *Being and Time*, Heidegger proposed that the way to set forth a "fundamental ontology" and explore the meaning of "Being in general" was through an interrogation or analysis of *Dasein*—the being or entity (which each of us is) that is "ontically distinguished by the fact that, in its very Being, that Being is an *issue* for it."[11]

"Dasein" is Heidegger's term of preference for human being—or, rather, for being human—since it was feared that humankind, also, had too long been interpreted as an entity or "Reality" like any other, a thing, a static substance, or oppositional subject.[12] Literally, "There-Being" or "Being There," "Dasein" can be seen as a tacit critique of Plato: It is right here, *there* where one stands, that authentic Being dwells, not "out there" or "up there" in some ideal Platonic realm.[13]

Descartes can be recognized in Heidegger's concern about an oppositional subject. While Kant, Hegel, and Kierkegaard may be present,[14] unlike any other, Descartes broods over the whole of *Being and Time*, especially through its trademark "Being-in-the-world."[15] Although Plato is reflected here anew, with its emphasis on this-worldly engagement, Heidegger is seeking to repair the sundered world of the Cartesian *cogito:* There is no bare subject without a world, no isolated ego that, somehow, must hazard a transit into an external world of objects. Thus, there is no need for a worldless subject to discover or prove the "Reality of the 'world'."[16] On the contrary, one is already involved in a world of significance, relationship, and concern.[17] Whether it proves to be authentic or inauthentic, Being-in-the-world is the basic and essential state of Dasein.[18]

The force that Heidegger wishes to convey in asserting that Dasein is "already" in a world is best highlighted with a more sequential rendering of *In-der-Welt-sein* as "In-the-world-being" or "In-the-world to be." This last construction does not signal a future world or afterlife; rather, it indicates that one is already situated in a world of context with the task and challenge of *Be*-ing. As Heidegger phrased it, "the 'essence' of this entity lies in its 'to be'."[19]

Here we see a further significance of the employment of the term "Dasein." According to Heidegger, any entity is either a "what" or a "who."[20] Dasein cannot be defined as a what, as some thing might be, since Dasein is neither a thing nor an object but a *who*. Thus, without the prejudiced content other terms might inject, "Dasein" is used to signify one's Being.[21] "[B]ecause we cannot define Dasein's essence by citing a 'what' of the kind that pertains to a subject-matter, and because its essence lies rather in the fact that in each case it has its Being to be, and has it as its own, we have chosen to designate this entity as 'Dasein', a term which is purely an expression of its Being."[22]

It is this that foundationally differentiates Dasein from the "what" of mere things or objects—in Heidegger's lexicon the "present-at-hand," which indicates a "substance" that is utterly lacking in concern about, comprehension of, or relationship to its Being.[23] Exemplified by things of nature, these are entities that "just occur" without the instrumental or functional involvement in Dasein's world that the "ready-to-hand," equipment and tools, possess. On the other hand, Dasein's Being is not that of instrumentality, either.[24]

In saying that Dasein has its Being to be, Heidegger is highlighting the fact that Dasein's world is a world of choice. Through its choices Dasein is opened to possibilities beyond its immediate understanding and present "actuality." Dasein, who can "be itself or not itself," "is primarily Being-possible."[25] Thus, Dasein is not monolithic, reified, or irrevocably actualized, a Self-thing persistently present-at-hand; rather, as itself, Dasein must "*become*—that is to say, *be*—what it is not yet."[26] "As long as Dasein *is* as an entity, it has never reached its 'wholeness'."[27]

Here we see two more indications of Dasein's character and of the significance of the term. Dasein is not "once and for all"; instead, and unlike anything present-at-hand, Dasein is incomplete and unfinished. This is a further consequence of its open structure. Moreover, as indicated by the characteristics of "ownmost" and "mineness," Dasein is individually constituted.

However, this does not bespeak solipsism or selfishness. Instead, it emphasizes the profound responsibility that one must bear simply by the fact that each has been "delivered over to" his or her own Being, as well as the fact that each, whether authentically or inauthentically, is uniquely concerned about his or her existence.[28] No one can live or assume life for another. "Only the particular Dasein decides its existence, whether it does so by taking hold or by neglecting. The question of existence never gets straightened out except through existing itself."[29]

"Existence" is Heidegger's term for the unique Being of Dasein, and "in each case Dasein is its Self only in *existing*."[30] Dasein's distinctive character or essence lies in its existence, and elsewhere, drawing the distinction between other entities and Dasein's special "essence," Heidegger is emphatic: "Entities of Dasein's kind of Being cannot be conceived in terms of Reality and substantiality; we have expressed this by the thesis that *the substance of man is existence*."[31]

If comporting oneself understandingly toward (or Being-toward) one's ownmost possibility is Heidegger's definition or "formal concept" of existence,[32] it will be recalled that death is this ownmost and uttermost possibility. It is precisely death, individualizing Dasein down to itself, that opens "a way in which the 'there' is disclosed for existence," so that Dasein might authentically *be* there.[33]

An ominous note may be recognized, however, since death also discloses that one's very Being is in issue. Thus, if "Dasein is its Self only in existing"[34] and exists only by comporting itself toward its ownmost possibility, then not only is Dasein's Being in issue, but its

existence is in jeopardy, and its there is in doubt. Dasein is a concernful being; the very basis of that Being is care.[35] It is no wonder, then,
that everyday Dasein is "the self-forgetful."[36] The eclipse of Being is
not due exclusively to the oversight of philosophers. Dasein is not
"there," and for this very reason Being is obscured and forgotten.

Foundationally, or proximally and for the most part, as Heidegger would say, Dasein is in an attitude of flight or evasive turning
away. What does Dasein evade? From what does Dasein flee? It is,
in fact, nothing at all—no thing, no "what"—from which it flees.
Dasein flees in the face of itself.

In turning from itself, Dasein loses itself in the collectivity, as
we have seen in chapter 2. Concomitantly, it turns toward, and
becomes submerged in, entities within-the-world.[37] This absorption
in the world of its concern relieves Dasein of the uncanniness or
"not-at-home" of Being-in-the-world; that is, the experience and
burden of not being at home is the primordial state of Being-in-the-
world.[38] Dwelling in the self-assured tranquillity of the "they,"
Dasein has fled into the "Being-at-home" of public, average everydayness that covers up its primordial and anxiety-producing state.[39]
As glimpsed in chapter 2, this dynamic of evasion and inauthenticity
is called "falling," although Heidegger is quick to distinguish this
from the notion of a fall from (theological) grace and from the concept of original culpability.[40]

The meaning of falling can be understood most easily if it is
recalled that Dasein is the being who comports itself toward its
Being. As fleeing is the inauthentic and average, everyday reaction
to and retreat from that Being—in contrast to the authentic comportment of existing—falling is the inauthentic contrast to the self-
standing or self-constancy of authentic Being.[41] One is unable to
stand before the facticity of one's own reality.[42] In the face of oneself and the onus of authentic Being-in-the-world, one simply collapses, escaping to the security, support, and relief of the "they."
Falling is a refusal—or inability—to stand forth (ex-sist), radically
individualized and nakedly oneself, into the burdens of being
real—embracing the brute fact that one is.

Not "situated" or "there" in its "not-at-home" (in the world), Dasein dwells in the comforting amnesia and "supposed freedom" of the "they's" publicness.[43] This closing off and covering over of Dasein's true condition or situation conceals Dasein from itself.[44] "This factical tendency to cover up, confirms our thesis that Dasein, as factical, is in the 'untruth'."[45]

What is desperately needed, therefore, is the dis-closure and unconcealing of the truth of Being, a dis-covering that lets Dasein exist—or choose to exist—in "the authenticity of Being-one's-Self."[46] Within the perspective of *Being and Time*, this takes place through the encounter with death, but it is precisely this that needs to be clarified.[47]

The ultimate intention of *Being and Time* is to arrive at a fundamental ontology, uncovering the meaning or sense of Being in general (not beings or entities but the Being of beings). The propaedeutic for this ontology is the existential analysis of Dasein. By coming to an understanding of Dasein (the only being, Heidegger postulates, that has an understanding of Being, since "it is disclosed to itself in its Being") and in making its existential structure transparent, Heidegger seeks a preparation for an insight into Being in general.[48] Thus, *Being and Time* is operating on two levels of concern simultaneously. Heidegger wants to "present Dasein in an ontically primordial manner for ontological analysis."[49]

In Heidegger's explorations, "ontological" refers to Being, while "ontic" refers to beings and, specifically, to Dasein as the subject of his inquiry.[50] "Existential" is to ontological as "existentiell" is to ontic. The "existential" refers to the qualities, attributes, or characteristics of the structure of Being. The "existentiell" is the ontic—that is, an entity's—manifestation or appropriation of the (theoretical) existential possibilities or attributes of Being; it is the understanding of oneself that "leads along this way" of existence.[51]

To achieve the "provisional task of exhibiting Dasein's Being," it is necessary to view Dasein in its entirety or wholeness, the concluding chapter of the first division announces.[52] Only through comprehending its Being as a whole can Dasein have any hope of understanding it authentically as a foundation for understanding Being in general.

Heidegger asks if there is not a distinctive "understanding state of mind" whereby Dasein is brought before itself in its structural totality.[53] Anxiety is the state of mind that satisfies "these method-ological requirements" giving a "phenomenological basis for explic-itly grasping Dasein's primordial totality of Being."[54] Anxiety discloses Dasein's basic state of Being-in-the-world as care, and Heidegger says that the phenomenon of care should "prepare the way for the problematic of fundamental ontology."[55]

"Care" is the unity of the fundamental ontological characteristics of Dasein's Being-in-the-world: existentiality (or existence), facticity, and falling.[56] The litany of "existence, facticity, falling" reverberates throughout the book. This simply means that, whether consciously or unconsciously—hidden, concealed, and covered over in Heidegger's discourse[57]—one is concernfully involved, whether authentically or inauthentically, in one's life. *Facticity* is one's given condition. *Falling*, the mode of inauthentic care, is the inauthentic reaction to that given, while *existence* is the authentic response of care to one's situation. Even-tually, temporality will be uncovered as the primordial ground, unity, and meaning of care and, thus, of Dasein and Being-in-the-world.[58]

However, at the end of *Being and Time's* first division, Heidegger is already questioning whether or not care is the most primordial disclosure of Dasein, leading him to wonder: "Has our investigation up to this point ever brought Dasein into view *as a whole?*"[59]

Heidegger opens the second division announcing that the *"exis-tential analysis of Dasein up till now cannot lay claim to primordiality."*[60] The reason is that, throughout the first division, the analysis had consid-ered no more than the *inauthentic* Dasein of the they-self and, there-fore, had comprehended "Dasein as *less* than a *whole.*" In other words, not the existence of authentic care, but the falling of inau-thentic care had been the focus. Heidegger emphasizes that the provisional interpretation of Dasein's Being will fail unless the pos-sibilities of its authenticity and totality can be brought to light. "Thus arises," he concludes, "the task of putting Dasein as a whole into our fore-having."[61]

The task of bringing "Dasein as a whole" into view is taken up in the first chapter of *Being and Time's* second division (II.1). It is in the search for this wholeness or totality that death, comprehended through "anticipation," is grasped as the ontological possibility whereby Dasein can be liberated to choose itself and take hold of itself.

The cue Heidegger follows is that every entity comes to an end that "limits and determines in every case whatever totality is possible." For Dasein, "Being-at-an-end" is death. "Thus the whole existing Dasein allows itself to be brought into our existential fore-having."[62] "Therewith," Heidegger concludes, "the possibility of Dasein's having an *authentic* potentiality-for-Being-a-whole emerges, but only as an ontological possibility."[63]

In spite of this statement, the reader is unprepared for the startling declaration that concludes the chapter: "Nevertheless, this existentially 'possible' Being-toward-death remains, from the existentiell point of view, a fantastical exaction. The fact that an authentic potentiality-for-Being-a-whole is ontologically possible for Dasein, signifies nothing, so long as a corresponding ontical potentiality-for-Being has not been demonstrated in Dasein itself."[64]

In Heidegger's mind, therefore, the chapter on Being-toward-death (II.1) has done nothing more than establish the ontological possibility of Dasein's Being-a-whole. This begs the question of whether or not Dasein can also exist *authentically* as a whole—as well as the criterion by which this can be evaluated. "Manifestly, Dasein itself must, in its Being, present us with the possibility and the manner of its authentic existence. . . ."[65]

In the second chapter of the division (II.2), Heidegger investigates the issue of Dasein's authenticity, seeking to discover if, existentielly, Dasein attests, "from its ownmost potentiality-for-Being, as to a possible *authenticity* of its existence.[66]

Shaken loose from the they (anticipating death), Dasein is thrown back upon itself, free at last to hear the call of conscience—the appeal of care itself—summoning Dasein's authentic Being.[67] Heidegger is at pains to distinguish the call of care from the ordinary understanding of conscience.[68] From Heidegger's perspective, conscience attests that Dasein is ontologically guilty, but this

"Being-guilty" is prior to an indebtedness or guilt arising from any action or inaction on the part of Dasein. Rather than challenge Dasein to rectify specific behavior and eradicate guilt, conscience appeals to Dasein to *be* guilty, to take up primordial Being-guilty, which constitutes authentic existence for Dasein.[69] The avoidance of this Being through fleeing or falling constitutes inauthenticity.[70]

While embedded in the "they," attuned only to the dictates of the mass, Dasein has been unable to recognize or hear its own deepest voice. The summons that abruptly arouses awareness, presenting Dasein's "ownmost potentiality-for-Being-its-Self," is an unnerving and constant threat to Dasein as an everyday element of the self-forgetful "they."[71] The call forward into this potentiality and possibility—its "bare 'that-it-is' in the 'nothing' of the world"—is a summons to *return to* and embrace the very self one already is, despite the fact that this self is covered over and closed off.[72]

The character of this Being that Dasein *is*, but generally fails to be, is called "thrownness."[73] This word is only part of a bizarre vocabulary that Adorno has justly called the "jargon of authenticity,"[74] but it possesses a certain logic of its own. Thrownness is a manifestation of the fact—or facticity—that Dasein is and has to be. Dasein has been thrown and delivered over to existence and abandoned to itself.[75] "That-it-is" evinces a quality of "alreadyness" over which one has absolutely no control, and it is this aspect of its existence that is particularly onerous for Dasein. Without consultation, election, option, or ratification, Dasein finds itself in Being, thrust into a situation beyond and prior to its efficacy. Dasein "has been brought into its 'there', but *not* of its own accord."[76] Heidegger adds that one can never get behind this thrownness so as to lead oneself into the "there."[77] In other words, Dasein can never establish its own basis or foundation, however much, in existing, it must take over "Being-a-basis."[78]

Heidegger's definition of guilt or the "formally existential idea of the 'Guilty!' " is *Being and Time's* cruelest exercise in bizarre jargon. "Guilty" is defined as "Being-the-basis for a Being which has been defined by a 'not'—that is to say," Heidegger clarifies with a pithy shorthand, "'Being-the-basis of a nullity'."[79]

In this definition, the element of a nullity or a "not" is, of course, thrownness, the fact that Dasein's Being is beyond itself, its own origination or constitution, with the impossibility of ever creating its own dispensation: Dasein's Being is *not* of or from itself. "Dasein is not itself the basis of its Being. . . ."[80]

Being-a-basis, nullity, thrownness, and guilt are synonymous. Implicit in this phenomenon is the profound impoverishment of finitude's radical limitation. The nullity of thrownness, however, is compounded and absolutized by the fact of death. Dasein is thrown toward death. It is no wonder that its Being is in issue, that awareness of thrownness is ordinarily closed off, or that "this nullity is the basis for the possibility of *in*authentic Dasein in its falling."[81] Dasein's situation—its "there"—is one of being helpless insofar as it *already* is and has to be, even into death. "'Being-a-basis' means *never* to have power over one's ownmost Being from the ground up."[82] Thus, Being-guilty constitutes the Being named care: "To be its own thrown basis is that potentiality-for-Being which is the issue for care."[83]

The second ingredient or element of guilt, "Being-the-basis of," simply indicates the fact that Dasein must assume responsibility for itself, taking over its Being and entering into this thrown situation of its "there."[84]

The character of responsibility is elucidated when Heidegger says that Being-a-basis means to exist *as thrown*.[85] It will be recalled that the inauthentic reaction to facticity is the flight of falling. The authentic response is *existing,* and to do so in full understanding of one's thrownness.[86] To exist means to *project* oneself into life toward one's ownmost potentiality-for-Being or death. Dasein's authentic responsibility—or ability to respond—to the call of conscience is manifested in hearing the call *resolutely,* reticently "taking action" as Being-guilty. In resoluteness Dasein embraces, or projects upon, its guilt ("which Dasein is as long as it is") and exists authentically.[87] Resoluteness lets oneself be summoned out of lostness in the "they" and brings the Being of the "there" into the situation of its "ownmost potentiality-for-Being-its-Self."[88]

In conscience, Dasein—as potentially authentic—is the caller and Dasein—as falling—is the one who is appealed to.[89] The "whence" of the call—the uncanniness of "Being-in-the-world as the 'not-at-home'"—is also the "whither" to which we are called back in being called forth.[90] While "the call comes *from* me," the call is not explicitly *by* me; instead, "'It' calls, against our expectations and even against our will."[91]

Unfamiliar and incomprehensible to the everyday they-self, the call strikes as an alien voice. "In its 'who', the caller is definable in a 'worldly' way by *nothing* at all."[92] Ignoring the *what* Dasein understands itself to be, misinterpreting itself proximately and for the most part "in terms of that with which it concerns itself," conscience summons Dasein to the "who" of a self "individualized down to itself . . . and thrown into the nothing."[93]

Remaining "empty in its what," the authentic self is a nobody and nothing "after the manner of the world."[94] This transformation into the null basis of resolute thrownness, with its revolution in identity from what to who, from some*thing* to nothing, is simply incomprehensible and without value to the common sense of the collectivity. Nevertheless, Dasein is radically deprived "of the possibility of misunderstanding itself": As *who*, I am there authentically in the world, no longer at home as a "what."[95]

The call of conscience, then, attests that we are guilty or basically null but appeals to us to resolutely assume responsibility for this primordial fact, entering into or projecting upon its possibility, our unique and ultimate potentiality. To do so is to exist authentically as the thrown (toward death) individual that each of us, in Being-there, is and cannot otherwise be.

William Richardson summarizes the emergence of authenticity: "There-being comes to its achievement in authenticity, insofar as it permits a strange uneasiness that steals upon it from time to time to estrange it from the ontic distractions that fill its every day, chooses to hearken to a voice that comes from within itself to tell it that it can transcend these beings unto Being but can never transcend its finitude."[96]

Chapter II.2 had opened with the concern that Dasein, because it was lost in the collectivity, had to be "shown" its possible authenticity or remain forever inauthentic. "In terms of its *possibility*,

Dasein *is* already a potentiality-for-Being-a-Self, but it needs to have this potentiality attested."[97] Authenticity was revealed through the distinctive disclosure of Dasein's conscience; with Dasein's response of resoluteness, "we have . . . that truth of Dasein which is most primordial because it is *authentic*."[98]

This existentiell authenticity uncovered in chapter II.2 must now be united with the existential totality or wholeness of Dasein's Being that was the concern of the first chapter of the second division. This takes place in chapter II.3 as Heidegger's logic unfolds itself, but it is easy for the reader to be impatient with the painstaking exposition. With little difficulty one has already perceived the unity of wholeness and authenticity. However implicitly, it is clear that the authenticity of finitude encompasses the entirety of one's life, from birth to death, and that the whole field of one's life, disclosed in Being-toward-death, necessarily comprehends the revelation of finitude.

In chapter II.3, Dasein's potentiality-for-Being-a-whole and its authenticity are explicitly united. It will be recalled that Dasein's (authentic) Being-toward-death, through which the whole of its life is comprehended, is realized by *anticipation*. On the other hand, Dasein's authentic disclosedness—that it is finite from beginning to end—is taken over through *resoluteness*, with Dasein reticent and ready for anxiety, projecting itself upon its ownmost Being-guilty in response to conscience's existentiell attestation.[99] This jargon simply means that Dasein, as authentic, moves forward into life at last accepting or taking responsibility for the fact that it *is*—beyond its determination and in spite of itself—and that only as such a contingent being can it truly exist.

Forgetting that thrownness was earlier characterized as being thrown into death (and, thus, a resolution to be guilty necessarily encompasses Being-toward-death), Heidegger asks, "What if it is only in the anticipation of death that resoluteness, as Dasein's *authentic* truth, has reached the *authentic certainty* which *belongs* to it . . . [so] that all the factical *'anticipatoriness'* of resolving would be authentically understood—in other words, that it would be *caught up with* in an existentiell way?"[100] Not surprisingly, the answer is affirmative.

"As *Being-towards-the-end which understands*—that is to say, as anticipation of death—resoluteness becomes authentically what it can be."[101] Only in anticipation of death is resoluteness completely and primordially itself, and only through resoluteness (taking over "in its existence the fact that it *is* the null basis of its own nullity") is Being-toward-death realized in an existentiell way.[102] Thus, Being-toward-death is attested from Dasein and not simply an "ontological projection" or "a fictitious possibility." Rather, "it is a *mode* of an existentiell potentiality-for-Being . . . which Dasein exacts of itself, if indeed it authentically understands itself as resolute."[103] Heidegger says that resoluteness harbors or hides Being-towards-death within itself.[104] Only as *anticipatory resoluteness* "is the potentiality-for-Being-guilty understood authentically and wholly—that is to say, primordially."[105]

Thus, anticipatory resoluteness discloses the "primordial truth of existence" that "must guarantee the understanding of the Being of Dasein"—and that provides, as well, the preparation for understanding Being in general.[106] In other words, through anticipation resoluteness grasps entirely the having been of its thrown nullity right to the end of death, bringing Dasein "back to its ownmost potentiality-for-Being-its-Self." Heidegger adds: "When one has an understanding Being-towards-death . . . as one's ownmost possibility—one's potentiality-for-Being becomes authentic and wholly transparent."[107]

Remaining open to the primordial truth of disclosed facticity,[108] Dasein is constantly faced with the revelation of its nullity. Threatened always with this anxiety-provoking situation, authentic resoluteness, to remain self-constant and situated *there*, cannot be a once-and-for-all commitment; instead, "authentic resoluteness . . . resolves to keep repeating itself."[109]

With the union of anticipation and resoluteness, "we have exhibited," Heidegger declares, "an authentic potentiality-for-Being-a-whole which belongs to Dasein . . . [and] have reached a way of Being of Dasein in which it brings itself to itself and face to face with itself, . . . dispersing all fugitive Self-concealments."[110] This openness to oneself opens the formerly closed and concealed

Dasein to the full horizon of its existing. This distinctive quality of anticipatory resoluteness, of Dasein's authentic Being, Heidegger calls "temporality."[111] Only as temporality is one authentically "there," embracing the *having been*[112] of thrownness into *futural* death through the moment of vision—or insight—of the authentic *present*.[113] "Only in so far as Dasein *is* as an 'I-*am*-as-having-been,' can Dasein come towards itself futurally," yet "only so far as it is futural can Dasein *be* authentically as having been."[114] Only as temporality is anticipatory resoluteness possible for and experienced by Dasein.[115] This threefold ecstasis[116] of openness releases one for—and *is*—the embrace of individualized finite Being. Resolutely understanding the radical and dual nullity of Being-guilty—thrust into Being without consent and cast out of existence without consultation—temporality, as authentic care,[117] shatters the grip of the collectivity.[118] With eyes at last open, one projects existence beyond the illusions of the "they."[119]

4

The Trauma of Death

Studies on Hysteria

. . . the Ocean of things lays siege to us.
—St.-John Perse, *Chronicle*

The purpose of the following scrutiny is to confront Heidegger's assertion that the encounter with death leads to authenticity. While it may be true that our being[1] is unto death, the realization of this profoundly elemental fact need not liberate one from the inauthenticity ingredient to, and tacitly mandated by, everyday collectivity. While such a deadly encounter may effect the appropriation of one's ownmost—or unique—facticity as Heidegger proposes, it should be equally apparent that a more dreadful reaction is also possible and much more likely to occur. If the appearance of death has the capacity to penetrate a narcissistic, erotic project with liberating consequences, the penetration can also be brutal and shattering. Rather than provide the essential parameter in an equation of authenticity, death may be apprehended as a massive, preempting threat, catapulting one more deeply into illusion and inauthenticity or, in Freud's terms, neurosis—and possibly psychosis.

Evidence of this is discovered in Freud's earliest cases, those published under the title of *Studies on Hysteria,* coauthored with Josef Breuer. To be certain, Freud was already operating under the assumption of a sexual etiology for neurosis.[2] Nevertheless, anyone conversant with the cases in *Studies on Hysteria* cannot fail to be impressed by the presence of death. In protean manifestation, death pervades all of the cases and is regnant in most. While it is impossible to examine the patients or to cross-examine Freud and, thus, impossible to know with exactitude what occasioned the pathology, it is clear on the face of these clinical reports that Freud's conclusions are not definitive.[3] While the following interpretations may challenge these conclusions, or rather their presuppositions, they do not repudiate the hypothesis of a sexual etiology for neurosis. Rather, and simply, they seek to show that such an etiology is not exclusive, that death is a concomitant in each of the cases, and that encountering death may compel one into neurosis as readily as any causation. In fact, both etiologies (the recoil from either sexuality or death) reveal precipitants that are penultimate and symbolic, reflecting the more radical and compelling datum of mortal *being* or finitude.[4] Either phenomenon—sexuality or death—has the power to unveil narcissistic illusion and dismantle the Eros of self-absorbed being, dethroning one's fictive omnipotence with soberingly rude finite reality.

In *Studies on Hysteria,* Freud is working with the hypothesis, first presented in the "Preliminary Communication," also coauthored with Josef Breuer and included in the volume, that psychical trauma can precipitate physical symptoms. The rationale for this conversion, Freud theorizes, is the splitting of thought and affect. An idea that is incompatible with the ego is repressed or excluded from consciousness while its excitations or affective energy, cut off from psychical association, are channeled along an erroneous path into somatic innervation. A splitting of consciousness results through the formation of an autonomous psychical group separated from the prevailing currents of the mind, with—implicit in this understanding—a truncation of personal agency.

ELISABETH

In the case of Elisabeth von R., his concluding study in this volume, Freud attempts to marshal the conclusion that Elisabeth's hysteria was due to a tender regard for the husband of her now deceased elder sister and the vital wish to become the widower's spouse. "So for a long time you had been in love with your brother-in-law," Freud triumphantly exclaims. This "incompatible idea," he reasons, "was resisted by her whole moral being. She succeeded in sparing herself the painful conviction that she loved her sister's husband, by inducing physical pains in herself instead. . . ."[5] Elisabeth's rejection of this gratuitous explanation, with an attendant outburst of emblematic pain, was regarded as an indication of strong resistance to uniting the repressed ideational group with the rest of consciousness. However, what was overlooked was the very force of Freud's assertion, which itself might be reason enough for the girl's outburst, not unlike a later and similar therapeutic blunder in the handling of Dora.[6] In wiser moments the technique of both incidents would have been eschewed by Freud since he came to the conclusion that precipitate communications were disastrously unprofessional.[7]

Whatever the contributory or complicating elements of Elisabeth's affection for her brother-in-law, this affection is not likely to have been the precipitating cause of the neurosis. Rather than being a split-off and repressed ideational group in Elisabeth's psyche, her relational posture to her brother-in-law was patently in everyone's awareness, including Elisabeth's own.

Prior to her sister's death, Elisabeth was cognizant of her own appreciation for this special in-law. She was sufficiently impressed by the quality of his relationship with her sister that she hoped to find someone of similar quality for her own marital bliss. The sister was no less aware of the mutual regard of her spouse and Elisabeth, and she encouraged their association. Most significantly, Elisabeth was able to recall and readily articulate the thought that shot through her mind as she stood at her sister's bedside, beholding the lifeless body and regretting that she had arrived too late to say farewell: "Now he is free and I can be his wife."[8] If pain and ambulatory incapacity have been the telltale indicators of Elisabeth's hysteria, then the absence of these criteria in the face of such a direct and spontaneous, but potentially alarming, avowal is a clear manifestation that her conflict or incompatible and repressed idea is not the relationship to her brother-in-law.

A deeper, more foundational split appears to be present. Had evidence not already accumulated in Freud's rehearsal of his sessions with the young lady, the question put to Elisabeth about her sister's death and the anguished rail journey from Gastein to the deathbed would have directed our attention: "I asked her," Freud recounts, "whether during the journey she had thought of the grievous possibility which was afterwards realized. She answered that she had carefully avoided the thought. . . ."[9]

In fact, there seems to have been a virtual conspiracy between Freud and the young woman to avoid the topic of death, including the reality of a deceased father. Never does he ask, "How did your father's passing affect you?" or "How did you feel, or what were you thinking, as you stood by his deathbed or at the grave site?" Toward the middle of treatment Freud does encourage the girl to go (alone) to her sister's burial site in order "to bring up fresh memories," but he fails to inquire about the thoughts and feelings evoked at her graveside vigils.[10] Moreover, in flagrant violation of his theory, her acknowledged resistance to facing the possibility of her sister's death, a virtual invitation for his exploration or intervention, is utterly ignored, passed over in silent complicity. In their sessions he never broaches the subject of her losses or of death's impact upon her life. Death remains always outside the therapeutic session and is never allowed to become an issue therein, while her father's specter broods over the entire account, scrupulously unattended.

At one point, seeking fruitlessly to bolster his theory of sexual etiology for this hysteria, Freud remarks that "I obtained no result when I tried to discover a psychical cause for [the pains]. . . ,"[11] overlooking the fact that the encounter with death, especially a parent's death, could inflict a sufficiently violent impingement on the young girl's psyche.

Freud's account of the therapy sometimes fluctuates as much as the spontaneous alterations of Elisabeth's condition that he recounts, but the inception of the girl's illness appears to have occurred at the moment her father was carried into the house, felled by a heart attack. Transfixed with fright, "she stood stock still as though rooted to the ground" as her father, vivacious man of the world and foundation of the family's social position and prestige, was carried, unconscious, to his bed.[12] This was the *first* of the "scenes with painful impressions" that she recounted, and eighteen months later her father would be dead.

A bold highlight is not needed to realize that a life-threatening illness, even death, was present at this threshold. It was death, itself, that Elisabeth viewed as she watched the comatose figure carried to his sickbed for what inevitably became a last confinement. It was this recognition that incapacitated her with paralyzing fright.

At some point during the six-month period immediately prior to her father's death, pains forced Elisabeth, herself, to bed for a day and a half, but she insisted that these had demanded no attention after quickly dissipating. While the onset of illness with chronic inability to walk was not realized until two years after her father's death, the focus of this original pain perduring throughout the illness and the treatment with Freud was a "fairly large, ill-defined area of the anterior surface of the right thigh."[13] This portion of the leg suffered the most intensive pain, and it was from there that it radiated most often.

Elisabeth's sessions with Freud elicited the discovery that the painful area was associated with her father. It was on this spot that the ill gentleman rested a badly swollen leg each morning as his daughter changed the bandage.

When Freud says, ignoring the traumatic intensity of a dying parent and the "painful impressions" that Elisabeth had revealed, that a psychical cause for her symptoms failed to appear, he is not wholly in bad faith, nor is he necessarily evading the recognition of death, whether for his own safeguard or for Elisabeth's. Whatever blindness to the profound specter before him, his young patient is understood, at least in part, in light of the reigning presupposition of the period. Hysteria was conceived as a woman's ailment and believed to be caused, if early Greek physicians were trusted, by a wandering uterus—the "inner woman" searching for personal and marital bliss in the reality of childbearing.[14] In consequence, Freud's (and, in part, Breuer's) brilliant understanding of the mechanism of hysteric symptomatology—that is, the conversion of psychical affect into somatically manifested pain due to the division of thought and excitation, with the former's suppression—was wedded to the traditional, if unscientific, hypothesis of a sexual etiology.

As characterized by Freud, the atypical hysterogenic zone of the thigh that Elisabeth presented could have alerted a detached scientific observer, which Freud sought to be, to the presence or possibility of etiology beyond the traditionally imputed sexual one, especially with the significant association that the changing of her father's bandages occasioned. The crippling right thigh symbolizes her participation in the inevitable body of death that threatened to force its consciousness upon her through the pathos of a dying father. Rejecting this ultimate awareness of her father's impending demise and, subsequently, its brutal realization as well as her own bequeathed ending, Elisabeth was necessarily confronted by painful, somatized affect, detached from the suppressed idea and petitioning for a recognition of these definitive realities. The power of repression, Freud has said in something of a tautology, is an indication of the intensity of resistance. Elisabeth's resistance was tenacious to the point that painful associations multiplied, partaking of the crippled thigh's emblematic sharing in the unbearable corpse, indicating that these subsequent traumatic occurrences in Elisabeth's life were associated with the realities of death, loss, and limits occasioned by her father.

In fact, both legs shared in the pathology. The painful right leg was associated with memories concerning both her father and a young male friend of her youth, while pain in the left leg was associated with recollections of *either* of her two brothers-in-law. Since Freud speculated that repressed sexual inclinations toward the young man paralleling conditions vis-à-vis the favored in-law were integral to Elisabeth's illness, it would be expected that the similar etiological conflicts should be associated with the same appendage. The fact that they are not strengthens the assessment that etiology is to be found elsewhere. The presence of the first brother-in-law, husband of Elisabeth's eldest sister, as an ingredient of the chronic disability further undermines Freud's hasty diagnosis and highlights a trauma of death, loss, and limitation. Not only was this elder in-law not an object of affection, he was disdained as a family antagonist.

For that matter, the widower himself was not exempt from family censure. However highly regarded otherwise, he was castigated for inflicting the severest blow upon the family, second only to the father's death. His wife, the beloved sister, "succumbed to an affection of the heart which had been aggravated by her pregnancy."[15] Since there had been childhood indications of cardiac disorder, the family was distraught that the marriage had been permitted in the first instance. Nevertheless, the surviving spouse was reproached for "having endangered his wife's health by bringing on two pregnancies in immediate succession."[16] Displeasure with the widower intensified after his refusal to allow Elisabeth and her mother to have custody of the surviving child. Thus, both in-laws stood in positions analogous to death as family antagonists.

It is not surprising that the young friend plays a role in Elisabeth's hysteria since he was profoundly associated with the father. An orphan, the youth was devoted to Elisabeth's father, Freud tells us, and the admired gentleman functioned paternally for the young man, counseling him in his career and, undoubtedly, in other instances as well. Recollections of one so closely identified with the deceased would be sufficient to evoke painful associations with her father, yet the associations are more richly determined than this.

Standing in the place of a son, the youth's surrogate role exactly parallels Elisabeth's position vis-à-vis her father "who used to say that this daughter of his took the place of a son and [was] a friend with whom he could exchange thoughts."[17] Thus, to recall the young man was to think of herself in the figure of a son, though solely in relation to a now absent father. Most important, this loss through death parallels Elisabeth's relationship with the young man, who represented all that was best and deepest in her relationship with her father.

In the egalitarian atmosphere shared by the gentleman and his precocious daughter, Elisabeth developed a heedless honesty of strong opinions and sure judgments. Ambitious plans gestated as well, with Elisabeth anxious for study or musical training. She became indignant at the prospect of sacrificing integrity and freedom of judgment to the traditional expectations of a nineteenth-century marriage. Her father recognized that these dispositions and intellectual powers deviated from the ideal of a young woman for that period, and he cautioned that she was unlikely to find a husband. With the young man, however, she was presented with someone who understood her, and the love that he offered held out the prospect that she would not have to abandon her strengths in the dreaded diminishment of a mindless contemporary marriage. In this hope, the young man reflected all that was treasured in her relationship with her father, even though he was not yet self-supporting and prepared for the financial responsibilities of wedlock.

As she dedicated herself to her father, awaiting a turn for the better, so, also, did she dedicate herself to the young man, expectantly awaiting him. As her hopes were disappointed when the ameliorating turn failed to arrive, so, too, were they destroyed by the young man. The wrenching loss suffered with the death of her father was paralleled by the unexpected termination—or death—of her relationship to the young man. This loss was sustained when life took him in new directions following her father's death. When the gentleman died his alter ego disappeared, too. It was this association that added power to the painful memory of the defunct relationship that, in its vitality, so mirrored herself in relation to her father, making it an ingredient of the painful right thigh and all it symptomatically recalled of the absent father.

The episodes with her favorite brother-in-law, the spouse of her eventually deceased sister, also derive torturous significance from associations with her father and, thus, with the mortality she was never able to face. A natural rapport with this in-law allowed as fluid a conversation as she had known with her father. Once again, she found the same collegiality and thoughtful engagement that she had first enjoyed with her father and had lost with his death.

Significantly, the two key episodes at the health resort that link Elisabeth's illness to the brother-in-law in Freud's mind are not exclusively concerned with him at all, and closer inspection reveals his role to be symbolic and mediating. There are two somewhat conflicting renditions for both of the major incidents at the resort. Initially, it is said that, although Elisabeth had been aware to some degree of prior pain for a short while, a bath subsequent to a half-day walk at the vacation site a few days earlier was the occasion of the first violent pain and the onset of her chronic condition. The walk was highlighted only because the family believed that the pains arose because Elisabeth had been overexerted and become exhausted on the path. The walk received greater importance in a second account when it was said that "she remembered being very tired and suffering from violent pain when she returned from the walk."[18] To this was added the fact that she was uncertain as to whether or not she had already noticed pains before this episode.

While the first account represents "superficial" memories at the start of treatment and the second presents recollections from a "deeper" phase of therapy, it is impossible to gauge the more accurate account since two renditions (both from the deeper period) of a second walk reveal similar discrepancies. Following Freud's own logic that Elisabeth would not have attempted a walk had she been suffering significant pain, we can discount the second report of violent pains following the initial walk because a few days later she undertook the second trek. Thus, it is more than likely that any pain experienced after the first walk was of a less than violent nature and passed speedily without alarm. This conclusion is strengthened by the more strenuous character of the second hike that negotiated a hill, apparently to its summit.

The second hike occurred in the early morning of the day following the departure of Elisabeth's sister and brother-in-law. Before the lovely hilltop view, Elisabeth became lost in thought. In the first account of this event she returned from her hillside meditation with violent pains. These made their definitive and perduring appearance that very evening after a warm bath. The second account has her experiencing pain at the conclusion of her hillside rhapsodies "when she stood up, but it passed off once more. It was not until the afternoon, when she had had the warm bath, that the pains broke out, and she was never again free from them."[19]

Whatever may have been the significance of the second excursion, both accounts point to the bathing episode as the pivotal occurrence that transformed her condition into chronic disability: "From this time on Elisabeth was the invalid of the family."[20] Thus, the bathhouse is the key to the entire matrix of events and to discovery of whatever associations link the discrete incidents of two walks and a bath, providing a conspicuous indication of Elisabeth's etiology.

Trying to ascertain what thoughts had occupied her during the bath, Freud learned from Elisabeth that "the bath-house had reminded her of the members of her family who had gone away, because that was the building in which they had stayed."[21] To rephrase this, the bathhouse was the dwelling in which the family, together anew, had *lived*. For Elisabeth, the dismemberment of the intact family excited delicate associations with a father who, irredeemably, had also "gone away."

Exploring the cause of the initial episode, Freud asked Elisabeth "what it was in the walk that might have brought on the pain." According to his account, she replied that "the contrast between her own loneliness and her sick sister's married happiness (which her brother-in-law's behaviour kept constantly before her eyes) had been painful to her." This parallels, in part, her thoughts on the hillside the morning after her sister and brother-in-law had left the resort. One account of those thoughts has her concerned with "her loneliness and the fate of the family; and this time she openly confessed to a burning wish that she might be as happy as her sister."[22] Another account simply says that she "dreamt once again of enjoying such happiness as her sister's and of finding a husband . . . like this brother-in-law of hers."[23] The fact that she is aware of such thoughts (about her loneliness and her sister's marital bliss) is, as already noted, one indication, supplemented by the unity of thought and affect (the "burning desire" of one episode and the painful character of the earlier one) that these conscious issues cannot, by definition, be the nucleus of her hysteria.[24] Rather, the enunciated concerns of loneliness and marital happiness appear to be screen memories, camouflaging her actual dilemma and the true crisis. The issue of a screen memory will be examined in due course, but, first, the shared associations that provide insight into Elisabeth's situation may be further explored.

In asking a leading question—what, *in the walk,* precipitated the pain—Freud may have inadvertently misdirected or prejudiced Elisabeth's response. The fact may be that nothing in the walk triggered the pain. Since the pain was experienced after their return, once the venture had been concluded, it is possible that some condition or event at the resort itself primed the painful stimulus. If, instead, the question is asked, "What condition or situation existed at the resort that might have troubled Elisabeth?" the answer is readily apparent. The holiday resort represented the reunion and, thus, unity of the three families[25] after difficult times. In the face of the father's absence, however, this gathering represented the actual disunity of the family. Returning to the hostel after the walk's diversion, therefore, confronted Elisabeth anew with the dire prospect that the family's integrity had been concretely shattered and could never be realized again. Aggravating this awareness was the fact of her eldest sister's early departure. As Freud phrased it, she "had already gone away,"[26] and the loss, Elisabeth knew, was virtually irrevocable since the sister's husband, anticipating a promotion, had moved his family to a remote Austrian village. This breech of cohesion, which coincidentally sharpened their mother's isolation, formed a primary reproach that Elisabeth leveled against the insensitive brother-in-law.

These somber considerations pressed with renewed vigor as, unaccustomedly alone after the holiday companionship, she faced the hillside view on her second, early morning climb. "Once again [she was] concerned with her loneliness and the fate of her family,"[27] and this bleak prospect was woefully compounded by her solitary journey to the very spot that had been shared so often with her sister and brother-in-law as a favorite haven. Only a void now marked their presence, the absence heightened by the recent departures.

Both losses, or departures, connect profoundly with the bath-house and its significance as the space wherein the vacationing family had reunited under the cloud of their father's premature "departure." As Elisabeth bathed, these loved ones could be present only in their absence and loss as those "who had gone away."[28] Not only were the family's ill fortune, shattered unity, and scattered presence associated with, because occasioned by, the same catastrophic loss, but any thought of absent loved ones would lead necessarily, if unconsciously, to a consideration, however resisted or repressed, of that paramount figure who was irrevocably away and present only as an absolute privation. What Elisabeth resisted with all her strength was the recollection of her father and the death that had destroyed her well-being and that of the entire family.

From this perspective, it is easier to apprehend Elisabeth's unhappiness as a screen memory. Her melancholy was neither prompted nor intensified by her sister's contrasting (marital) bliss. It was, in fact, diminished to the measure that her sister's happiness proffered an external focus for her disenchantment. Otherwise, the discord she experienced would have to be sustained wholly within, and the tension of such disharmony might be sufficient to rent her utterly.

The extent to which being married or unmarried bears upon Elisabeth's health, if at all, reflects not her sister's situation but the vital relationship with her father. We recall that Elisabeth had developed, by reason of this relationship, a headstrong and independent character that her father warned was unlikely to attract a spouse. It is precisely because of these traits and this character, which thrived and matured vis-à-vis the gentleman, that she is presently unable to secure the anticipated boon of marriage. It is clear that the poor girl cannot assign this incapacity—or responsibility for it—to her father. The dear man is dead, and this death is the greatest misfortune for both Elisabeth and the family. To attribute culpability in his direction would be villainy. Elisabeth, therefore, is imprisoned in a conflict between loving her father and blaming, perhaps hating, him. Since censure is unthinkable, the conflict is transposed to the living, herself contrasted in misery to her sister and her sister's happiness. Above all, with this slight of hand serving as a screen, the recollection of death is banished from consciousness and confrontation with it avoided, since to blame the father would recall his passing and the provoking trauma.

In fact, Elisabeth's loneliness appeared before the problematic of her unmarried state. Though decisively constituted with her father's death, it was initiated by the isolation at his bedside. The definitive mark inflicted with the death arose from the resolution Elisabeth, herself, forged at the deathbed. There she determined to do everything possible to restore her family's unity and lost prestige. Needless to say, this very dedication to virtually unattainable goals assured Elisabeth's segregation from the normal life and activities of a young woman.

If a closer look is taken of the pledge fashioned in the wake of her father's death, a revealing discovery emerges. As previously recognized, the father's demise occasioned the family's own. Position eroded and prestige eclipsed, social isolation compounded the family's jeopardy. For the daughter who "jealously guarded everything that was bound up with these advantages" wrought by her father, the gap that had been created by her family's truncated existence was an especially severe blow.[29] Reacting to "the breaking-off of so many connections that had promised to bring her interest and enjoyment,"[30] Elisabeth stepped forward to fill the gap, determined to stem any danger, repair the misfortune, and restore her family's former glory.

She assumed responsibility for rebuilding the lost happiness or, at least, providing a substitute for it. When the eldest sister's husband conducted himself irreverently toward her ailing and widowed mother, insensitive to the family's need for unity, it was Elisabeth alone who defended the family integrity, indignant at his callous behavior and chagrined at her sisters' apathy. It was she, as well, who most zealously fought to preserve the familial intimacy that had formerly existed. In short, at her father's deathbed, Elisabeth resolved, as defiantly as she could, to rebuild a new life for herself and her family.

Scrutiny reveals that Elisabeth had taken on the role of the absent father and was now standing in his place. She had shouldered the

burdens and assumed the functions of the family head, so identifying with these responsibilities that, not surprisingly, she is paralyzed,
unable to take a step on her own behalf. Powerless to move forward
into her own life, she, herself, is thwarted. A second look reveals that
Elisabeth is attempting to undo, if not her father's death, at least the
ill effects of that occurrence, with its diminishment of and insult to
her narcissistic advantages. Through repression and through her
endeavors, she is locked into—and thus blocked by—a double denial
of that upheaval. An alert reader may have recognized that her identification is actually with death.

The paradox is that although Elisabeth resists admitting death to
consciousness, such energy is expended in its repression that she is
enthralled to it. Bound up and by this unconscious struggle, she is
not free for life. Instead, and incapable of the psychic burdens of
reality, her existence is reduced to a compulsive substitute for
mature, human living that resists mortality and the vicissitudes of
the finite. Her life is sacrificed to death. By the time the actual hysteric conversion takes place, identification is complete. For the two
years prior to meeting Freud, Elisabeth—identifying with the
aggressor as Anna Freud[31] would later phrase it—has been an incipient corpse, suffering from painfully impaired mobility, "functional
paralysis" as identified by Freud.[32]

This defensive evasion manifested itself from the very onset of
misfortune. Elisabeth's cry that she cannot take a step forward orig-
inated in the experience of being rooted to the ground at that terrifying moment when her stricken father was paraded before her:
how can one take a forward step in the face of the forbidding prospect of one's mortality and death, glimpsed in the visage of a father?
Freud, himself, had a sense of this when, at the close of treatment,
he observed that the path was now open for Elisabeth. The utterance is unintelligible in Freud's habitual context of frustrated
erotic interest since the hypothetical interest, the widower, was
unquestionably out of the picture by this time. Elisabeth's mother
had underscored to Freud that, for numerous reasons, she and family advisors did not find this match a suitable one.

From the beginning, then, death blocked Elisabeth's path, usurping her life through the unthinkable trauma. Defenses circumvented, or attempted to circumvent, this life-insulting blow. Her reaction could be anticipated—narcissistic recoil toward security and Erotic recoupment of the plundered life.

In the face of imminent death, denial ensued: the thought of its encounter was split from its affect—anxiety—and repressed. Into her resistance all the energy of the split-off affect necessarily and naturally flowed, pouring into the activities of denial and recoupment that maintained narcissism's illusion of omnipotent control.

This provides an understanding of why there was no pain—or memory of pain—until the vacation. Freud had conjectured that bodily pain was present from the beginning of Elisabeth's trauma but that it simply was not recalled. However that may be, it is also probable that the intensity of Elisabeth's defense absorbed the entire quota of affect. In other words, activities prior to the vacation were wholly somatic—her total embodied being thrown into the effort—expending all of the released energy, and no conscious pain surfaced.

Once the failure of her enterprise became apparent and defenses evaporated, the trauma—with death at the threshold of awareness—was admitted indirectly to consciousness through somatic expression as the only remaining tactic that might ward off direct exposure to the threatening realization.

Prior to the holiday, Elisabeth was already experiencing helplessness, inability, the frustration of her hopes, and the collapse of her desires; moreover, she was "embittered by the failure of all her little schemes for re-establishing the family's former glories."[33] When the holiday placed all defensive endeavors in abeyance, the energy was channeled, with no other outlet, into bodily symptoms. Pain, attended by disability, ascended.

United at the holiday resort, the von R. family "hoped that Elisabeth, who had been exhausted by the anxieties of the last few months, would make a complete recovery during what was the first period of freedom from sorrows and fears that the family had enjoyed since her father's death."[34] The recovery failed to materialize. Instead, Elisabeth's condition worsened, taking its acute, incapacitating form.

Writing of the turning points in life, John S. Dunne has noted that if the ultimate crisis is death, the penultimate crisis is the apprehension of death. "Here the temptation to panic and seize control of life becomes most acute."[35] In the face of death, as we have seen, Elisabeth single-handedly attempted to coerce her life and the family's fate. Contrary to family expectations, the freedom of holiday leisure vacated nothing but Elisabeth's desperate endeavors, stripping her utterly of control. Bereft of protecting illusions, Elisabeth faced existence—and the death she had avoided for two years—beyond immunity, exposed to the mortality of a nakedly vulnerable self. Reality, disclosing limits, constraints, contingency, and failure—in a word, finitude—and inherently traumatic for narcissistic being, impinged relentlessly upon Elisabeth during the mountain interval.

This burden and crisis of freedom did not rest solely upon a spacious leisure, incapable of supporting Elisabeth's rigorous denials. Freedom's possibility, Kierkegaard tells us, is heralded by anxiety. This is so because freedom is not the ability of doing this or that or, more radically, the ability of choosing good or evil. The possibility of freedom is the very possibility of a self, of becoming and being a self, for the self is freedom. Largely—and perhaps for a lifetime—infantile, childish, unconscious,[36] the self is a relation that—if ever at all—first relates to itself in anxiety and, in the face of its anxious possibility, succumbs and collapses.[37] Thus did Elisabeth, her*self,* collapse.

Recalling a cue from Freud that, at the end of treatment, the path lay open for Elisabeth,[38] we can recognize that aggravating the collision between self and death—and initiating the process of self-encounter that eventuated in the pain of defensive conversion—were the very paths that Elisabeth and her family so innocently and thoughtlessly hiked.

Kierkegaard reminds us of a simple yet powerful association for the human psyche: in common parlance, there is a "universal, generally accepted metaphor that compares life to a way."[39] This way of life is a deadly way. To walk the way or path of life is to trod a path that leads unavoidably to the grave. Even paths of glory, Thomas Gray reminds us, lead but to a grave.[40]

To walk the mountain paths, then, and however unreflectively or unconsciously, was to share in this elemental sensitivity to the human situation. This primordial relationship, however, was richly overdetermined for Elisabeth through associations with her father and connections to him through the person of her sister's husband. On the ominous day that all the family somehow sensed was pivotal for her hysteric conversion, Elisabeth walked these fatefully significant paths with the young in-law who surreptitiously linked her anew to a deceased father and, thus, to death.

On the portentous walk—with Elisabeth's sister, sick and confined to bed, having urged her spouse to join the group for Elisabeth's sake—the brother-in-law evoked recollections of the egalitarian atmosphere Elisabeth had known with her father. The two, it will be recalled, could engage in the profoundest conversation with complete accord. Unwittingly, Elisabeth found herself traversing paths in unconscious association with her father.

In traveling with her father, she trod the way of her father. For Elisabeth, it was a deadly path that suffered not only the grave but the burdens of mortality—the way of the earth, the path of ephemeral finitude. Such marks define the way and all those who find them*selves* upon it, even those who resist its recognition, including the omnipotent personality of Erotic narcissism. The lesion of mortality is the ultimate narcissistic wound.

"The awareness of [one's] mortality," John S. Dunne writes, "is a tragic sense of life; it is a consciousness that deprives [one] of the illusion of immortality that can go with living merely in the here and now."[41] The "illusion of immortality" perfectly describes the Erotic dynamism and its narcissistic enterprise. This infantile consciousness (remaining substantially unconscious, as Freud has noted and Searles has underscored), effectively experiences itself as immortal, product of Eros's insatiably self-oriented aggression for life, striving and struggling to be ever greater. To suffer the way of the earth, that is, to move from narcissistic omnipotence and immortality to a vulnerable mortality—or to be threatened by

awareness of such a possibility—would exact a diminishment or rel-
ativizing of oneself among the multiplicity of realities that would be
equivalent to death, terminating the secure structures of an impregnable power that comprehends no absolute beyond itself. It would be a
vital if precarious exodus to hazard this passage, embracing the earth,
usurping nothing of another's but sharing the path of life with all.

Elisabeth exemplifies the hazards of this challenge. When the
intrusion of death uprooted her life and its anticipated course, she
recoiled from the shock, grasping for stability by experiencing herself as rooted to the ground—vain security against the intransigence
of death. The attempted self-grounding was itself uprooted, if
unconsciously, by her experience of the way, which represented an
incipient passage beyond defenses and, consequently, an uprooting
of security.

"[W]hen living becomes an earnest matter," Kierkegaard says,
alert to the crisis that life inevitably discloses, "then the question
becomes: How should one walk, in order to walk the right way on
the way of life?"[42]

"[I]f one is willing to walk alone and willing to be in need," John
S. Dunne writes, as if in response to Kierkegaard's observation,
"one travels the way."[43] One necessarily travels alone—that is,
responsibly standing on one's own feet—even if, like Elisabeth, one
travels with companions or, also like Elisabeth, one finds intimacy
in shared agreement. One walks alone because no other, as Heidegger realized, can walk for you. In the company of many, the com-
mencement is, nevertheless, an individual one, risking alone. If one
embarks upon this way, Kierkegaard's "right way," Heidegger's path
of authentic being, one must walk in need because one is, oneself,
the way of finite contingency, scarred head to toe with mortality,
endlessly open and incomplete. One must walk in need because
"the willingness to be in need enables one to take the way into the
human circle."[44] Dunne's prescription of neediness is identical to
Kierkegaard's diagnosis for humanizing change: instead of being
master of one's fate, "become one in need."[45]

In Kierkegaard's view, not to know oneself, one's deepest and
authentic self, is utter delusion. What he calls the real or deeper self

"seems . . . to be so far distant that the whole world seems much closer."[46] The world, in fact, appears "as favorable as possible," and it is as if "they are just waiting for each other, as it were: the happy self and the favors of fortune. . . ."[47] The fortunate or first or inconstant self (all of which Kierkegaard applies to this master of fate) believes itself to be in possession of everything necessary to achieve its ambition.

Already similarities with Elisabeth's circumstances are discernible, but with insights virtually anticipating her predicament, Kierkegaard continues his analysis: Nevertheless, the deeper self is relentless and refuses to withdraw, attending to the first self like a "physician at the bedside of the sick," or at a deathbed, as he subsequently remarks.[48] The physician begins with antidotes that any offering resistance must experience with anxiety "as a shocking delusion," for instead of the whole world one gains only oneself; instead of mastering life, one becomes a needy petitioner; instead of being able to do all things, one discovers that one "is capable of nothing at all."[49] It is as though, Kierkegaard says, the deeper self barred the way of the fortunate self, interfering with its outward movement, with aspirations and yearnings for success in its pursuits. The outcome, Kierkegaard adds, is that the first self, powerless to take a single step forward, "cannot move from the spot."[50] Anticipating what Freud would call repression, Kierkegaard says that the first but inconstant self must either yield to its authentic being or "silence" it, continuing "to kill the deeper self, to render it forgotten."[51]

Elisabeth did not yield. Exposure in traversing the way of the earth proved too great a danger, promising to bring her, anew, face to face with realities she could not yet confront. This tragic or hopeful passage, this possible emergence into a genuinely human reality, was initiated for Elisabeth by the enigma of death and its catalytic potential. There is, as Heidegger says, something profound about death that, when it confronts our life, we cannot evade without serious peril. Nevertheless, as Heidegger did not admit, that same revelation can be overpowering, leading one to evade, resist, or repress the encroaching presence and whatever truth it promises or threatens to uncover. As we see with Elisabeth, *pace* Heidegger, the encounter with death need not lead to authentic life nor lead one into the human circle. Instead, it can hurl one into the evasion and flight of neurosis, if nothing worse.

Elisabeth short-circuited the exposure to death and concomitant realization of mortal being, attempting to seal the lesion of authenticity through self-sustaining hubris and repression, the portal of awareness guarded by neurotic illusions. Nevertheless, the wound would not heal. Despite denial and defense, human needfulness perdures. One remains always in need, helplessly open to the vicissitudes and vexations of the finite, against which all defense is simply sham. Repressing the recognition of death and the realization of mortality, Elisabeth repressed as well the possibility of emerging into a new if vulnerable self, a more open, compassionate, and conscious way of being human. Without experiencing and feeling the rending truthfulness of death, her way—she herself—was barred, an obstacle to authentic life in the human circle. She traded the painful vision of reality for a body in pain, symptom and symbol of the finitude she could not consciously embrace. In multiple if varying measures, the reality of death is present in all of the major cases of *Studies on Hysteria*.

ANNA O.

The case of Anna O., a sole presentation by Josef Breuer, Freud's coauthor, most resembles Elisabeth's because, like Elisabeth, Anna was a young woman of extremely gifted intellect who suffered hysterical conversion after nursing her dying father.[52] To some extent, Breuer's case represents the overwhelming of fact by theory, with Breuer failing to assess the leverage of death. Breuer's favored hermeneutic for understanding hysteria was the hypnoid state.[53] The mental splitting of hysteria, he believed, was caused by the absence of communication between various states of consciousness. Excitations arising during the peculiar mental condition of a hypnoid state "can easily become pathogenic because such states do not provide opportunities for the normal discharge of the process of excitation."[54] The products of hypnoid states were supposed to penetrate into "waking consciousness" with the disruptive force of unassimilated foreign matter. Breuer speculated that exhaustion from lengthy hours of dedicated nursing had diminished Anna's consciousness, creating the split of a hypnoid state. Armed with his presupposition, Breuer never considered the phenomenon of death or its possible traumatic impact.

LUCY

In the case of Lucy, strong correspondences with additional elements of Elisabeth's situation come into view. Paralleling Elisabeth's deathbed resolution, Lucy bound herself by a deathbed promise that effectively placed her, not unlike Elisabeth, in the role once occupied by the deceased. To the dying woman, a distant relative of her mother, Lucy pledged—she told Freud—that "I would devote myself with all my power to the children, that I would not leave them and that I would take their mother's place. . . ."[55]

The pivotal episode of the case occurred in the context of Lucy's ambivalence about leaving the household and abandoning her charges. At the moment of ostensible crisis, Lucy was supervising the children at play. They were cooking in the schoolroom of the estate when a letter arrived from Lucy's mother. Jocundly, the children tore the letter from Lucy's hands, insisting that it was for her birthday, two days hence, and that it should not be opened until then. The smell of burnt pudding, suddenly apparent as the children's cooking experiment went awry during this affectionate interlude, persisted as a recurrent olfactory hallucination, although Lucy had otherwise suffered a total loss of smell. Freud concluded that the agitation precipitating trauma and hysteric conversion was a conflict between opposing affects, the desire to leave versus a regret for relinquishing this nurturing service and the endearing, vulnerable children.

In puzzling out the loose ends of the case, Freud rightfully observes that "it was not until this trauma, or at any rate this small tale of trouble, that the girl had acquired hysteria."[56] This underscores that the dilemma over staying or leaving was not a sufficient psychological issue to be the traumatic catalyst. Lucy had lived with the uncertainty of this alternative—and with the fact that in giving notice she had reneged on her deathbed pledge—without these deliberations occasioning the least degree of neurotic symptomatology. Rather, as the olfactory sensations attest, the schoolroom drama, itself, is the venue that alone can properly reveal Lucy's conflict.

The associations that neither Lucy nor Freud perceived were simple but profound ones. Lucy's mother, alive and present via her letter, contrasted rudely with the absence and loss of the children's mother, stolen from them by death. It was this intrusion on the part of death, occasioned by the letter and proving incompatible with "the dominant mass of ideas constituting the ego," that Lucy "had sought intentionally to leave in obscurity and had made efforts to forget."[57] The children, who had already suffered the loss of one mother to an untimely death, were now, Lucy unconsciously realized, on the verge of experiencing that death anew through the loss of a second, much beloved, if surrogate, mother. Considering the consequences of a projected departure, Lucy was forced to behold once again the unwelcome aura of death, underscored by the letter's arrival from her living mother.

However, with Freud, we can ask why the trauma would be signaled by a smell, "why, out of all the sense-perceptions afforded by the scene, she had chosen this smell as a symbol?"[58] The smell of burnt pudding was the most appropriate and accessible mnemic symbol, to use Freud's technical term. As the advent of death fouled her well-ordered life, or—to use the proper metaphor—as the stench of death assailed her, rising in consciousness, the offending organ was blocked. Lucy suffered a general loss of smell, while the noxious odor and reality were wished and whisked out of mind, thoroughly masked by the smell of burnt pudding. Not only did this smell taint the air at the threatening moment of recognition when death struck Lucy's awareness anew, it was also especially suitable since burnt pudding signified the failure of what otherwise might have been a successfully sweet enterprise. In light of this trauma, what hitherto had been relatively inconsequential events, dealt with successfully, now became recast and reconstrued, melding with the single traumatic issue, all necessitating Freud's aid.

A chronology of the significant events leading up to, and encompassed by, the schoolroom trauma reveals that Lucy's first years in the household caring for her little charges were a routine but happy service. This contentment was altered by an intimate exchange of views with the children's father. They spoke cordially and collegially about the children and their upbringing, and he confessed his dependence upon her for their well-being. From that moment, a love for him was conceived.

Her feelings were challenged after an undisclosed passage of time when a lady acquaintance of the gentleman kissed the children on their mouths as she concluded a visit. Lucy was privately reprimanded for permitting such a thing. The father's diatribe concluded with the threat that, if this were ever to happen again, the children would be entrusted to another's care. Lucy was crushed. "I must have made a mistake," she mourned to Freud. "He can never have had any warm feelings for me, or they would have taught him to treat me with more consideration."[59]

A few months later, and two months before the letter from Lucy's mother arrived, a similar episode occurred when a frequent visitor, the father's chief factory accountant and a valued friend, attempted to kiss the children as he left the house following a workday luncheon. This time, when the father flared up, shouting at the grandfatherly gentleman, Lucy felt a stab at the heart, stunned by his violent rudeness.

Finally, Lucy gave notice after failing to receive a vote of confidence and "as much support as I had expected" when she protested misrepresentations that the rest of the staff, joining in a "little intrigue" against her, had made to her employer, the children's father. In spite of giving notice, and though she thought she should leave the house, she did not depart. "I was in this state of uncertainty at the time, and thought I should be leaving the house; but I have stayed on."[60] In spite of everything, in spite of the father's misconduct, the servants' vendetta, and in spite of both love for the widower and its "unfulfilled wish"—to note a concern of Freud—she remained, testament to her love for the children and lack of conflict about their father and the "loss of his love." None of the incidents proved disabling. None gave rise to neurosis. None demanded thera-peutic intervention or left a telltale mnemic symbol of conversion. None drove her from the home or led her to break her promise. Until the letter's arrival, with the resultant schoolroom trauma, stay-ing and leaving were not problematic; they were not in issue. To the contrary, in the face of an inclination to go, she maturely chose to stay without psychic detriment of any kind. Under the specter of trauma, however, everything is reinterpreted and charged with a new valence. Significant possibilities of earlier events, once latent, now suffered the ominous hermeneutic of death.

It is clear, highlighted by her fellow servants' rebuff, that Lucy fancied herself beyond a proper station, whatever actually character-ized her relation to the children's father. There is no reason to doubt the staff's unanimous perception, and Lucy appears to con-firm that appraisal by annoyance with their idle trivia. Her aspira-tions offer greater corroboration and clearly betray her. "You're afraid of their having some inkling of your hopes and making fun of you," Freud offers. "Yes, I think that's true," Lucy easily affirms, elucidating further: "I am only a poor girl and he is such a rich man of good family. People would laugh at me if they had any idea of it."[61] In truth, Lucy is sensitive to these challenges because she, her-self, knows her pretension is laughable, with visionary possibilities of success. In actuality, Lucy has been engaged in the fabrication of an illusory self at the expense of the children's father and, more profoundly, at her own expense, for she is in the process of identi-fying with a possibility that bears only the remotest congruence with reality.

It is a classic instance of the Erotic impulse, a narcissistic self striving—or aggressively lusting—to become ever greater to its exclusive advantage, others simply functioning to sustain or facilitate this blind and unrestricted avarice. It is the establishment of this imaginary and hegemonic self that the staff has keenly discerned.

The threat directed toward her after the visitor's kiss and the sober awareness wrought by the widower's conduct do not disabuse her. Instead, the incipient awareness gives way to narcissistic impul-sions; she stays on, grasping for the mirage, with the servants' rebuff, perhaps, only steeling her resolve to please and, thus, win the gentleman. The stab at the heart during the second incident with the grandfatherly accountant indicates that she has not yet faced the impossibility of her self-deceptions but that, instinctively, she apprehends her illusory self-aggrandizement is at risk, perhaps already receiving a mortal blow.

Nevertheless, the events and the situation are not acknowledged aright until death intervenes, rearing its omnivorous head through associations prompted by the arrival of her mother's letter. What is jeopardized by the threatening awareness is not so much the love of the widower as a new and hoped-for existence, the status and security that might otherwise be hers.

With the assumption of her duties, Lucy had set about, not unlike Elisabeth, to obliterate the memory of death for both herself and the children. Becoming their mother—in fact as well as in service—would effectively accomplish the task. The marriage would further supply the self-enhancement Lucy unconsciously craved. In one grand anabasis she would conquer death, banishing it from the children's lives as well as from her own, gain status, overcoming indigence and personal ignominy, and realize a wealth of security, once and for all.

The awareness and reinterpretation that death forced upon Lucy incapacitates. Though she has long resisted letting go of—even facing—her sustaining illusion, truth is unveiled with death, compelling her to recognize the failure of an enterprise that is essentially a failure of her*self*. Unexalted—without prospect of elevation—she cannot bear to stay because to do so is to accept a statusless, finite, mundane self, one among peers. It is no more, but no less, than the unpretentious existence of being human. In crying out, "I couldn't bear it any longer in the house,"[62] she is telling Freud that the crisis of death has left her vulnerable as a real—not illusory—self, without rank apart from the common humanity she is only nascently learning to share.

Amid the cleansing poverty and pain of disillusionment, she can begin to understand and address the needs of others. For too long her service with the children was chiefly an exercise of self-enhancing

Eros. Glorified by the children's adulation and affection, she had basked in narcissistic splendor. Her departure would enforce a second and perhaps crueler loss upon her charges. To her credit, this she could not inflict. With her decision to remain, Lucy has been on the threshold of seeing the children, not as objects for her own aggrandizement, but as others truly deserving in their own right, apart from assuaging her needs. She may not yet have been able to cross that threshold, entering fully into selfless presence on behalf of the children, but she refused to flee. Instead, if unconsciously, she submited to the compromise—albeit conflicted—formation of conversion, staying yet repressing the deadly threat she, herself, experienced.

By the time Lucy—happy and transfigured—visits Freud for their concluding session, she has worked though the crisis of reality and limits that death had thrust upon her. "And what do you think of your prospects in the house?" Freud asks. "I am quite clear on the subject. I know I have none, and I shan't make myself unhappy over it. . . ."

"And you are still in love with your employer?"

"Yes, I certainly am, but that makes no difference. After all, I can have thoughts and feelings to myself."[63]

Now, apart from any reference to herself or to her own needs, she is able to view her employer's merits for their own value, on their own terms, despite some gauche deficiencies. In fact, having acknowledged her own limitations, she can perceive his limitations as well, without finding her employer repulsive. The fact that she chooses to remain in the household inspires the certainty that she has moved beyond self-indulging child care. Were this a fairy tale, it might be added: "And they lived happily ever after."

KATHARINA

A fourth case that Freud presents involved a chance meeting during a mountain trek while vacationing. Her sulky, unhappy look betrayed the disposition of a strong, well-built girl of perhaps eighteen. Freud conjectured that she must be suffering from neurosis, "for nothing else could very well be the matter" with this otherwise robust mountain specimen. With an admission, "The truth is, sir, my nerves are bad," Katharina opened their therapeutic dialogue. The symptom that most alarmed her was shortness of breath. "I get so out of breath. Not always. But sometimes it catches me so that I think I shall suffocate."[64] In response to Freud's questioning, she amplified: "First of all its like something pressing on my eyes. My head gets so heavy, there's a dreadful buzzing, and I feel so giddy that I almost fall over. Then there's something crushing my chest so that I can't get my breath." To another question she responded: "My throat's squeezed together as though I were going to choke"; and to an additional one she concluded: "I always think I'm going to die." One remaining element completed her description of what Freud diagnosed as an "hysterical attack the content of which was anxiety": "I always see an awful face that looks at me in a dreadful way, so that I'm frightened." She could not recognize the face, answering "No" when Freud asked, " [I]s it a face that you've really seen some time?"[65]

The calamitous events that ultimately led to this mountainside collaboration are such that might have impelled Freud's original seduction theory.[66] At the age of fourteen Katharina experienced the first of apparently several sexual advances by her father. At an inn in the valley below the mountain hostel her family managed, an inebriated father climbed into bed with his already sleeping daughter. "You don't know how nice it is," he replied to Katharina's remonstrations. Leaping to the door, she remained there until he returned to his own bed. She revealed "yet other experiences of somewhat later date: how she had once again had to defend herself against him in an inn when he was completely drunk, and similar stories." Although on these occasions she also felt pressure on her eyes and chest, it was clear to Freud "from the way in which she reported having defended herself . . . that she did not clearly recognize the attack as a sexual one." "Not at the time," she replied to Freud's direct question as to whether or not she had understood what her father was attempting.[67]

This recognition arrived as the climax to a series of observations that there was "something between" her father and Franziska, a cousin. On that occasion Katharina had discovered her father in bed, lying atop Franziska. Some climbers had found their way to the hospice, and Katharina, seeking her cousin to cook, had come to her father's room as a last resort. Finding the door locked, she glanced innocently through a window in the passageway and made the astounding discovery. Repelled from the window, she clung to the wall for support and found, as from time to time thereafter, that it was impossible to get her breath.

She was frightened but, even at sixteen, "didn't understand anything at the time."[68] Three days later she suffered nausea, ceaselessly vomiting for three days in apparent reaction, Freud suggested, to the disgust she felt when looking into the room. "Yes, I'm sure I felt disgusted"; but she added: "It was too dark to see anything; besides they both of them had their clothes on. Oh, if only I knew what it was I felt disgusted at!"[69]

Noting a change in her daughter, Katharina's mother coaxed a report from her, and "there followed some very disagreeable scenes" between the parents.[70] It was, as Freud observed, a period of "more and more agitating scenes."[71]

Reflecting on the case, Freud surmised that Katharina had not been alarmed—or disgusted—by the sight of her father and Franziska but by the memory that the sight had awakened. "When she caught sight of the couple in intercourse, she at once established a connection between the new impression and these two sets of recollections" regarding her father's approaches toward herself.[72] "[S]he began to understand them and at the same time to fend them off."[73]

In spite of their implied resolution, Freud's superb observations beg the question: what was understood and what was being fended off? To his query about her thought processes "when you had your first attack, what you thought about it—it would help you," Katharina had to respond, "Yes, if I could. But I was so frightened that I've forgotten everything."[74] Nevertheless, with regard to the discovery of her father and Franziska that, as Freud speculates, must have initiated her own sexual awareness, she answered: "I always kept thinking about it."[75] Moreover, recollections of her father's earlier advances toward herself came readily to mind and were effortlessly articulated. In fact, Freud found that this young woman shared none of the prudishness of his urban clientele who regarded the natural—that is, sexual—with shame.[76] What is clear, consequently—and all the more so because Katharina had confided the Franziska episode to her mother, largely abreacting the trauma as Freud notes—is that it is not the sexual content or illumination that continued to trouble Katharina. Indeed, to the extent that three days of vomiting indicated a hysterical reaction to the onset of sexual understanding, this passed quickly, as Freud also notes, never to return. The sexual scenes, apparently, were occasions for some other impingement of a far more unsettling illumination. To state the obvious, the idea that Katharina was too frightened to recall was the very thought that struck with such repelling intensity as to force a defensive splitting that led to somatization of the unrepressed affect in the perduring symptoms affecting eyes, chest, and breathing. It was the very idea that could not be shared with her mother because it remained blocked from Katharina's consciousness, already repressed. These symptoms, mnemic symbols of the foundational disruption and its repressed idea, help unveil the traumatic intrusion.

The pressure on her eyes indicates, of course, both the harsh reality that continues to threaten her, pressing for recognition, and its tendency to render Katharina unconscious—giddy and almost falling over. The nonnurturing, strangling character of the constricted throat, in tandem with the more primal crushing sensation of the chest, indicates the fatal blow to, or the life-threatening impact upon, her existence.

"I always think I'm going to die."[77] There is no reason to doubt Katharina's experience or this anguished admission, but this describes the feeling that seizes her, not the seminal and conflicting idea. Nevertheless, death is precisely the idea that oppresses her; it is she, her*self*, who is oppressed. Freud tells us as much when he says she is suffering from an anxiety attack. As his second and mature view of anxiety alerts us, anxiety is a signal to the organism that it is in imminent danger.[78]

We have already observed with Lucy what an undermining blow the termination of a relationship can be when the relation is—in some sense—a fundamental one sustaining the core understanding of one's self, however illusory that interpretation may be. The revelation of Katharina's father's misadventures—fulfilling the intimations of his earlier indiscretions—not only signaled a finish to this foundational father-daughter relationship but to the matrix of family stability and to the very person Katharina had understood herself to be in light of these basic givens. In Heidegger's language, what suffers a veritable death is a whole *world*—the sum and ground of all relational significance and lived meaning, of and including the self it creates and that, in part, creates it. Katharina faced a void that marked the extinction of life as she had hitherto known it. What pressed for recognition was the dawning awareness that the illusory amniotic sac of a secure, trustworthy universe was irrevocably ruptured. In short, what Katharina felt imperiled was all that she knew herself to be.

This interpretation of her condition is corroborated by two elements of the recurring symptoms. An apprehension of immediate danger is signaled by her sense that "someone's standing behind me and going to catch hold of me all at once."[79] Emblematic of personified death, this stalking threat of an abrupt seizure is associated with death by Katharina, herself: "I always think I'm going to die."[80] In addition, there is the terrorizing face Katharina is unable to identify. It is not Franziska's, as Freud at first surmised, nor is it the face of Katharina's father at any of his lascivious moments. Rather, it is the contorted face of his exposure, "when all the disputes had broken out" and he "gave way to a senseless rage."[81] Incensed, he blamed Katharina for the divorce, the unhappy dissolution of his marriage and convenient, well-established life. It was this violent mask, which "kept threatening he would do something to me," that she beheld. "I always ran away from him, and always felt terrified that he would catch me some time unawares."[82] These dire threats reinforced and magnified the vulnerability of an evaporating life in a shattered world that she had experienced from the start, transmuting all insecurity into the sense of an ominous stalker promising imminent peril.

As she had fled her father, she continued to flee a recognition of the burdens decimating her world until the fortuitous meeting with Freud at the new hostel across the valley from the traumatic site. Concluding her stories, she was—Freud amazingly witnessed—transformed, "the sulky, unhappy face had grown lively, her eyes were bright, she was lightened and exalted."[83]

With the help of another, she discovered the links between the felt presence of death consuming her life and the sources of the destructive dynamism that, unfaced, could never be remedied. In part, this successful alliance was possible because she and her family had already made the therapeutic move to a more wholesome environment. In part, it occurred because of her courageous sharing. With another, she could hazard the connections and discover that she had not been annihilated in the process. Something precious in her life might have been irretrievably lost, but in journeying to the origins of her distress, she learned that whatever had perished, she, herself, had not. Vitally, she had endured; now, thanks to this fortunate collaboration, she could prosper.

EMMY

The case of Emmy, forty-year-old widow of a wealthy industrialist, is, in fact, the first of Freud's own cases to be treated in *Studies on Hysteria*, and it was, he tells us, "the first case in which I employed the cathartic procedure to a large extent."[84] Throughout her sessions with the nascent analyst, as throughout her life, death is rampant. From earliest youth, the impressionable age of five, she was often besieged by brothers and sisters throwing dead animals upon her.[85] At age seven, unexpectedly viewing a sister dead in her coffin proved frightening, as did the experience, at nine, of coming upon a dead aunt's coffin at the moment the cadaver's jaw suddenly fell open. In between, at the age of eight, she was routinely hounded by a brother terrifyingly draped as a ghost. These scenes lingered indelibly in her mind's eye, apprehended with all the vividness of reality. Even when these events were recounted in sessions with Freud, she "twitched all over and took on a look of fear and horror."[86] In addition, dreams wherein she laid out the dead in coffins also appeared during her treatment.

When she was nineteen, a brother died. She then suffered bizarre, theriomorphic visions apparently related to this death, which would later alarm her anew. Four years earlier at fifteen, she had discovered her mother lying on the floor, victim of a stroke. The woman did not die at this time, but four years later, not only was her son—Emmy's brother—dead, but she, herself, as well. Not surprisingly, Emmy once again suffered the burden of discovery.

The psychological death of madness also intruded into this unsettled life. In addition to an alarming encounter with one acquaintance suddenly gone mad, Emmy, fifteen and struck speechless by the shock, witnessed a cousin's removal to an asylum for the insane. The scene often "appeared before her," undoubtedly with the disturbing reminder that madness vitally threatened the entire family, especially since her mother once suffered confinement "for some time."[87] Most unnerving, perhaps, had been a recurring incident at a health resort. Terribly ill after her mother's death, Emmy had retreated to the haven out of necessity, but even here safety and rest were not assured. On several nights, entering her room by mistake, a lunatic reached her bed.

Emmy's life was under siege. Nowhere was she secure. Death, in physical or psychic forms, approached wherever she sought refuge. Prior to her brother's death, she had felt particular alarm, fearing contagion and terrified that his "horrible disease" could be hers. Soon after, she nursed a second brother whose serious consumption threatened its own contamination.

The climax of this morbid history was yet to come. At the age of twenty-three, Emmy married an older, accomplished, and well-positioned gentleman. After only a few short years, this able and extremely gifted person was dead, victim of a coronary.

The horror unfolded as a two-stage catastrophe, not unlike her mother's demise. In this instance, however, Emmy was present on both occasions to receive the full force of the blow. Initially, while vacationing on the Riviera, her spouse had "suddenly sunk to the ground and lain there lifeless for a few minutes but had then got up again and seemed quite well." Not long afterward, as she lay in bed following postpartum, he rose "all at once" from a nearby breakfast table, "looked at her so strangely," took a few steps forward, then collapsed.[88] Doctors could not revive him. Complicating this devastation, the infant, their second child, was seized by a serious illness. Through part of its six months' duration, Emmy, herself, was confined to bed with a high fever. Employing hypnosis, Freud asked which event in her life had produced the most lasting effect on her and arose most often in memory. Her husband's death, she replied. This reiterated her lament to Freud upon their first meeting. Then she reported that, with varying degrees of severity, she had been constantly ill since the death, and she told Freud that she attributed her own illness to this event.

This lady, who "still looked young and had finely-cut features" and possessed, not unlike Anna O., an "unusual degree of education and intelligence," suffered from a variety of symptoms.[89] Depression, insomnia, tormenting pains, hallucinations of animals and corpses, and a general fear of anything unexpected, sudden, alien, or new do not exhaust the litany of her woes. Even in the nursing home, wherein Freud had placed her to gain some respite from her daughters and to facilitate his daily visits, Emmy felt unsafe. Whenever anyone opened the door or unexpectedly entered her room, she became violently alarmed. With a preliminary knock, excitement did not cease altogether; even Dr. Breuer's visit "frightened her to death" on one occasion.

Expectations of misfortune continually haunted her. Fearfulness on her own behalf extended to progeny as well. She was concerned, Freud learned under hypnosis, that "something might happen to her children, that they might fall ill or lose their lives."[90]

Nevertheless, Emmy's condition "improved so rapidly, that she soon assured [Freud] she had not felt so well since her husband's death." After seven weeks of treatment, Freud allowed her to return home, armed with hypnotically induced maxims "to protect her from relapsing into similar conditions."[91]

Seven months later Freud learned from Breuer that after several healthy months, Emmy, overcome by violent self-reproaches, had suffered a breakdown from "a fresh psychical shock," apparently connected with the failure of a therapeutic intervention on behalf of her elder daughter. Freud's reaction was that Emmy, "by an act of the will as it were . . . undid the effect of my treatment and promptly relapsed into the states from which I had freed her."[92] He was yet to discover, after she returned to Vienna "and put herself once more into my hands," that Emmy was in better condition than reported and that "much of what I had accomplished the year before was still maintained."[93]

The work of the renewed treatment dealt with "disagreeable impressions" suffered in regard to her daughter's treatment, to Emmy's own stay at the sanatorium and, to a greater extent, with confusion or "storms in her head."[94] Emmy's recourse to the local sanatorium had "failed completely," necessitating this second therapy with Freud one year after their first encounter.

In a few weeks these problems were disposed of, but Frau Emmy remained in Vienna under Freud's observation "for some time longer." During this period, eating disorders were resolved that, in large part, hearkened back to feeding episodes when the matron cared for her ill brothers.[95] Freud pronounced that "the therapeutic effect of these discoveries under hypnosis was immediate and lasting."[96]

In the spring of the following year, Freud visited Frau Emmy at her home, staying several days. "She seemed reluctant, however, to be communicative under hypnosis," and Freud suspected that she was in the process "of withdrawing once more from my influence."[97]

After the visit, Freud heard that her daughter's condition, a continuing source of distress and agitation for his former patient, eventually undermined the matron's health, and three years later Emmy sought hypnotic treatment with a doctor in her vicinity since she was unable to journey to Vienna.

It was the persistence of Emmy's problems that led Freud to assert that the numerous traumatic factors that were originally adjudged to be sources of her "pathological ideas" could no longer be accorded etiological significance.[98] Instead, he was "now of the opinion that there must have been some added factor to provoke the outbreak of illness precisely in these last years, considering that operative etiological conditions had been present for many years previously."[99] The widow's presumed sexual abstinence was accorded explanatory prominence, for "such circumstances are among the most frequent causes of a tendency to anxiety."[100] Among all the "intimate information" Emmy had disclosed, "there was a complete absence of the sexual element, which is, after all, more liable than any other to provide occasion for traumas. It is impossible that her excitations in this field can have left no traces whatever. . . ." Freud concluded with the suspicion that Emmy "had not won her victory over her sexual needs without severe struggles, and that at times her attempts at suppressing this most powerful of all instincts had exposed her to severe mental exhaustion."[101]

Apart from the fact that such speculative reasoning, long after the therapeutic sessions, is egregious—since any number of other elements might also be absent—there is, on the record, ample indication of why Emmy's symptoms might persist.

"My therapy," Freud instructs us, "consists in wiping away these pictures[102] so that she is no longer able to see them before her. To give support to my suggestion I stroke her several times over the eyes."[103] As the young practitioner later acknowledged, at the time of this treatment he was "completely under the sway of Bernheim's book on suggestion and I anticipated more results from such didactic measures than I should to-day."[104] Although he claims that he also "investigated the genesis of the individual symptoms so as to be able to combat the premises on which the pathological ideas were erected," it is clear that therapy at this early moment in his career was dominated by "assurances and prohibitions, and by putting forward opposing ideas of every sort."[105] Moreover, Freud noted that Emmy's situation provided the first occasion to employ the technique of Breuer's hypnotic therapy, frankly admitting: "I was still far from having mastered it; in fact I *did not carry the analysis of the symptoms far enough nor pursue it systematically enough.*"[106]

This naive therapy, alone, would be a sufficient cause for the persistence of any and all ills. It is not surprising that Freud could reflect, during his visit to Frau Emmy's home, that "in spite of all my improving suggestions there had been little change in her fundamental character."[107] Anew, Freud admits that the analysis of

Emmy's states of delirium "was not exhaustively carried out" and that "the definitive cure of a case of hysteria such as this would have to enter more thoroughly into the complex of phenomena than I attempted to do."[108]

These admissions, on their own, might beg the question of etiology. Perhaps if Freud had gone deep enough or far enough, sexual causation might have been revealed. It is impossible to know, but militating against this eventuality is an additional element of the record.

While Freud found Emmy to be "an excellent subject for hypnotism," he also found that, although generally submissive to his authority and willing to please, the lady could be as closed mouth in somnambulism as she would be in ordinary consciousness when his questions were found disagreeable.[109] At one point, Frau Emmy grumbled that Freud "was not to keep on asking her where this and that came from." Instead, "I was to let her tell me what she had to say."[110] This was not simple catharsis, for, as Freud observed, "the impression made by her mental behaviour during somnambulism was, on the whole, one of an uninhibited unfolding of her mental powers and of a full command over her store of memories."[111] In other words, what was most therapeutic and successful about the treatment anticipated the hallmark methodology of psychoanalysis: this was (as his editor Strachey himself footnoted) perhaps the earliest appearance of free association. As Freud observed, Emmy's conversation "often leads on, in a quite unexpected way to pathogenic reminiscences of which she unburdens herself without being asked to. It is as though," Freud notes in apparent delight, "she had adopted my procedure and was making use of our conversation, apparently unconstrained and guided by chance, as a supplement to her hypnosis."[112] With Emmy's "compulsion to associate similar to that prevailing in dreams,"[113] some trace of sexual etiology would have emerged had it existed; yet Freud discovered none.

What did emerge was a pervasive culture of death regnant in her psyche but inaccessible to waking consciousness. While Emmy was aware of the impact of her husband's death and attributed etiological weight to that calamity, she was unable to make connections with the traumatic skeletons and deeper fears ravaging her unconsciously. During their sessions, ample material presented itself, begging to be addressed, but Freud did not—or could not—confront the pathology, and the necrophobia remained intact, tyrannizing the woman utterly.

While Freud came close, acknowledging at one point the traumatic precipitating causation of Emmy's youthful encounters with death and the devastating impact of her spouse's collapse, he failed to attend to these indications, making no exploration of their depths.[114] As a result, he failed to recognize the profound unity of all of Emmy's fears. He treated discrete symptoms only, while the etiological core fouling her life remained neglected and impervious, losing none of its power to haunt this victim in imperious, inexhaustible disguise.

5

Primordial Finitude

Inhibitions, Symptoms, and Anxiety

Who knows his birthplace yet?
—St.-John Perse, *Exile*

A difficulty with the foregoing interpretation, it might be argued, is Freud's belief that the "unconscious seems to contain nothing that could give any content to our concept of the annihilation of life."[1] That is, since the unconscious knows nothing of death, for nothing like death could have been experienced, "it would seem highly improbable that a neurosis could come into being merely because of the objective presence of danger, without any participation of the deeper levels of the mental apparatus."[2]

These remarks appear at the conclusion of an impromptu consideration of the war neuroses:

> If anxiety is a reaction of the ego to danger, we shall be tempted to regard the traumatic neuroses, which so often follow upon a narrow escape from death, as a direct result of a fear of death (or fear *for* life) and to dismiss from our

minds the question of castration and the dependent relationships of the ego. Most of those who observed the traumatic neuroses that occurred during the last war took this line, and triumphantly announced that proof was now forthcoming that a threat to the instinct of self-preservation could by itself produce a neurosis without any admixture of sexual factors and without requiring any of the complicated hypotheses of psycho-analysis. . . . In view of all that we know about the structure of the comparatively simple neuroses of everyday life, it would seem highly improbable that a neurosis could come into being merely because of the objective presence of danger. . . .[3]

Perhaps this is the most scurrilous utterance in the whole of Freud's corpus, compounded by the admission that "not a single analysis of a traumatic neurosis of any value is extant."[4] It is impossible not to imagine that if Freud, himself, had been a battlefield target subject to lethal fire, his theory would have suffered immediate revision.

Who can say what the unconscious does or does not "contain"? To argue that the unconscious contains nothing to support the concept of an end to life would seem to overlook the phylogenetic contribution, at the very least. At its most extreme, the assertion appears to subvert any notion of a death instinct that *Beyond the Pleasure Principle* had proposed. To urge, moreover, that objective danger cannot occasion anxiety impresses one as preposterous, although the statement is mitigated, if not fully countered, by Freud's subsequent reflection a page later:

In addition, it must be remembered that in the experiences which lead to a traumatic neurosis the protective shield against external stimuli is broken through and excessive amounts of excitation impinge upon the mental apparatus; so that we have here a second possibility—that anxiety is not only being signaled as an affect but is also being freshly created out of the economic conditions of the situation.[5]

Indeed, the initially, if not exclusively, conscious encounters with death that Emmy experienced would appear to be sufficient to propel one into the flight of neurosis. Not merely an abstract "concept," but a very concrete phenomenon of alarming proportions, the death that Emmy beheld, for example, was not the antiseptic propriety of a contemporary funeral home. Instead, she witnessed the pallid corpse-white of death, the first flaking of nose, lips, or eyelids, and the unnerving smell that remained all-too-briefly subtle. Freud's own remarks about death in *The Interpretation of Dreams* ("the horrors of corruption, of freezing in the ice-cold grave, of the terrors of eternal nothingness—ideas which grown-up people find it so hard to tolerate"[6]) betray a significant affective dread that would prompt most individuals to defense.

Nevertheless, there is a truth in the view that without an experience of death at the deepest levels of the psyche, by which Freud means the unconscious, death—or its possibility—cannot be perceived or known as anything other than a "naught" that is powerless to affect our mental lives. If Freud's assertion is allowed full weight and acquiescence is granted to the proposition that death, as a terminus to bodily life, cannot directly arouse anxiety and neurosis, we are forced into a deeper exploration that can only enrich our understanding.

The best place to begin this exploration is with Freud's indications in *Inhibitions, Symptoms, and Anxiety* of a primeval traumatic experience and of a resultant primal repression:

> Anxiety is not newly created in repression; it is reproduced as an affective state in accordance with an already existing mnemic image. If we go further and enquire into the origin of that anxiety—and of affects in general—we shall be leaving the realm of pure psychology and entering the borderland of physiology. Affective states have become incorporated in the mind as precipitates of primaeval traumatic experiences, and when a similar situation occurs they are revived like mnemic symbols.[7]

"It is highly probable," Freud continues, "that the immediate pre-cipitating causes of primal repressions are quantitative factors such as an excessive degree of excitation and the breaking through of the protective shield against stimuli."[8]

Under the qualified and tentative influence of Rank's book, *The Trauma of Birth,* Freud provisionally considers birth as the primal trauma: "In man . . . the act of birth, as the individual's first experi-ence of trauma, has given the affect of anxiety certain characteristic forms of expression"; nevertheless, he cautions against placing undue stress on this and further reflects that "biological necessity demands that a situation of danger should have an affective symbol, so that a symbol of this kind would have to be created in any case. Moreover, I do not think," he concludes, "that we are justified in assuming that whenever there is an outbreak of anxiety something like a reproduction of the situation of birth goes on in the mind."[9]

While in the ensuing pages Freud vacillates in his regard for the birth hypothesis, he ultimately dismisses Rank's thesis that birth is the prototypical experience of anxiety. His former colleague had sought to demonstrate, in particular, that the earliest anxieties of infant phobias replicated a traumatic birth. After considering the possibility, Freud definitively rejects the suggestion, delivering this fatal blow: "I am driven to the conclusion that the earliest phobias of infancy cannot be directly traced back to impressions of the act of birth and that so far they [and, thus, the roots of anxiety] have not been explained."[10]

Prior to this conclusion in pivotal chapter 8, Freud had delivered telling fusillades in his examination of Rank's thesis. Already Freud had argued that birth could not be associated with the primal trauma, although "in the act of birth there is a real danger to life," because it cannot be supposed that "the foetus has any sort of knowledge that there is a possibility of its life being destroyed." Psy-chologically, the objective danger "says nothing at all to us. The danger of birth has as yet no psychical content."[11] To some extent this mimics his remarks about the war neuroses, although with greater cogency vis-à-vis the infantile mind. While it is true that "far too little is known about the mental make-up of a newborn baby,"[12] not only does the foregoing statement appear to be a just assessment, but so too does an earlier objection to the seminal valence of a birth trauma. There Freud considered the postulate that birth is anxiety producing because it is, objectively speaking, a separation from the mother:

> Now it would be very satisfactory if anxiety, as a symbol of separation, were to be repeated on every subsequent occasion on which a separation takes place. But unfortunately we are prevented from making use of this correlation by the fact that birth is not experienced subjectively as a separation from the mother, since the foetus, being a completely narcissistic creature, is totally unaware of her existence as an object.[13]

To the question, "What is a 'danger'?" of sufficient traumatic force to evoke anxiety, birth as a passage appears not to be an answer: "The danger of birth has . . . no psychical content."

If the neonate suffers no trauma because it is unable to comprehend the possibility of a deadly reversal in the thrust toward life, it nevertheless can be overwhelmed by the reality of existing, "aware of some vast disturbance in the economy of its narcissistic libido. Large sums of excitation crowd in upon it, giving rise to new kinds of feelings of unpleasure. . . ."[14]

The full significance of this threatening impingement is not underscored for another two pages. Although Freud has already rejected the notion of a birth trauma caused by separation from the mother, he is on the verge of considering it anew when these considerations are suspended: "But a moment's reflection takes us beyond this question of loss of object."[15] Freud realizes that the absence of a nurturing figure becomes traumatically significant only because a prior condition is already operative. This alarming and preexisting condition is one "of a *growing tension due to need*," in the face of which an infant is helpless.[16] Without succor, the state of need escalates to unbearable summits of discomfort.

For the infant, the onus of these excitations—without possibility of mastery or discharge—is "analogous to the experience of being born" and is a repetition of the original situation of danger. What both situations, the nonsatisfaction of incapacitating need and the original, anxiety-provoking trauma, share in common is "the economic disturbance caused by an accumulation of amounts of stimulation. . . . It is this factor, then," Freud concludes, "which is the real essence of the 'danger'."[17]

While Freud compares the state of needfulness to that of birth, it is clear that he is not pointing to the passage or separation of birth that is ingredient to Rank's hypothesis. Instead, what he expressly highlights is the concrete situation following birth that is the notorious impotence of the human species. It is not the event of birth, itself, but the overwhelming condition of uncontrollable need and intruding helplessness that provokes anxiety. As Freud will emphasize in the *Outline,* his concluding synthesis, internal excitations, that is, "instinctual demands from within, no less than excitations from the external world, operate as 'traumas'."[18]

What, at one level and from one perspective, is "mere" biology or physiological excitation, from a parallel vantage is the human being, itself, *being* itself.[19] What the excitations manifest is the very way one *is* finitely embodied. The vast and systemic "economic disturbance" that all must suffer indicates the catastrophe of incarnate vulnerability aware of itself. What overwhelms the infant is neither excitation nor stimulation, nor even tension. What overwhelms the infant is *itself,* irrevocably swaddled in finitude. This swathe, which can never be unraveled, is the oppressing contingency we are and never can escape—the mysterious riddle, as Heidegger has indicated, of a being who is in issue—or, perhaps more alarming, of a question in being whose issue is in doubt.

If we return to Freud's point of departure with the understanding that he has pointed away from the process and event of birth by focusing on internal excitations, it is apparent that the primal trauma is situated more remotely than proximally to the act of birth than Freud's continuing birth references suggest.[20]

Freud corroborates this when he says, concluding his dismissal of Rank, that anxiety phobias of infancy are not directly related "to impressions of the act of birth. . . . A certain preparedness for anxiety," Freud explains, "is undoubtedly present in the infant in arms. But this preparedness for anxiety, instead of being at its maximum immediately after birth and then slowly decreasing, *does not emerge till later, as mental development proceeds*, and lasts over a certain period of childhood."[21] This provides the first indication of where the element that Freud deemed essential for the onset of trauma is to be discovered.

Although "inclined to think that [primal] anxiety is based upon an increase of excitation" and that states evoking the signal of anxiety are a "reproduction of some experience which contained the necessary conditions for such an increase of excitation," Freud rejected a "purely physiological account" as inadequate. Instead, he was "tempted to assume the presence of a historical factor which binds the sensations of anxiety and its innervations firmly together."[22]

If a purely physiological explanation is insufficient, birth would be disqualified, perforce, since it ushers the infant into a universe of stimulation, but with awareness virtually nonexistent or minimal at most. Possessing woefully immature psychic structure and cognitive power at best, the bundle of newborn impulses remains a chaos without ordered and subjective effect. The requisite foundation for an experience of anxiety is simply nonexistent. What is needed, then, is not the necessary condition for "an increase in excitation"—this, it can be surmised, abounds aplenty—but a catalyst that provides sufficient binding power to sustain a cohesive historical experience. For anxiety, birth might be a sine qua non, but it is not an efficient cause.

As adumbrated, one ingredient of the anticipated historical factor would have to be a consolidated awareness or consciousness. The notion of binding adds an organizing valence since, in the context of Freud's requirements, binding means to pull together, establishing order and unity. This provides the definitive pointer.

"The ego is an organization and the id is not," Freud underscores at the inception of chapter 3.[23] The ego represents both functions: it is an organizing faculty and the power of perception and consciousness. Thus, the historical factor precipitating the primal trauma is the advent of consciousness with the positing of the ego.

Of course, it is impossible to determine precisely when the trauma takes place. While it can be said that the dawn of consciousness is a more or less gradual awakening during which the needs of the infant's system impose an ever-increasing burden, at some point the summation of excitations and the press of awareness through maturing ego functions converge with traumatic impact for the fragile and tentative organism. Repression results. Although Freud lets it slip from view in his intensive investigation, these traumatizing excitations are subjected to a primal repression.

It does not require great speculation or much imagination to observe the reciprocal influence taking place. Dawning consciousness gives the excitations their imperiling force, provoking anxiety, while, coincidentally, mounting anxiety impinges upon the evolving consciousness and organizing tendencies. It is likely, in fact, that the incipient ego is given an urgent developmental thrust by the escalating distress of its primal impotence.[24]

Thus, we can comprehend the relationship between the ego and anxiety, why and how Freud says the ego is the seat of anxiety and, abandoning an earlier view, that anxiety arises in the ego and produces repression.[25] The rudimentary ego, apprehending the excitations as endangering, is irrevocably cast—or traumatically deformed—by that very danger into a defensive structure, ever vigilant for the possible return of the repressed and the terrible possibility of succumbing anew to the vicissitudes and incapacities of the finite.[26]

The primordial repression helps to illumine Freud's "body ego" language in *The Ego and the Id*.[27] Initially, the nascent ego is convergent with the whole of its bodily sensorium, the entire field of incipient awareness. With the primal repression, awareness is emancipated as the ego recoils from bodily constraints, and the self grows opaque to itself as the body is eclipsed. With this primordial cleavage, the foundation of the mind-body dichotomy is created.

Impaired vision or perception—selective consciousness and diminished quality of awareness—is an eventual casualty of repression that extends beyond the human entity to the surrounding environment. Others are eclipsed, even abused, as Eros impels the organism toward the quantifiably greater, ever enhancing its domain. Its unconscious, consuming compulsion, pushing beyond infirmity and misfortune, is a desperate attempt to bury forever the impediment of finitude, revealing Eros as an emblematic trace of the primordial repression—as is the infant omnipotence Freud addresses in other contexts. Since the infant is anything but potent, omnipotence can only indicate a reaction formation in the face of the powerless indigence of primordial incapacity—the foundational ignominy of finite being—that has been banished from sight. Eros is the infantile writ enduringly.

A comparison between certain relationships in *Inhibitions, Symptoms, and Anxiety* (ISA) and in *Beyond the Pleasure Principle* is additionally instructive. In *Beyond* (BPP), death is opposed to life. This is only at first glance, although it remains faithful to Freud's own summary formulation. Closer inspection shows that death is actually opposed to the tensions or *excitation* of living. In ISA a weaker opposition between anxiety and an undisclosed danger (anxiety *about* danger) leads propaedeutically to an articulated anxiety about the excitations or tensions of *need* and, finally, to the stronger conflict between repression and these excitations of embodied finitude. Side by side, the oppositions of the two works look like this:

BPP	ISA
death vs. excitations	repression vs. excitations

From this several things are evident. First, in light of the subsequent work, *Beyond* has overstated the opposition, literally providing overkill. This is doubly so since the mechanism of death in *Beyond* is not opposed to quintessential life, although Freud continues to speak of life and death instincts clashing, but only to that life fraught with excitations and burdened by tension. Most important, it is apparent as well that repression is parallel to death vis-à-vis the embodied life of excitation and serves an analogous function. Repression, however, does not merely provide a schematic parallel, analogously opposing stimulations. Instead, repression *is* de facto death to the life of excitation and need—the concrete manifestation of being finitely human. Thus, the realm of the unconscious has had an experience of death and has been its matrix, if not (in integral though unknown ways) its actual agent. Nevertheless, the dynamic of repression is more complex and profoundly valenced than a diagram can reveal.

In *Beyond*, Freud had attributed the organism's forward movement into a life of vexation to decisive external circumstances since the quickest route for the inherent death instinct would be a retreat to the recent inorganic past. He hazarded unconvincingly that the organism's maintenance of a prolonged life of stimulation was occasioned by its search for a "death of its own," free from external causes. This function was attributed to the ego's self-preservative instinct. So unconvincing was the attribution that Freud repudiated the suggestion a few pages hence, leaving the hypothesis begging for a rationale. In light of ISA, however, it can be seen that this movement through time by the human organism is realized under the aegis of repression quieting the vexations that had initially traumatized.

In light of *Beyond's* thesis, it would be expected that the internal canceling of tension should issue in the peaceful extinction that is death's nirvana. To the contrary, a virulent form of life is provoked in contrast to the contingent vulnerability initially suffered by the infant organism. This self-constituting act of repression parallels the structure Freud had proposed for the death instinct. In *Beyond,* Freud postulated that life, itself externally imposed upon inorganic matter, would be sloughed off in favor of the effortless bliss of the prior inanimate state. In the context of ISA's historical factor (consciousness), it can be seen that existence before this axial event would be analogous to the inanimate, inorganic status as a condition of unawakened bliss. The action of repression, paralleling death and extinguishing the life of tension, returns the organism to its initial state beyond the ravages of reality, with nirvana sought—not as inorganic death—but through an effortless, unperturbed life. Rather than extinguish itself, the virulent organism strains to extinguish all impediment, whether of internal need or external constraint. This is the irresistible, self-enveloped Erotic drive.

Seeking a secure position beyond the impotence of primal trauma and mirroring *Beyond's* death instinct, Eros presses forward as a body of resistance and death, recoiling from its original life and struggling to eradicate the subsequent afflictions of mortality, hostile to others whenever jeopardy presents a face.

This reveals why Freud had difficulty in *Beyond* with his dual drive theory. The opposition between death and Eros seemed to collapse before his eyes in the consolidation of the two. The complete logic and ramification of this conjunction was not realized until *Civilization and Its Discontents* transmuted the death instinct from a nirvana principle intending bliss to aggressive Thanatos targeting others.[28] This inevitably resulted since narcissistic Eros does not simply place itself at the expansive center, striving to be ever greater; it can only secure the illusion of this primacy, maintaining an equally illusory exemption from turmoil and tension by aggressively opposing any other who might curtail or endanger it. Since every other can displace it as the central axis, all must be construed as potentially antagonistic: one lives in opposition, safeguarding hard-earned gains, apprehensive and defensively misperceiving all as a challenge. Primal repression, thus, closes one in upon oneself. Expansive omnipotence and aggression, or conflict in the face of threatening others, are complements of the self-surviving, narcissistic existent.

It may be recognized, as well, that the termination of Eros would not necessarily issue in the organism's oblivion. What could result, instead, is the reemergence of the indigenous body of excitation. This would exact the demise or diminishment of Eros while restoring the organism's primordial reality. According to *Beyond's* definitions, this proclivity for the initial state of affairs is the distinguishing characteristic of an instinct. Moreover, the tacit instinctual opposition intensifies exponentially with the recognition that Eros would not graciously relinquish its regime. In fact, its natural dynamism would resist, vigorously opposing any encroachment.

With this antithesis we see a reconfiguring of the conflict model of the psyche in a reassertion of the dual drive theory that had seemingly vanished. This is nothing other than Eros contesting with the return of the repressed: as Eros struggles to move definitively and absolutely beyond the primal trauma, the organism attempts to embrace the repressed, endeavoring to fully recover the integrity of its primal state, realizing its given, original self, however finite and fragile that may be.

Whether this is called an instinct of transcendence or an Exodus principle, the identical potential is indicated: a trajectory beyond the aggressive solipsism of Eros, opening oneself to a vaster relational world of difference, differentiation, stimulation, tension, the new and the unknown—an experience of all that can be ego-dystonic or, more hopefully, ego-transforming, with an open-ended comprehension that embraces the greatest diversity.

This openness to the alien facticity of the relational world is possible only in consequence of a proportional relatedness to all that is hidden within. Others can be accepted as one affirms the otherness of oneself, opening to, however incrementally, the repressed reality of authentic, primordial facticity—or thrownness in Heidegger's parlance—which necessarily alerts Eros to an alteration of its status. It is this prospect of diminution, with a potential for demise, that is the situation of danger signaled by anxiety.

It is here that we can understand the purchase death exerts with incomparable force upon the psyche. The incompatibility of Eros with any reduction of its hegemony and the unconscious action of repression combine to articulate how death precipitates sufficient intervention by the unconscious to occasion neurosis.

It will be recalled that Freud was of the opinion that the deeper or unconscious recesses of the mind would likely have to come into play for neurosis to intervene. Militating against this interplay was Freud's judgment that the unconscious could know nothing of a threat to or possible extinction of life, having had no experience of death.

It is, in fact, the unwaning vigilance of the unconscious against any potential for a reversal of its primordial defense that predisposes it to jeopardy from any force beyond its province or purview. The very fact that the unconscious lacks an experience of death is precisely what renders it vulnerable and gives death its power. Since biological or material death remains untested, the enigmatic phenomenon is interpreted by the unconscious in terms of the functional death it does know, its own powers of repression that so devastatingly extinguished the traumatic excitations of finitude, giving rise to omnipotent and reality-denying Eros. Whatever death might mean or be, it signals an end to the only life (born in the matrix of instinctual reaction) the unconscious psyche has tolerated. If what it has constituted through repressive force can be reversed, with its unconscious action apparently and potentially countered by the agency of death, then death must loom as a danger to be received with the greatest apprehension. Beyond the powers of repression and immune to the manipulative energies of Eros, death must threaten the return of the repressed, promising a decisive collapse of unconscious structures and the repressive, Erotic dream of impervious security.

While intimations of cognitive powers on the part of the unconscious might be resisted, one needs only to recall that *The Interpretation of Dreams* established to Freud's satisfaction that the unconscious is capable of the profoundest mental functioning that merited, however analogously, to be called (unconscious) thinking. Nevertheless, however essential the unconscious depth may be for the production of neurosis, this does not imply that it, alone, is sufficient for neurosis to appear. Consciousness is undoubtedly an integral factor. Thus, it may be that initial awareness of the presence and significance of death is supplied by conscious functions that provoke excitatory responses that, in turn, trigger action on the part of the unconscious.

It may be emphasized that no reference is made to consciousness as an isolated system; a rigid dichotomy between the conscious and unconscious should not be entertained. While, it is true, the topographic model of *The Interpretations of Dreams* absolutely segregates the two insofar as the unconscious cannot become conscious, it does not address the relationship of the organ of consciousness to its foundational roots. In ISA, Freud gave a mature assessment after cautioning against taking conceptual abstractions too rigidly:

> We were justified, I think, in dividing the ego from the id, for there are certain considerations which necessitate that step. On the other hand the ego is identical with the id, and is merely a specially differentiated part of it. . . . In repression the decisive fact is that the ego is an organization and the id is not. The ego is, indeed, the organized portion of the id. We should be quite wrong if we pictured the ego and the id as two opposing camps. . . .[29]

With regard to the inner world, the ego undoubtedly conflicts at times with the unconscious id, which is simply to say that excitations that were repressed in the primal trauma are forever banned if the ego's defensive sense is alarmed. With regard to the external world, however, the ego may ally itself with unconscious recesses to ward off the specter of mortality that initially was forced from view. Freud sums this up in an earlier but related context of ISA, saying, "[T]his view implies a concession to the ego that it can exert a very extensive influence over processes in the id. . . ."[30] In other words, born in the midst of trauma, the organ of consciousness bears—without intervening remedial action—the imprint of repressive defense. It clings to its matrix, in complicity with the unconscious, to resist the emergence of the repressed.

In sum, death is alarming precisely as an unknown element and external force that, eluding control, jeopardizes Eros's narcissistic project. Augmented by imputed repressive powers, it threatens the work of primal defense, signaling the return of the repressed and challenging the unconscious into neurotic flight. Death, thus, can be a reckoned factor in neurosis, forcing the unconscious into play in multiple ways—which are integrally a single vector—by reason of the primal repression that, itself, has created an avenue through which death gains meaningful entry.

Death (Heidegger's ontological possibility) does not so much reveal something novel as create an opportunity for one to recognize what the embodied self has proclaimed (Heidegger's ontic disclosure) since birth. If most close off this possibility, refusing to apprehend the authentic human situation, it is only a continuance of the primordial recoil from finitude. Recognizing the ill-equipped, infantile psyche that was confronted by an indigenous life of need, the automatic reflex of repression (Heidegger's fleeing) is understandable, as is the ensuing life ruled by the pleasure principle's demand for immediate discharge of any tension. The essentially infantile dominant of such a psyche, in which life is less lived than reduced to a series of reactions and recoils, justifies Kierkegaard's assertion that most persons remain a child for the whole of life.[31] If the return of the repressed reveals a deeper desire to appropriate one's original and authentic existence, it is evident why, in Kierkegaard's understanding, dying away from immediacy is the corrective of, and transition from, an infantile psyche to the mature one he calls a self.[32] This is the very Exodus principle of transcendence, opening beyond the wishful and immediate satisfaction of unchallenged existence where depth and growth are incontestably absent.

Distinguished from the engagement with death, Kierkegaard's "dying away from" suggests a much less catastrophic encounter. Indeed, the very language indicates a process that is an incremental and deepening repetition over time. Such a gradual opening to the reality of mature vision presents the hope and possibility that the child may be weaned and an authentic adult may come to be. If one can transcend the impulsion of narcissistic immediacy and embrace the needy finitude it seeks to escape, one does not return merely to individual origins. One embraces the neediness of all, the earth of genuine humanity, with the possibility in mutual openness of authentic sharing.

6

Dynamics of
Rejection and Retrieval

Freud and Heidegger

To march forward, bearing the burden of eternity, to
march forward, bearing the burden of humanity. . . .
—St.-John Perse, Nobel Address

Before turning to some of Heidegger's mature reflections to amplify
the hermeneutical image Kierkegaard has offered, let us pause
momentarily to recognize some of the convergences between Freud
and Heidegger that have already emerged, although more or less tacitly.

Both Freud and Heidegger perceive a primordial and generic
self-evasion. Freud of course speaks of this in a metaphor of depth
as repression, whereby an aspect of the self is thrust from view in
reaction to a traumatic engagement of oneself at the threshold of
consciousness. Employing the metaphor of another dynamism,
Heidegger speaks of fleeing from oneself.

Each thinker corroborates the other. Heidegger warrants
through the structure of falling the ontological possibility of the
primordial repression apprehended by Freud. Freud, on the other

hand, concretizes Heidegger's ontological understanding, pinpointing the ontic inception of the drama that is already underway as Heidegger opens *Being and Time*. The archaic and foundational character of the repression explored in *Inhibitions, Symptoms, and Anxiety* (ISA) helps to clarify why inauthentic Being, which Heidegger avows maintains itself proximally and for the most part, is intransigent and so resistant to change. Both affirm that an existential structure established prior to consciousness and the onset of language is extremely difficult to locate, or even recall, for ameliorating reconstruction. Not merely a part or an aspect of the personality, but the self in its wholeness or potential wholeness is segregated, banished, and essentially terminated.

The metaphors of repression and flight are complementary. Their common element testifies that one cannot face—or be—oneself. It is certain that Heidegger's "fleeing" is not a geographic evasion in the first instance but, like repression, an interior one. The convergence of perspectives is consolidated insofar as Heidegger speaks of covering up and concealing the authentic self—images that parallel the dynamic of repression: "Dasein covers up its ownmost Being-towards-Death, fleeing in the face of it."[1] Identifying repression with flight, Freud unites the two perspectives in his concluding synthesis.[2]

Both Freud and Heidegger recognize that resistance to the unwelcome material is manifested through forgetfulness. In the light of ISA, the forgetfulness that *Beyond the Pleasure Principle* considers in terms of the specific neurosis of an Oedipus complex or "some portion of infantile sexual life"[3] can be recognized as grounded in a more constitutive forgetting.

Both Freud and Heidegger assert the indispensable necessity of recovering one's "original face" if human being is to be restored as an authentic whole. This demands, each recognizes, that the forbidding element of oneself be uncovered. Both speak with roughly the same accent. While *Beyond* focuses on the compulsion to repeat in terms of neurotic resistances to remembering—and reexperiencing—the cutoff material, Freud also indicates that the return of the repressed is the genuine repetition that must be realized for a successful analysis.[4]

For Heidegger, too, "repetition" describes the resolute appropriation of closed-off facticity that he hopes can be effected.[5] This facticity is one's "thrown" Being as finite, as ISA recognizes in the infant organism's recoil from its first conscious experience of embodied finitude. The terrible cost of this psychophysiological nirvana exempt from excitation is the conflictual division of oneself.

Freud, speaking in more dynamic terms, stresses the repressed's attempted ascent to consciousness, while Heidegger, speaking less dynamically, simply says that, from "the depths of its uncanniness" and "with an alien chill," conscience summons or calls.[6] Both perspectives bear the common insight that the cutoff material actively seeks integration; when Heidegger emphasizes that the call comes "from me" though "not of me" but, rather, "'it' does the calling," one familiar with Freud cannot help but hear the id evoked. However much this linkage may be an interpolation, it is a peculiarly rich association, suggesting that the psychophysiological caldron of the id is antithetical only to the rigidly defensive ego and that the id represents—in some aspect at least—one's potential wholeness. Emblematic of all manner of alien and threatening impulses, the id tends to be specifically associated with the chthonic and the sexual. Perhaps stronger associations are suggested when Heidegger says that Being-true, the authentic way of Being for Dasein, is "uncoveredness" or "Being-uncovering."[7] This unveiling of and encounter with one's naked self, one's "bare 'that-it-is',"[8] exposing vulnerable finitude, perhaps casts light on the virulence of sexuality as an etiology of neurosis.[9]

Not surprisingly, both Heidegger and Freud perceive the cultural organism as, in some sense, a product of the primordial evasion and suppression of one's facticity. Social bonding, predicated upon this flight, is thus a playing out of the inscrutable logic of one's unconscious reaction to the initial trauma of discovering oneself. This bonding is a symbiosis and merger of necessary and defensive convenience in a desperate but unsuccessful struggle to secure refuge in the face of the absolute contingency each remains in spite of denials. Through its massive quantification, the collective identification—unconsciously banishing memory of individual vulnerabilities—hopes to stand against the overwhelming trauma of existing.

The symbiosis of this "union," however, is not genuine relation-ship; it is unconscious expediency. It is the expediency of mutual advantage, but the mutuality persists only as long as the bonding perdures to and for one's own self-promotion and only so long as vulnerability is not exposed by another. All are united, paradoxically, by the cohesion of self-interest and the urge to avoid one's self.

In Heidegger this is clear enough. Fleeing the guilt of thrown finitude, one falls into the collective "they," *das Man.* An alternative rendering of *das Man*, a scholar underscores, is (the) One.[10] Together with the Robinson-Macquarrie translation as the "they," a fuller understanding of the collectivity is obtained. The translation of *das Man* as the "they" emphasizes the fact that inauthentic Dasein has abdicated responsibility, the power of decision and self-choice, to the Others of the collectivity and, thus, is self-alienated and appropriated into the misunderstanding of the "they."

"The One" underscores the fact that, for whatever reason, Dasein has become so thoroughly absorbed into and merged with the inauthentic collective mentality that its individuality has been effectively eradicated. From Freud's perspective in *Beyond*, the cohe-sive agent of this social organism is Eros, characterized by Roth as "the urge to merge."[11] The driven and precipitant character of this bonding is indicated within Heidegger's perspective by the "falling" that fleeing in the face of oneself exhibits. In Freud's understanding, this fleeing of oneself, initiated by repression, is maintained by resis-tances to the unmasking of forgotten or unconscious material. The definitive episode of this drama plays itself out by immersion in the cultural arena, through submission to the pedagogy of the latency period, following the narcissistic wounding of the oedipal crisis. Inevitably, the structures and energies of repression are incorpo-rated into the life of the culture.

In *Civilization and Its Discontents*, Freud sounds somewhat like Heidegger as he attributes the emergence of social bonding, what he elsewhere called the "phenomena of their narcissistic organiza-tion,"[12] to guilt: "Since civilization obeys an internal erotic impul-sion which causes human beings to unite in a closely-knit group, it can only achieve this aim through an ever-increasing reinforcement of the sense of guilt."[13] Some will recognize, and others will suspect, that the context of this remark is a discussion of the primal crime that first occupied Freud in *Totem and Taboo* (1912–13). While that study has been criticized today,[14] especially concerning its focus on totemism, it was based upon the best researches of the time, with particular debt to Charles Darwin.

While anthropology and archaeology must assess Freud's data and conclusions in light of their expertise, what is of special value for these considerations is the fact that the mythohistorical legend of *Totem and Taboo* resonates with Freud's clinical experience. In other words, Freud was attracted to this borrowed notion because it exhibited a certain harmony with and contributed an explanatory valence for the data he was uncovering in his explorations of the human psyche. This myth—along with others in his repertoire—helps to elucidate the issues that focused his attention.

The essence of the myth of the primal crime is based upon Darwin's notion of a primal horde in a primitive age of our species that was dominated by "a violent and jealous father who keeps all the females for himself and drives away his sons as they grow up."[15] At some moment, the exiles banded together to kill the tyrant and thus end the patriarchal oppression. The act was consummated with the consumption of his remains, through which "each one of them acquired a portion of his strength."[16] While the father had been feared and loathed as a "formidable obstacle to their craving for power and their sexual desires," he had been envied, Freud says, and admired as a model. These more affectionate traits provoked a reaction of guilt to the patricide.[17]

The guilt of which Freud speaks is not the ontological guilt of Heidegger's concern but the product of an ontic act. Since, not unlike Heidegger's dynamism of falling, Freud drops us into the middle of a drama already in progress, it might be suspected that there is some antecedent catalyst impelling the events. This will come to light in due course, but what immediately attracts attention is the figure of the father. The primal father, in many ways, manifests the ultimate logic of the Erotic drive as it strives to enhance an ever greater organism. With an absolute focus on itself, the Erotic organism cannot conceive of either limiting the self or of a limited self. After first securing its (symbolic) turf, then expanding the terrain, it moves toward dominating the entire field, much as the primal father tyrannizes the scene, confiscating anything and everything of value. Claiming all for himself, the primal father evinces the compulsive hoarding of resources—and ultimately of oneself—that the Erotic orientation represents in its desperation for security. His expulsion of the sons symbolically sums up the hegemony of Eros that aggressively pursues its uncontested reign as an absolute center beyond need and contingency. Ingredient to this, as Freud has pointed out, is the instinctive aggression that narcissism directs toward any rival or threat.[18]

In *Totem and Taboo*, this natural inclination comprehends the entire male population. The sons' overturning of their father's tyranny is, in fact, its preservation. The violent father generates violent sons whose "craving for power," thwarted only by his superior position, is finally realized through his vicious, destructive legacy.

The primal crime, however, is but a reflection of the original and more primordial transgression against oneself—the lethal self-rejection of repression. This is the ontological substratum of what otherwise appears to be an isolated ontic deed. The original violence against the nascent self provides the dynamic rationale for both the father's hostile conduct and the sons' equally hostile response.

The bond or "social organization" that proved the father's undoing did not simply result from the transgression, as Freud avers, but in truth evoked it, manifesting the propensity of Eros to eschew finite individualization through collective quantification. While the primal father's uncontested domain represents the ultimate logic of Eros to which all unconsciously aspire, what Freud calls the narcissistic social organization[19] is an expedient and compromise formation. One way or another, Eros will preserve the primal repression that seeks to definitively escape finite vulnerability. Where the hoarding of resources cannot be absolute, the power of numbers substitutes the illusion of omnipotent invincibility.

The violent deed, however, serves an additional function. As Freud not infrequently emphasized, the organism experiences inner tension as more onerous than outer excitation.[20] Thus, the interior conflict resulting from the self-mutilation of primal repression is assuaged through its enactment in the parricide. Once externalized in the slaying, one's inner division can be denied more effectively even as it is institutionalized in ritual celebration as a victory for freedom and the foundation of a necessary union. This is precisely the totemism that Freud says emerged from the crime. While totemism, exogamy (which Freud claims is an additional fruit of this lethal act), even the crime itself, are earnestly contested or refuted by many, such issues are not the focus of these considerations. Rather, the congruency displayed by the mythological elements with Freud's psychological system is what is of significance here.

While it might be argued that devouring the slain father is a non-essential embellishment, a scrutiny of this fantastic ingredient reveals that it simply mirrors the psychologically rapacious Eros, which would devour finitude through its infinitely replenishing conquests.

Whatever might be said of these repugnant elements, the presence of an antagonistic father is not tangential to the Freudian perspective, nor was it a late addition to the essential core of psychoanalysis under the influence of extraneous sources. Through the mythological malice of Kronus, this hostile father casts its first shadow as early as *The Interpretation of Dreams* (1900) in the foundational articulation of what will become known as the Oedipus complex. What stands out in this primal rendition, although destined to be eclipsed by a more sexual emphasis in the subsequent version, is precisely the intergenerational conflict later glimpsed in *Totem and Taboo*.[21]

The Interpretation of Dreams presents Kronos, "the violent old man who devours his children," as typical of a certain contemporary father "who was a hard man, liable to fits of rage."[22] Freud found the myth of the devouring and murderous Kronos metaphorically illustrative of a patient's crisis. Earlier, in an extended discussion that distinguished between the "cultural standards of filial piety" and "the real relations . . . between parents and children," he spoke of primeval mythology that "gives an unpleasing picture of the father's despotic power and of the ruthlessness with which he made use of it."[23] Like the desperately oppressed sons of *Totem and Taboo*, Zeus slew his villainous father and succeeded to his rule, although here there is a greater vindication of self-defense than in the legend of the primal horde. Although it will be lost from view in Freud's consideration of Oedipus and the complex that bears his name, in *The Interpretation of Dreams* Freud underscored the analogy between contemporary paternity and the ancient titans: "Even in our middle-class families fathers are as a rule inclined to refuse their sons independence and the means necessary to secure it. . . ."[24]

This refusal to share, hoarding the riches of life, that is viewed through the unyielding patriarchs of both *The Interpretation of Dreams* and *Totem and Taboo* is reconfigured in Freud's study of Little Hans.[25] Although the case was presented in ISA as an exemplary instance of, and evidence for, the Oedipus complex, the facts beg the question of whether the concept was not misapplied in this situation. Prior to that issue, however, the possibility arises that the very notion of an Oedipus complex is simply redundant. In the classic oedipal theory that childhood sexual impulses are directed at one's mother (in the situation of a male like Hans), with jealousy and hostility directed toward one's father, there is a mirror image of the myths of the violent primal father and the murderous Kronos. The hostile reaction of a child to a parent is comprehended within the parent's hostility toward the offspring. In fact, since parent-directed hostility is simply the Zeus reaction or pole in the Kronos-Zeus myth of hostile generations, it can be argued that the Oedipus complex is an unnecessary proliferation of theory.[26]

Nevertheless, the facts of the case suggest an amplification of psychoanalytic understanding that enriches the perspective already gleaned from the intergenerational contest. What is manifest in Hans's situation is that hostility toward his father is not the primary datum; it is derivative and twice removed. Hostility toward the mother is derivative as well. The primary focus of Hans's wrath is his sister, and the instigating event is her birth. The little child refuses to share his place and space. Hans will not be relativized; he insists on retaining an absolute position. Here, then, ill-named after

Oedipus, is an enlargement of the sphere of rejection and refusal, that of sibling-directed hostility. In this context, if we continue to think of an Oedipus complex, henceforth it will simply indicate this second dimension of hostility and hoarding.

A third "myth," the "Family Romance," reveals another direction of hostility and a third magnitude of rejection.[27] Here the child renounces the status and situation of the parents. Unlike the Kronos-Zeus myth, the repudiation does not occur within a context of enmity and strife. Instead, it reflects the omnipotent psyche seeking a circumstance other than the relatively impoverished particularity of its native condition. Wistful for a more illustrious derivation than its actual parents can provide, a child fantasizes origins of august and glorious pedigree. In this is reflected narcissism's dissatisfaction with anything but regal privilege. Like the young Hans, one refuses to share the space of life in any position other than an ultimate one. While the parents are the primary focus of one's rejection in this romance, there is a tacit rejection of oneself as well.

Three myths or legends that Freud finds characteristic of the human condition articulate the repudiation of others in the refusal to share: progeny, progenitors, and peers are all disavowed. We might expect to find a fourth myth, equally representative of the human situation, wherein one refuses to embrace one's own life, especially since this would make explicit the self-rejection implicit in the "Family Romance." Indeed, it has already appeared in Freud's use of Aristophanes' myth in *Beyond* to interpret the rejection and clinical evasion of one's actual human situation for the illusion of blissful, preoedipal contentment. The myth told of gods dividing a fantastic primordial creature to produce the concrete human individual known to history. Renouncing one's actual situation, individuals of the human species, the myth records, forever strive for the illusory existence.

These four myths, in varying degrees, are exemplary of Freud's understanding of the human situation as he came to know it in the clinic. Together, all document a species in conflict with itself. This refusal or inability to share the human reality or suffer the penury of finitude reflects the inauthentic, in Heidegger's terms, or the pathological, in Freud's, that plagues the earth.

Is there a resolution to this unhappy circumstance? Did Freud recognize an exit from the crisis that might open into the possibility of a shared world? I believe he did. Since his career was devoted to uncovering the pathological recesses of the psyche and exploring their dynamics, it could be expected that the resolution only gradually appeared and that Freud, himself, was only dimly aware of the insight that his researches were awakening—although implicit from the inception of his psychoanalytic science. Whether aware or not, Freud reveals a clue.

In *Beyond*, the myth of Aristophanes provided an interpretive key for understanding the drives as conservative tendencies that seek an earlier state of affairs. If, as has been proposed[28] (supported by Jones's characterization of the book as a free association), *Beyond* presents itself in dream-like convolutions, Aristophanes' myth becomes part of that dream's manifest content, beneath which can be discovered a latent content. Freud's clue leads precisely in this direction. In *Beyond*, he was perfectly clear about the fact that the myth was *Aristophanes'* contribution to (Plato's) *Symposium*. On later occasions, however, attribution was awarded to Plato. In "Why War?" he spoke of instincts "which seek to preserve and unite—which we call 'erotic', exactly in the sense in which Plato uses the word 'Eros' in his *Symposium*. . . ."[29]

While philosophers may debate what exactly in Plato's dialogues represents his own thinking, three basic possibilities exist.[30] One extreme might propose that no content from the dialogue is presented as Plato's own teaching; instead, the philosopher is attempting to demonstrate a model of philosophizing or a mode of living.[31] Another might urge that no specific discussant within a dialogue represents Plato's thinking; instead, Plato's perspective somehow comprehends the breadth of views presented. By far the most common understanding—whether correct or not—and the most likely association for Freud, himself, would be that Plato's perspective is enunciated through Socrates. In this case, a reference to Plato's myth from the *Symposium* would have to refer to Socrates' oration therein.

The most surprising and striking phenomenon that greets the reader of the *Symposium* is that Socrates offers a perspective that he received through Diotima's instruction at some point in his youth. The assorted issues this creates cannot be explored here.[32] Instead, given Freud's association, let us focus immediately on the myth that Socrates appropriated from Diotima's insight and presented with his own assent.[33] Diotima highlights the origin of Eros in the union of Poros and Penia (203B). Although it can mean way or passage, *poros* is usually translated as resource (that is, the wherewithal of both savvy and means or plenty); *penia* is poverty or need.

At a feast celebrating Aphrodite's birth, Poverty came to beg but remained in the shadows of the gate. Overindulging on nectar and inebriated, Resource retreated to Zeus's garden and fell asleep. Observing this, and determined to abolish or alleviate her destitution, Poverty lay with Resource and conceived Eros.

As the son of Poros, Diotima explained, Eros is courageous and intense, a lover of wisdom who, seizing the initiative, is sagaciously impelled toward the good and the beautiful, although not without resourceful scheming. Nevertheless, Diotima emphasized earlier, it is only because Eros, as a child of Penia, is lacking in the good and the beautiful and remains ever in need that these boons are desired at all and must be forever sought (202D). What is striking in this account is the radical and enduring poverty of Eros. Unassailable need is integral to its very identity.

If, recalling Freud's conflation of Aristophanes and Plato, this perspective informs the recuperative dynamic of Aristophanes that *Beyond* presented, it is transparent that the elusive half from which one is separated, and that desperately begs recovery, is the neediness of contingency and finitude that the primordial repression attempted to eradicate but succeeded only in thrusting from view. If the truncated being is to be renewed and made whole, this inescapable facticity and all it grounds must be uncovered and embraced.

As Diotima explained, it is the function of Eros to unite the divine and the human, the mortal and the immortal (202E). Psychologically, this can be understood as reuniting the sundered and dichotomized human being. The divine pole represents the recoil from mortal being that is preserved through immortal narcissism's infinite struggle to omnipotently distance itself from the vulnerability of human need.

The efficacy of Eros, Diotima asserts, creates a harmony of body and soul (206B–D); and this can be interpreted as one's becoming consciously mortal and willingly embodied.

This integrative transformation, which Diotima calls beautiful as well as harmonious, provides the indispensable foundation for a life of creativity. Without this unification, one cannot beget, whether physically or psychologically. All of us, Diotima says, are pregnant in body and soul (206C), but a self who is not in harmony remains divided, shirking into itself, refusing or unable to give creativity birth (206D). This ugly disharmony is apparently coterminous with aggression since the person who grows more beautiful, that is, more and more whole or unified, becomes gentle and delights in being productive. Diotima thus shifts the focus of Eros from the quality, beauty, or merit of the object to the creative valence and quality of the loving being: Eros, she proposes to Socrates, is giving birth in beauty (206E). Since this includes procreation and progeny, it underscores the life-giving sharing that contrasts profoundly with the self-assertive hoarding of the primal father, who must be emblematic of what would be for Diotima the ugly, divided, and violent soul. The integrated being—no longer divisive or repressed, with psyche and body now in harmony and giving birth—treasures its offspring, whether of body or mind, and nurtures the new life, sharing the beauty and bounty it has realized (208B, 209C).

This new life of openness and sharing is impossible without the reappropriation of one's finite and contingent being—one's poverty and need—or, as Diotima puts it, without the emergence of wholeness through the union of soma and psyche (206C).

The healing potential of reclaimed finitude, without which there is no authentic humanity, that emerges from the interface of the myths of Diotima and Aristophanes is precisely what Freud has signaled by the return of the repressed in *Beyond the Pleasure Principle*. Initially called the compulsion to repeat, Freud was astonished to witness this ameliorating dynamic short-circuited and usurped by the wounded and intransigently defensive ego—which had emerged within and was scarred by the crucible of repression—in the rejection of its concrete personal reality. Thus, *Beyond* initially recognized the contest between the ego and the reemerging material. Nevertheless, the full significance of the repressed, fighting for consciousness and for integration, was obscured when it was construed solely within the narrow range of oedipal issues that both symbolized and obscured the profounder realities.

In light of the primordial repression uncovered in ISA, the foundational and global significance of the repressed and its drive to emerge becomes apparent. In that archaic conflict, the entire human being is affected and placed in issue. Conscious mortal life is challenged and in doubt from the liminal moment separating human existing from the merely organic. Struggling to exist, yet intimidated and overwhelmed, the human paradox seeks both to emerge and to obliterate itself as the embodied event of finitude. What hangs in the balance is exactly the issue Heidegger underscored: can a human being *be*, wholly and authentically—undivided and unrepressed—and will a human being emerge into conscious mortal life? With the attempted return of repressed finite being, the issue is joined.

In the thrust of the returning repressed, relentlessly seeking to restore the truncated being to original integrity, the Exodus principle, adumbrated at the close of chapter 1, can be discerned. This unsettling but restorative resurgence presents a counterforce to Eros as well as a second principle, opposing the pleasure principle, that Freud vainly pursued in *Beyond*.

7

A Shared World

Exodus and Beyond

> . . . made of the one and the many . . . epic of all. . . .
> —St.-John Perse, "For Dante"

"Exodus" aptly names this second principle and dynamic since it constitutes a liberation of ourselves—and of others—from the oppressive Egypts of our self-captivity. This is the dual bondage of narcissistic captivation and the enslavement of oneself to a less than whole, self-conflicted existence.

This second drive exhibits the elements that characterize a drive according to Freud's surmise in *Beyond* (a conservative inclination, seeking an earlier state) and bears the hallmark of a second principle, opposing the pleasure principle, in that it endures unpleasure to negotiate reality. The emancipation of the repressed—or, actually, the incipient integration and liberation of the self as a whole being—promises to reestablish the psychological situation that existed at the threshold of consciousness prior to the repression of finite facticity.

This dynamism is clearly antithetical to the pleasure principle because embracing the needy "earth of our humanity" requires one to go directly into and through the trauma of excitation and tension to reappropriate the vector of human reality cut off by repression. Enduring the vulnerability of this contingency, one becomes a limited being subject to all the vexations and vicissitudes of the finite. This principle counters the pleasure principle, moreover, insofar as the drive demolishes the secure structures of Erotic self-aggrandizement that defensively perpetuate the pacification of tension first effected in the primordial repression. As *Beyond* asserts, resistance from the narcissistic ego maintains the divisive repression.[1]

Since opening oneself to all that had been cut off and buried initiates the life of a whole human being, this second dynamic *conserves*, through its recovery, the integrity of finite Being, no longer alienated from itself. This is the meaning of Heidegger's individualization. "Individual" does not indicate an autonomous, isolated being. On the contrary, that is the character of Erotic, narcissistic Being under the guise of collective socialization. Rather, "individual" signifies, in the etymological sense of in-dividual, the state and condition of being no longer split or divided. This is the reality of being—or becoming—whole and united within oneself. If the drive conserves, it is nevertheless not conservative as a pleasure-principled Eros. In conflict with this, it opens to the future, exposing oneself to the new, unknown, and unexpected, *beyond* the protection of an impregnable, exclusive self-environment.

This dynamic exodus beyond narcissistic entrenchment or, as Heidegger would stress, this ecstatic opening into the clearing of finite freedom[2] transcending inauthentic and alienating structures of ego-syntonic defensiveness is an emergence beyond the crisis and eclipse of otherness and the resultant fall into undifferentiated merger.

In the first, incipiently conscious, encounter with ourselves that provoked the crisis, we ourselves proved to be the primordial other that propelled us from incipient integrity. Facing this formidable terror, uncovering and reclaiming the other we are, is the only path to encountering the otherness of a broader world. With this retrieval one ventures into universal terrain that everyone shares in particular, unique, and individual ways. The disarming and vulnerable "there" of human indigence, aware of the needs of others in the neediness of all, is fertile ground for relationship and mutual acceptance. However, this journey into the unknown, unfamiliar, and alien is not a facile one. Heidegger says authentic Being is ready for anxiety.

Manifest thereby is the fact that the Exodus principle is the only genuine reality principle, since Freud admitted in *Beyond* that the reality principle he was then able to comprehend was but a modified pleasure principle. Authentic (finite) Being, Heidegger says, is open to accidents, adversities, and the blows of fate. This is a reality principle that is not singularly concerned with one's own advantage, a mere and more comprehensive pleasure principle, but a principle that is open to reality in all its guises and manifestations, however much beyond our control or adverse it may be. The Exodus dynamism, therefore, is the human being's drive to be real, emerging from illusion and concealment to engage all phenomena, whether of fortunate or unfortunate circumstance.[3]

In contradistinction to Eros and the pleasure principle, the Exodus principle is not conserving but generous and donative in its self-openness, not hoarding but sharing. Neither does it dominate; it relinquishes the imperialism of a narcissistic self. All are liberated to be uniquely themselves. This is the import of Heidegger's understanding of phenomenology: letting others be revealed and perceived in their own light.[4]

While the drives of these two principles are initially, and perhaps proximately and for the most part, antithetical, it can be seen that, at least potentially, the two can work in concert if a certain balance and integration is realized in the human being. The tension of existence, as Freud noted, is very real and mercilessly exhausting. Alternatively, therefore, "thrusts" or advances beyond the self could alternate with pauses for rest and recuperation, stabilizing and integrating, not so much the "gains" of life as the more and more comprehensive openness to and embrace of the otherness of reality. In this reality principle, the self not only can endure what Heidegger calls "the blows of fate," but it is assisted by them in being more profoundly emancipated from dependency and illusion, individualized more and more as the unique openness only it can be. In sum, the healing dynamic that Freud vaguely glimpsed, latent in *Beyond* in the myth of Aristophanes and revealed by his own associations, opens to a shared humanity through the discovery and acceptance of oneself that unites divisions of our elemental earth.

It would be helpful if this second dynamic—the liberating integration of repressed finitude—could be viewed in a corroborating analysis. This is possible through Marie Cardinal's report of her own psychoanalysis, albeit presented under a patina of fiction. "I was running away from myself," the analysand comments, in what resembles a gloss on *Being and Time*.[5] She lived in a world where "[t]he most ordinary words and gestures were pretenses, disguises, masquerades."[6] Home and school conspired to efface her uniqueness as she was subjected to the brainwashing of a scrupulous enculturation.

> I had been fashioned to resemble as closely as possible a human model which I had not chosen and which did not suit me. Day after day since my birth, I had been made up: my gestures, my attitudes, my vocabulary. My needs were repressed, my desires, my impetus, they had been dammed up, painted over, disguised and imprisoned. After having removed my brain, having gutted my skull, they had stuffed it full of acceptable thoughts which suited me like an apron on a cow. And when it was verified that the graft had taken, that I no longer needed anyone to control the waves which welled up from the depths of my being, I was let go. I could live freely.[7]

Thanks to this processing she had become "more or less worthy of my mother, my family, and my class."[8] Nothing was left to her. "Who was I? No one. Everything I was, was destroyed, and in its place was zero, this beginning and end. . . ."[9] Her personal perspective was eclipsed: "I had no vision of my own. . . ."[10] Moreover, "everyone . . . had submitted to the very same fate."[11] The final episode of this tragedy befell the mother who had so faithfully tutored her in the "hypocrisies and lies"; her mother, Cardinal tells us, remained afflicted to the very end and succumbed at last to mental illness, afraid to emerge from the artful illusion. Her mother lacked "the words and the gestures of rebellion . . . THEY had never taught them to her."[12]

For Cardinal, psychoanalysis was an experience of opening her eyes on her "agonizing desert," but the resistance to this opening was formidable and amazingly powerful. Refusing to suffer the forgotten injury anew, her resistance guarded something that "had wounded me, which had done me great harm, which had stolen my identity and shattered my life."[13]

Healing was slow. In spite of progress, after a year she remained enclosed and "so fast asleep in my cocoon."[14] As she opened measure by measure to her secret terrors, she discovered not so much the anticipated horror as a child's fears. Gradually awakening to these realities, she began "to clear the newly conquered terrain. My space became increasingly enlarged."[15]

As her strong resistances were confronted and transcended, she became less afraid of being "face to face with myself."[16] In due course, she discovered that, "in fact, I had encountered myself for the first time. Until then, I had always organized the scenes of my past in such a way that others—my mother, in particular—had the leading role. I was merely the submissive performer, a nice little girl who was being manipulated and who obeyed."[17]

The process of retrieval and transformation began with the emergence of a healthy embodiment as she gradually won "the freedom of my body."[18] This precipitated an incremental discovery of her self, and "little by little, my character emerged in all its individuality. I had become a person."[19]

Able, now, to think of herself as "an independent person and an individual,"[20] a true exodus was under way as she emerged from her defensive cocoon into a world of agency and relationships. Instead of artificially induced symbiotic attachments, she began "constructing genuine relationships among the various members of the family," which gradually led her into an ever-expanding circle of involvement with society at large.[21] "Increasingly, I became able to talk with others and to listen to them. I was able to attend meetings and to go on my own from one place to another. . . ."[22] She discovered an impatience to know and encounter everything: she was growing open to all.[23]

The greatest lessons, however, were learned through her children. She was now at their disposal, open to them and able to comprehend their needs, while yet realizing that she could not be responsible for them ultimately. They were distinct and distinctive; she had to recognize them as individuals with their own identities. "They were not me, and I was not them."[24] She had to know them as the unique beings they were. As the process of healing permitted her to differentiate herself from the environment, she became increasingly able to discern others and attend to them as independent existents, rather than as ingredients of her ill-defined self.

Thus, the passage of recovery led from bodily integrity to identity as an individual self who was able, increasingly, to differentiate others as persons with their own value. As she, herself, was released from bondage, she was able to release others, distinguishing them from her prior confusion through mature relationships to independent peers. Concurrently, she was increasingly able to expose herself to the greater and once fearful world.

Heidegger articulates this second dynamic as anticipatory resoluteness, the recovery and repetition—as noted in chapter 3—of the factical thrownness of finite, individualized "having been," the prior situation or earlier state of affairs of Freud's concern. Experienced as Being-guilty, this given finitude initially precipitated a falling flight into the haven of inauthentic *das Man*, the collective "self-forgetfulness" of the "they."[25]

Dwelling at home in *das Man*, seeking relief and refuge from its thrown individualization, Dasein is alienated from, and not-at-home with, its authentic self. When, however, Dasein is authentically itself, *there* in its factical situation, it is not at home in the world. The ultimate significance and cause of this homelessness is that Dasein will die. Having no abiding dwelling place in the world, the clubish security of the "they" is exposed as illusion: Dasein is only in transit, in unceasing exodus. This homelessness illumines, as well, the fact that Dasein's identity and self-understanding cannot be extracted, gleaned, garnered, borrowed, or distilled from the world or anything therein, even though Dasein "gets its ontological understanding of itself in the first instance from those entities which it itself is *not* but which it encounters 'within' its world."[26]

This erroneous identification is the basis of Dasein's interpreting itself as a "what" rather than a "who" and of the consequent perception of others in a similarly misguided fashion. With such an inauthentic self-understanding, Dasein "misses itself," while "its place gets taken by what is present-at-hand within-the-world, namely Things," or with the mere instrumentality of the ready-to-hand.[27] As a "Self-Thing," life is quantified as a "business" or "something that gets managed and reckoned up."[28] Undoubtedly, like Kierkegaard's seducer, each manipulates and seduces others to one's own best advantage, for one's own peculiar success. The "they" is so involved, Heidegger says, "in order that it may be able to rid itself of an understanding of Being"; it is the "fugitive way" of saying "I."[29]

Anticipatory resoluteness opens up the possibility of an authentically existing self that had been concealed and closed off in the self-forgetful collectivity. The accoutrements and camouflage of *das Man* are unveiled and dispersed through the radical disclosure and resolute appropriation of one's original finitude. Transcending the entrenched recalcitrance of the "they," one emerges and stands forth—existing—into what Heidegger's "Letter on Humanism" eventually will call the clearing of Being, transparently individualized to one's "bare 'that-it-is'," beyond the fictive "I" of the they-self.[30]

To be at last freed from absorption in the "they" and from identification with things may allow one to be authentically and wholly all he or she is, but authentic, individualized being is not a species or instance of autonomous, sequestered self-interest. This is manifest by the radical poverty or dispossession of authentic Being, through which genuine relationship first becomes possible.

As inauthentic, even Dasein's use of utensils and things, the ready-to-hand or present-at-hand, had been misguided. The authentic present of a liberated self "permits us *to encounter for the first time* what can be 'in time' as ready-to-hand or present-at-hand."[31] Nevertheless, the deepest significance of Dasein's individualized transformation is illumined by emphasizing a nuanced sense of *eigen* (the root of *eigentlich*, usually translated as "authentic" existence) as "owned" existence.[32] Free from self-alienation, one is free to embrace—possess or own—one's unique life and self. This life, this self, however, is constituted, as we have seen in chapter 3, by a double nullity, defined by the finitude of its origin and its end. To own or "possess" oneself, therefore, is to *be* this nullity, thrown back upon oneself as utterly dispossessed: one possesses nothing and no one in owning and possessing oneself.

In a more positive idiom, it can be said that while Dasein is totally dis-possessing, empty of possessions or "whats" and exercising no mastery over others, it is open to all and remains open for all. This openness is the character of Dasein's temporality—its finite Being—that is ecstatically open through the three ecstases of present, future, and having been. "Dasein, as temporal, is open ecstatically."[33] Thus, the authentic Being of Dasein's anticipatory resoluteness is the open and finite world of temporality. The shared world is a world of finitude, the world of individualized Being.[34] "Only by authentically Being-their-Selves in resoluteness can people authentically be with one another. . . ."[35]

Dasein is called forth to that self who *is* Being-in-the-world, and this is a world that is always to be shared with others.[36] The shared world, then, is one wherein another is no longer regarded as a "what"[37] and appreciated only to the extent that he or she may serve my existence as an object to be used, abused, or overlooked according to my dispositions and needs. Instead, and at last, others are recognized, respected, and valued as Being-there with us.

As authentic, Dasein is freed for itself and, concomitantly, freed for its world.[38] There is no dichotomy or barrier between authentic self and authentic world. One is not closed off from the "external world" or isolated as an inner self or "free-floating 'I'."[39] Resoluteness toward oneself—existing authentically—"first makes it possible to let the Others who are with it 'be' in their ownmost."[40] Jealously and ambivalence are cleared away.[41]

No longer are others dominated by or made to orbit dependently around oneself.[42] Authentic care is restored to each that all may discover their own trajectory in transparent self-understanding, independent and free for unique worlds.[43] In sum, "[r]esoluteness, as *authentic Being-one's-Self,* does not detach Dasein from its world . . . [since] resoluteness as authentic disclosedness, is *authentically* nothing else than *Being-in-the-world.*" That is to say, authentically individualized, one is opened (or dis-closed) "into solicitous Being with Others."[44]

This capacity for sharing the world emerges because Dasein journeys "right under the eyes of Death" to take up the truth of its own "there."[45] "Only Being-free for death . . . pushes existence into its finitude," individualizing Dasein.[46] As free for death, Dasein comprehends itself in "its own superior power, the power of its finite freedom . . . and can thus come to have a clear vision," with an understanding of itself as Being-with and, consequently, of the potentiality-for-Being of others.[47] This power of Being-there is a "powerless superior power," the loyalty of finite existence to its own self that through repetition becomes more and more liberated from illusion.[48]

Being-there is a paradoxical power, indeed. It is powerless insofar as it submits to a definite and circumscribed world,[49] consciously embracing its own limitations with the recognition of death's absolute boundary that reduces one to the irrevocable condition of human neediness. With death's power exorcising the lust of self-assertion, whatever illusion of omnipotence may have deluded one's life is dissolved. Any power one may have possessed over others is abdicated as the narcissistic position of a central or sole existent is relativized in the clarity that one exists among many.

Nevertheless, it is an uncommon power to be human in profound simplicity, beholding reality, oneself and others included, without disguise or evasion. It is a power to be integrated and undivided, to be genuinely oneself, allowing—and aiding—others to be

wholly themselves. It is a power to be down to earth, relinquishing
the illusion of hegemony in the freedom to share.

If death is the power that transforms and humanizes, we are
reminded anew that our examination of *Studies on Hysteria* and *Inhibitions, Symptoms, and Anxiety* led to the caution that death might
prove to be a more sinister force, provoking a less than authentic
reaction. Although Marie Cardinal supports this caveat when she
notes that "death with its putrefactions" was enlisted by her resistances "in order to better guard the door" of repression,[50] she nevertheless experienced the process of healing as a death that issued
in rebirth: "I think that a well-conducted analysis must lead to the
death and the birth of the subject in question, securing his own
freedom and truth."[51] While "his own" recalls the "ownmost" of
Heidegger's authentic Being, her continuing remarks evoke special
interest.

"There is an inestimable distance," she noted, "between the person I was and the person I have become, so that it is no longer even
possible to compare the two women. And this distance between
them only increases, for the analysis never comes to an end, it
becomes a way of life."[52]

Cardinal's arresting metaphor of the healing process as a death to
a formerly repressed and truncated self is only heightened by these
elucidating remarks. If the distance between the debilitated and
integrated selves only increases throughout a lifetime, never coming
to an end, then the process of integrating recovery is not a discrete
or once-and-for-all event. Instead, the creative and liberating death
that issues in the birth of a new, incipiently whole being is integral
to the entire transformation and, integrally, a way of life enduring
a lifetime. This ongoing distancing reminds us of Kierkegaard's
"dying away from immediacy," underscoring the reality that
the transformation of any human being is necessarily slow and
undoubtedly a gradual, incremental passage. The revolt that escaped
Cardinal's mother is not a manifest repudiation of cultural life, but a
revolution of the psyche. As Heidegger maintains, neither one's
world, nor others, nor oneself is exchanged or repudiated in the dis-
closure of authentic Being.[53] Rather, the therapeutic "distancing" is

indicative of psychological growth—a revolution in relating to one-self and, thus, to others.

The passage or process may be, in fact, the reverse of what Heidegger imagined. Instead of death as the limit of Being that leads to an authentic life, it may well be that death as a beginning, within life, leads to a gradual acceptance of death as an end. If the return of the repressed maintains a constant pressure to emerge, it may be that (with an inscrutable measure of undetermined good fortune) one is able little by little, yet more and more, to face the repressed horrors that ultimately turn out to be, as Cardinal discovered, a child's fears. This is not to say the horrors are not for-midable and absolutely threatening. To the contrary, a death was necessary, Cardinal learned, to transcend brokenness precisely by facing and accepting it. What dies is the split self of primordial repression—the only self one consciously knows—and its divisive ways of perceiving and interacting with the larger world. The para-dox is that Eros maintains what appears to be life but, instead, is a body of death—the living death of primordial repression—while the death of the second drive, the Exodus principle, opens one to all that had been split off by dissolving barriers to one's primordial earth. Undoubtedly there is a quantum leap when facing death becomes possible, apprehended as Heidegger proposes, but its preparation is slow and tentative, following the rhythms of facing the terrors of finitude hidden within. After the threshold of this leap, a certain reciprocal influence or dialectical interchange mutu-ally informing and transforming each must be realized.

In fact, we can glimpse this incremental process at work in *Being and Time* if we focus less on death and more on Heidegger's empha-sis of the repetitive character of the appropriation of finitude. The resolution of "coming-back to one's ownmost Self"[54] is "repeti-tion" for Heidegger, paralleling Freud's initial compulsion to repeat, which became better enunciated as the return of the repressed. Nevertheless, it is clear that this appropriation of "coming-back" is not a single instance but an ongoing repetition because Dasein's authentic Being *is* as having been; it is the "temporality of that repe-tition which is *futurally* in the process-of-having-been."[55] There can be no doubt of the repetitive character of Dasein's authenticity when Heidegger speaks of becoming "*more* free of Illusion"[56] and asserts: "The *more* authentically Dasein resolves . . . the *more* unequivocally does it choose and find the possibility of its existence, and the less does it do so by accident."[57] Indeed, "[a]uthentic resoluteness . . . resolves to keep repeating itself."[58]

In *Being and Time*, this resolution inescapably transpires through anticipation of death, but in the later Heidegger, death as one's limit-situation is lost from view, while death as an ongoing, integral passage of healing and transformation, such as Cardinal has highlighted, is tacitly in evidence. Let us explore some of the riches of Heidegger's later thinking.

8

Celebrations

Opening Horizons and Heidegger's Way

> . . . on death itself shall we live . . . .
> —St.-John Perse, *Chronicle*

In *Being and Time* (BT) death disclosed finitude. Biological death, apprehended in anticipation as the conclusion and goal of life, unified the whole of one's existence through the disclosure of temporality and the appropriation of thrown facticity. In the later writings, it may be said, death is no longer the goal of life but the means of life. Falling from explicit view, death is discovered within life as the path and way to Being or presencing. Once again, as in BT, death necessarily discloses finitude, but as is appropriate, death is a more silent, invisible presence in the later works. There is still an indication of finitude as beheld in BT insofar as later writings either state or intimate that we do not think because one thinks only by Being-there, present and in issue: face to face with Being finite. We do not think because we are not present, present to ourselves, faced with the issue we are in Be-ing. However, while such works as "What

Calls for Thinking?" *On Time and Being,* and *Discourse on Thinking* maintain lingering connections with BT, a more stunning and profound elucidation takes place.

In "What Calls for Thinking?"[1] a bold and often torturous exploration, Heidegger's overarching concern is framed by a central and recurring assertion: "Most thought-provoking in our thought-provoking time is that we are still not thinking."[2] This gives rise to two core questions: What is it to think and what is it that calls us to, or directs us into, thinking? An accompanying and often repeated concern, therefore, and the purpose of the essay (or the series of lectures it introduces in the original context) is that we "learn thinking."

Parenthetically, it must be noted that Heidegger dismisses what has traditionally passed for thought, insisting that it must be radically unlearned if one is to enter the "neighborhood" of thinking. The facile identification of philosophers or the study of their thought with thinking is repudiated: this only perpetuates the "stubborn illusion" that *we* are thinking. While science is respectfully saluted in its proper place, the misidentification of science and thinking is equally dismissed. Recalling BT's critique of everyday, inauthentic discourse, it is not surprising to read that customary views, common understandings, current speech, and obvious meanings are especially misguiding.

In "What Calls for Thinking?" Heidegger does not say, as he would in BT, that we forget Being; rather, he says that we do not remember and heed that which heeds us protectively. More foundationally, Heidegger eschews this pervasive lapse that will not hold on to that which "holds us there" and "keeps us in our essential being."[3]

Not only do we not remember "what really must be thought," we are disinclined from it as well.[4] The disinclination arises naturally, perhaps, because what holds us and remains to be thoughtfully engaged has withdrawn from us since the very beginning and continues to do so.[5] Nevertheless, this very withdrawal develops and keeps a nearness that inscrutably touches and concerns Dasein, claiming us essentially. It is precisely in the mysterious way of escaping that this elusive reality keeps near, inclining toward us, summoning and appealing, calling us to come even as it withdraws. Although we may not remember it, it re-members us, from an alienated being—lost and scattered, as BT would say, amid the beings—toward the reality of a unified whole. "The event of withdrawal," writes Heidegger, "could be what is most present in all our present, and so infinitely exceed the actuality of everything actual."[6] To incline toward this withdrawal is where and when and how we first think and become "who we are."[7]

How, then, do we approach the neighborhood of thinking and enter the withdrawal? In saying that thinking must be learned, Heidegger indicates that a certain inertia must be overcome and our fundamental misdirection reversed.[8] Disposing all we do to the summons that addresses our very being, it is imperative to "set out from where we are."[9]

The way is provided by the withdrawing call itself, and until we open ourselves to its summons, we remain blind to our essential nature or embedded in the greater delusion that, while deprived of sight, we see.[10] If we respond to the call, we are led into "what is always problematical, always worthy of questioning," in the discovery that we, ourselves, are the text and texture of the question.[11] Only by faithfully questioning within this problematic do we think, orienting ourselves and all we do toward essential being: "only . . . by thoughtful questioning are we . . . on the way."[12]

There can be no steady progress toward this way, however. An obvious path into the heart of withdrawing is not to be found, nor can one happen upon it unaware or inadvertently. The fact of questioning, itself—indicating that everything is challenged and uncertain—underscores the discontinuity of the way.

Steady progress is understandably precluded if we recall the truncating primal repression that divides us from ourselves. An accidental or facile transition from alienated to unified, essential being is impossible. We recall that Cardinal characterized the therapeutic movement from repression to incipient integrity as a revolution and a death. Thus, the ultimate discontinuity, which exploration alone uncovers, is signaled by the alarming fact that no bridge can assist one over the widening void that both rebuffs and beckons.[13]

It is by a leap, alone, that one enters the way, plunging into the withdrawing abyss.[14] Abruptly, all is different and strange, Heidegger tells us. One is confounded all the more because the withdrawal continues its escape. When the leap is taken and "we follow the calling, we do not free ourselves of what is being asked," Heidegger notes. On the contrary, "the question cannot be settled now or ever."[15] The way, he insists, can never be left behind or traversed once and for all. One remains underway and on the way only by questioning; as we proceed, "the question becomes in fact only more problematical."[16]

Before the leap, the vortex is such that we are already in its pull, however unheedful, disinclined, or unaware we may be. The leap overcomes this resistance and places us in relation to the enigma.[17] It is a relationship, impervious to Promethean stealth, that must be welcomed and received with open and empty, nongrasping, hands.[18]

Prior to the leap it can be said that we are merely drawn along or, more accurately, dragged along in spite of ourselves and our conscious or unconscious opposition. Following the leap—and facing the elusive presence—we are with-drawn into the depth of its mysterious event.[19]

To be drawn toward and into this way is to bear in our uttermost being its very mark or stamp. With this character one is human, pointing to the withdrawal and drawing deeper into the nearness of its appeal.[20] This is a summons to come, a call to enter into presence—or presencing, since the venture is never complete. To enter more profoundly into the calling word is to be named, as well as claimed, by this defining reality that one is, yet more and more becomes.

So named, and restored to oneself, one can, as a pointer to the withdrawing, summon others to share in the shelter and healing of this essential event that holds all "there," letting each return to the "self-belonging" and rest of one's own identity.[21]

In spite of Heidegger's esoteric context, convergences with Marie Cardinal's experience of therapeutic transformation may be apparent. It will be recalled that Cardinal spoke of the distance between the debilitated self she had been initially and the healed, progressively whole person she was becoming. That distance, she emphasized, only increased with time—and never ended because the process of amelioration and integration was a way of life and a life-time endeavor. Cryptic and naive as Heidegger's language may be, the ceaseless withdrawing graphically portrays this distancing as it articulates the transformation in dynamic, processual aspect.

Like the two poles of Marie Cardinal's experience, an old or former self and a new and evolving being are in evidence. It is not difficult to perceive that this passage toward unified and essential being, overcoming a prior disinclination, comprehends—underscored by the indispensable leap—a disjunction that parallels the therapeutic reorientation that Cardinal experienced as a death.

This seemingly more radical change than BT's permutation from inauthentic to authentic Being is ramified by the "Conversation on a Country Path."[22] In a nocturnal dialogue between Heidegger, a scientist (possibly Werner Heisenberg), and a scholar (probably Eugen Fink), the trio spoke of the "historical change of the human being to an ego."[23] The discussants agreed that the ontological priority of human being was usurped at an undetermined moment by the emergence of ego—however necessary (it might be added) that emergence must have been. This parallels Heidegger's remarks in the "Letter on Humanism," convergent with the disposition of BT, that "Being is the nearest. Yet the near remains farthest from the human being. . . . [A]t first [one] fails to recognize the nearest and attaches himself to the next nearest. He even thinks that this is the nearest. But nearer than the nearest, than beings, and at the same time for ordinary thinking farther than the farthest is nearness itself: the truth of being."[24] In other words, although nearest and most intimately one's own, human realization or *being* human would necessitate an unceasing recovery, a return to origins that is impliedly symbolized by a journey into the uttermost regions.

Meanwhile, the discussants acknowledged, the ego misrelates to phenomena with objectifying manipulation. Calculative thinking—which has a proper place but is abusively thoughtless as an exclusive mode of operation—supplants a more humane disposition.[25] To an ego "the world . . . appears as an object open to attacks of calculative thought," with utility and economic possibility the only calculus.[26] The cruel twist is that by its "calculated intention" the ego falls into bondage to the very objects that appear to be serving its needs.[27] "Our inner and real core" is no less shackled by this servitude.[28] The pervasive "business" orientation of inauthentic Being, which regards life as "something that gets managed and reckoned up," as highlighted by BT, is wedded to this calculative orientation in the "Letter on Humanism" when Heidegger speaks of the "calculative businesslike way" we, as tyrants, exert "domination over beings."[29]

What is needed, Heidegger urges during his country dialogue, is "the possibility of dwelling in the world in a totally different way."[30] This implies a restoration from ego to human being or from *homo* to *humanus*, which the "Letter on Humanism" describes as a descent from the privilege and possession of a lord to the poverty of a shepherd or guardian.[31]

This arduous descent from the pinnacle of lordship and mastery, "climbing back down into the nearness of the nearest,"[32] can be amplified with additional scrutiny of the withdrawal.

Heidegger stresses that, as a pointer to the enigmatic and distancing nearness, one is a sign that "points not so much at *what* draws away as into the withdrawal."[33] Pointing to "what draws *away*" is not incidental; it is one's essential being. One *is* this "away." The call to come is precisely a call to venture farther and farther into this mysterious reality, forever departing our former and familiar ground. We arrive only to be summoned and to set out anew, transcending the self we have been to approach more profoundly the "humanity of *homo humanus*."[34]

Since our Being is always beyond us—and ever eluding our grasp—we are forever incomplete and unfinished. While this highlights the finitude of one who is "richer in contingencies"[35] and powerless to master or dictate the human situation, it underscores as well that our essential Being is this transcending, pointing always beyond itself, perpetually letting go and taking leave.

Such leave-taking into the unknown is the very definition of death. Relinquishing the secure and known certitudes of an established self, one hazards the void between what one was and who one might become. "Adventurer-like," Heidegger writes, "we roam away into the unknown,"[36] exposing ourselves to annihilation in the uncertain beyond. Nevertheless, this voiding of a former self analogous to Cardinal's experience of therapeutic death is the very stamp of the withdrawal, issuing in the same creative transformation that Cardinal realized as a new birth of emerging integrity, deepening awareness, and enriched concern for the well-being of others. Marked by the withdrawing's opening expanse, one becomes "more void," with increasing room for all as an ever-deepening and more inclusive whole.[37] One is released from the tyranny of a narcissistic focus for the perception of life in its rich diversity.

In the "Letter on Humanism" this way of existence is the "clearing of [B]eing" that lets "beings . . . appear in the light of [B]eing as the beings they are."[38] This inherence in the clearing and truth of Being as the "there" that guards the release or liberation of beings in the space of its shepherding care is, for Heidegger, the essential quality of our *humanitas*.[39] It is "the human way 'to be'."[40]

"If we think of Dasein not as an organism but a *human* being, we must first give attention to the fact that Dasein is that being who has its being by pointing to what is. . . . Dasein is the being who is in that it points toward 'Being', and who can be itself only as it always and everywhere refers itself to what is."[41] This attention to reality and "relatedness to what is"[42] Heidegger calls meditative thinking. It is this reflective way of being, "which contemplates the meaning that reigns in everything that is,"[43] that Heidegger has in mind when he charges that we are no longer disposed toward thinking. Indeed, he laments, we take refuge from this meditative, open being in the entrenched self-enclosure of an ego, pointing to nothing but ourselves.[44] This "closure of the healing dimension," refusing to share the space of creation, is the "sole malignancy," he maintains.[45]

Heidegger's perspective converges with the psychoanalytic understanding of Ernest Becker, whose insight enriches whether or not his existential recasting of Freud's legacy is subscribed to wholly. One is inclined to isolate "a manageable world," Becker writes, "uncritically, unthinkingly" throwing oneself into action, accepting the "cultural programming" that indicates where to look and how to see. One "doesn't bite the world off in one piece as a giant would, but in small manageable pieces, as a beaver does."[46]

The congruences with BT's inauthentic *das Man* are magnified when Becker adds that one learns "not to stand out; [one] learns to embed [one]self in . . . things and cultural commands," living in a "secure dependency on [the] powers around . . . [and] least in possession of [one]self."[47] The constricting of the world is due, Becker asserts, to illusions, character defenses, and the "expansive organismic striving" fed by limitless incorporation of things from the world that is the very definition of narcissism.[48] What is most germane in the present focus, however, is Becker's affirmation that an abiding world of openness is possible—and even requisite for a posture of maturity.

To encounter life's facticity beyond narcissistic solipsism, "to see the world as it really is" and open oneself to a greater and greater relational whole, "being-cognition" is required. Borrowed from Abraham Maslow, Becker defines the term as "openness of perception to the truth of the world."[49] While recognizing that the dangers of emerging from ego defenses are substantial, Becker underscores, in unison with Heidegger, that beholding reality "makes thoughtless living in the world . . . an impossibility."[50]

It may be hoped that one will be able to echo Cardinal: "My space became increasingly enlarged."[51] In harmony with her experience, however, Becker cautions that the realization of being-cognition constitutes a rebirth that is facilitated only through a necessary death.[52] Heidegger's advance over Becker lies in his understanding of the ongoing and, therefore, gradual nature of this essential and transforming passage. The incremental advances into deepening otherness and greater openness, which the withdrawing represents, keep one from being overwhelmed by the shattering absoluteness of death that precipitated the neurotic reactions Freud reported in *Studies on Hysteria*. Engaged with the onus of living, only gradually—with experience and reflection—does one, or might one, recognize that the transcending encounter has been an initiation into what Kierkegaard calls "dying away from immediacy," the qualitative transition from symbiosis to individuation, illusion to reality, sleep—or unconsciousness—to awareness, childhood to maturity. In due course, through deepening awareness and relational valence, one is able to comprehend biological death directly and more and more fearlessly.

In "What Calls for Thinking?" Heidegger spoke in passing of the "event" of withdrawal and, at one point, emphasized that "Withdrawal is an event."[53] *On Time and Being* (OTB) identifies the phenomenon exclusively as the "Event," *Ereignis*, although it has been translated as "Appropriation" and the "event of Appropriation," in part following indications from Heidegger, in part due to the Event's dynamics.[54] As the withdrawal with-draws, "The Event appropriates."[55] Richardson places a Heideggerian hyphen in e-vent to remind the reader that it comes from e[x]-venire: to come out, to come from, to come forth. The strong exodus character of this dynamic is thus emphasized: we do not simply come into openness and presence—presence to Being, as the "Letter on Humanism" emphasized—but we come *from* and *out of* the alienation, oppression, and illusion of our self-encapsulated, narcissistic Egypts into the reality of dis-closure and encounter.

In BT it was Dasein who appropriated authentic Being through resoluteness or resolve; in OTB Dasein is released by the appropriating Event to the "there" of a human presence.[56] This statement about release and the appropriating event harkens back to the *Discourse on Thinking* and its "Conversation on a Country Path," which parallels releasement (*gelassenheit*) and appropriation.[57] In this dialogue Heidegger says that, in one's being, one is "released to" the Region and its regioning insofar as one "is *appropriated* initially" to it.[58] Regioning, or the opening of openness, is the abiding expanse and expanding abide, the nearness of distance and the distance of nearness, that reveals even as it withdraws and is veiled even as it approaches.[59]

Concretely understood, it can be interpolated that, in the "distance of nearness" a symbiosis or fusion with the other is impossible. No longer viewed as an object that can be appropriated and assimilated to ourselves and our own ends, things are freed for their own identity and perceived as the realities they are in their own right. With regard to other persons, genuine relationship is at last possible, for in the "nearness of distance" space for the other in his or her uniqueness is valued above all else. Respected as integral persons, quite apart from one's calculative ego, true intimacy becomes a possibility in this ontological and psychological openness. The paradoxical character of healthy, authentic relationship is that people can relate only if each is free and independent of the other, with his or her own integrity as an incipient whole. Symbiotic mergers only confuse and conflate (non)identities.

Amid the otherwise "perilous situation" that humanity "is threatened today at its core," releasement and appropriation grant the promise of a "new ground and foundation," with the "vision of a new autochthony."[60]

Although Heidegger continues to speak of the realm of openness in OTB, the opaque and cryptic "regioning" is discarded. While reference to releasement also disappears, it can be seen in the "letting-presence" of Being, granted or "sent" by *Ereignis*.

The gift quality and dimension adumbrated in the *Discourse on Thinking* ("Releasement . . . would be a receiving of the regioning"[61]) and made explicit in the "Letter on Humanism" ("The 'gives' names the essence of being"[62]) is underscored with a central focus as OTB affirms the gift-giving character of *Ereignis*. Of the Event, Heidegger declares: "It gives."

Although it is clear that OTB is attempting to explore anew, beyond earlier articulations, and to express the inexpressible, the explanatory comment of the "Letter on Humanism" concerning BT applies a clarifying force in this new context as well.

Interpreting *"es gibt"* (as in the statement "being is" or "'there is' being"), Heidegger prefers the literal translation of "It gives," remarking that "the 'it' that here 'gives' is being itself. The 'gives' names the essence of being that is giving, granting its truth. The self-giving into the open, along with the open region itself, is being itself."[63]

The "open region" is reminiscent of the *Discourse on Thinking*, while evoking *Being and Time*'s understanding that the truth of being is dis-closure. Heidegger admits, continuing the "Letter," that in his thinking "it gives" ("es gibt")

> is used preliminarily to avoid the locution "being is"; for "is" is commonly said of some thing which is. We call such a thing a being. But being "is" precisely not "a being." If "is" is spoken without a closer interpretation of being, then being is all too easily represented as a "being" after the fashion of the familiar sort of beings that act as causes and are actualized as effects.[64]

On Time and Being reaffirms these distinctions: "[I]s Being a thing? . . . *Is* Being at all? . . . The lecture hall *is*. . . . But where in the whole lecture hall do we find the 'is'? Nowhere among things do we find Being."[65]

The "is," which is the giving or "sending" of being that brings beings to light, remains transparent. If "Being means presencing, . . . show[ing] itself as letting-presence" or "the unconcealing of presencing," Heidegger discerns that the epiphany is obscured by what is manifested: "In unconcealing prevails a giving" that "gives only its gift, but in the giving holds itself back and withdraws."[66] This self-withdrawal "in favor of the gift which It gives" has led to a lacuna in Western thinking, which mistakes the gift for the giving. The "It gives," or giving as such, has not been addressed but only being, misconstrued and conceptualized in terms of the beings that are disclosed.[67]

In order to think more primordially and ponder being explicitly, Heidegger is forced "to relinquish Being as the ground of beings in favor of the giving which prevails concealed in unconcealment."[68] In other words, OTB will thoughtfully explore the "It gives." How, Heidegger queries, is the "It gives" to be thought? In fact, It gives Being; It gives time; and It gives the relation that "holds the two toward each other." The two must be thought together, for "Being and time determine each other reciprocally."[69]

Common interpretations and representations of traditional thought are impediments that must be overcome to enter into explicit

thinking. If Being means presence and presencing, "presence" traditionally has been construed as a present "now" distinguished from
the future and from the past. "But the present understood in terms
of the now is not at all identical with the present in the sense in which
. . . guests are present. We never say and we cannot say: 'The celebration took place in the now of many guests'."[70]

A similar situation exists with regard to time. As in BT, Heidegger cautions that he is not speaking of time as commonly apprehended. That is, the unity of present, past, and future cannot be
represented in terms of "the now" and, as usually interpreted, perceived as a "calculable sequence of nows."[71] Rather than a mere or
immediate present, real time speaks of presence, which "differs so
vastly from the present in the sense of the now." Heidegger underscores that "we are not accustomed to defining the peculiar character of time with regard to the present in the sense of presence."[72]
Presence does not coincide with the present immediacy; presencing—"the approaching that reaches us"—prevails in the future
and the past as well as in the present.[73] With these caveats, Heidegger has prepared his reader for the opening of time-space.

The "unifying unity" of future, past, and present lies in the reality
that "they offer themselves to one another." That is, the presencing
granted within each is offered, and in this mutual giving the time-
space of true time opens up. Creating room for the unfolding of
space as it is generally conceived, time-space is the "openness which
opens up in the mutual self-extending."[74] As a unity of the multiple
"reaching out and opening up of future, past, and present," true
time is revealed to be three-dimensional, "three interplaying ways of
giving, each in virtue of its own presencing."[75]

The origin of this sharing is not attributed to any one of the
dimensions. Instead, "the unity of time's three dimensions consists
in the interplay of each toward each. This interplay proves to be the
true extending, playing in the very heart of time," that issues in the
"opening of openness."[76] It is a fourth dimension that, in truth, is
the first—the original, incipient giving that determines all.

This extending that opens up "the four-dimensional realm"—the
"It gives" of true time—recalls the "Region" highlighted in the

Discourse on Thinking. Regioning, as the opening of openness, expands into an abiding of all that has freely turned toward it and no longer bears, as a consequence, any character of opposition. Beyond contention, all rest in a releasement to origins, which restores the original integrity and "very nature" of each.[77]

Similarly, the presencing that "It gives" determines—and restores—the integrity of humankind. "Being as presence . . . concerns us humans in such a way that in perceiving and receiving it we have attained the distinction of human being." Only "standing within the realm of giving" that is the fourfold opening of time-space constitutes acceptance.[78]

As a constant receiver of the gift, one is appropriated to the "It gives" of *Ereignis*, which brings one into "one's own" as it assimilates him or her to the interplay of its own self-withdrawing openness.[79] Thus appropriated, Dasein "belongs to the Event."[80]

Initiated into this realm of multidimensional and deepening encounter, Dasein opens up in "the way . . . It gives Being."[81] This burgeoning, ever renewed ontological time-space reveals a twofold emancipation. The "sending" of Being that characterizes the giving of *Ereignis* underscores the letting go and letting be of the foundational human poverty enunciated in the "Letter on Humanism." In other words, the letting-presence of Being shares without imposing itself and gives without domination. It does not circumscribe its gift, nor constrict or restrict the interplaying sphere. Belonging to this inscrutable, elusive, and original self-effacing dis-closure, one becomes and *is* an e-vent in the Event that grants the epiphany of each, allowing all to be originally themselves.

Thinking, then, of this ontological spaciousness, let us simply conclude by saying that to stand forth, out of our closure and into its light, is to venture far out, as Kierkegaard would say, risking—and perhaps racked by—existence, ex-sisting. Beyond the defensively acquisitive fiefdom of an immediate horizon, it is a yes to a new and ever unknown, transcendingly inclusive region beyond the security, comfort, predictability, and inertia of one's particular "Egyptian bondage." As for Abraham and the Israelites of Antiquity, it is a constitutive, life-giving, and enduring Exodus through which we, ourselves, become a gracious opening wherein others might enter and refresh themselves, disclose themselves, discover themselves, or pause in whatever way they may wish.

In *Being and Time*, this realm of multidimensional presencing is anticipated in the authenticity of temporality. In BT, this ecstatic openness has the special quality of *spielraum*.[82] Literally, "playroom," this is the room or space that one, as authentic, *is*. As "Dasein-with," it is the "unshakable joy" of a shared world celebrating the Being of others as uniquely other, delighting in the distinctive, irreplaceable presence of each.[83] The playroom of temporality—or the interplaying gift of the Event—is an epiphany of all life, liberated from the oppressive illusions[84] of a narcissisticly closed self even as we, ourselves, are released for a more humane existence.

In this clearing and unburdening[85] of Being, one realizes that, "as the gift of the It gives, Being belongs to giving."[86] This is the incarnation of a new autochthony that shares, in a world of openness, the earth of our humanity. Each is a gift-giving space for the other, letting all be present as guests of the celebration.

9

Embracing the Earth

Kierkegaard and Kenosis

> For many times were we born, in the endless reach of day.
> —St.-John Perse, *Chronicle*

Perusing *Being and Time,* a reader familiar with Kierkegaard may come to the conclusion that Heidegger's commanding work is a gloss (rich, creative, and original but a gloss nevertheless) on the writings of this sagacious Dane.[1] It is a greater marvel, and a far greater surprise, to discover a Kierkegaardian antecedent to Heidegger's later thought, especially one that adumbrates the uniquely mysterious *Ereignis*. Nevertheless, such an entry is uncovered in Kierkegaard's journals:

> Only omnipotence can withdraw itself at the same time it gives itself away, and this relationship is the very independence of the receiver. God's omnipotence is therefore his goodness. For goodness is to give oneself away completely, but in such a way that by omnipotently taking oneself back one makes the recipient independent. All finite power

makes dependent; only omnipotence can make independent, can form from nothing something which has its continuity in itself through the continual withdrawing of
omnipotence. Omnipotence . . . can give without giving up
the least of its power, i.e., it can make independent . . . independent of that very omnipotence.[2]

In addition to the startling anticipation of Heidegger's dynamic
withdrawal, this passage highlights a limitless source, analogous to
the mysterious *Ereignis,* that inexhaustibly grants finite being its
integrity, while eschewing self-imposition in the very act of
bestowal. Although Heidegger was scrupulously unconcerned with
the godhead, this uncanny prefiguring of his ostensibly original
thinking—conceivably its inspiration—produces considerable
pause.

Curiously, although there is no evidence Heidegger was aware of
it, the phenomenon of a withdrawal appears several centuries
before Kierkegaard in the cosmogony of Isaac Luria, sixteenth-
century rabbinic and Kabalist mystic (1534–1572).[3] Luria was at the
center of a religious community in the town of Safed in upper
Galilee. Among the questions he faced was how there might be anything other than God if God were the All in All. Luria's response
was that the divine All withdraws power and presence, creating a
primordial space to make room for the creaturely other. However
naturalistic or naive this conception might be, its insight is significant and profound. Obviously, Luria is not contemplating the simple geography of two- or three-dimensional withdrawing. Rather,
this is the generosity of shared Being, delighting in creation through
its voluntary dispossession. The *zimzum* or withdrawal of the primordial creative act, without which finite being could not exist,
constitutes an abandonment or self-abdication that opens space in a
creative Being-with that realizes self-transcending otherness.

The absolute presence of the All in All is analogous to the dominating tyranny that the "Letter on Humanism," among other works
of Heidegger's later period, is concerned to see transformed into the
shepherding guardianship of a more authentic humanity. As seen

heretofore, Dasein's inauthenticity suggests that the desire to be fully and most uniquely one's self, *eigentlich* or ownmost, "proximally and for the most part" misinterprets itself. Making (everything) one's own is confused with Being all one's own. A misplaced possessiveness or misplaced identity results as a consumptive Eros seeks to make all my own and my own (self) all. The simple equation "all is me" or "I am all," with the desire to be "all in all," results in the blind absorption of narcissism. It is a tenuous and needful identity demanding, and dependent upon, everything to make it secure. Voiding the lordship of this kind of life was the implicit challenge and call of the "Letter on Humanism" and subsequent works of Heidegger's mature vision.

Luria corroborates Heidegger's seminal insight of an ongoing self-effacement that opens space for others, but this ratification remains at the macrolevel of cosmic process. An affirmation of more human proportions, however, can be discerned more than a millennium and a half earlier in a fragment from the earliest moments of the Christian dispensation:

> Have this mind among yourselves, which you have in Christ Jesus, who, though he was in the form of God, did not count equality with God a thing to be grasped, but emptied himself, taking the form of a servant, being born in human-likeness. And being found in human form he humbled himself and became obedient unto death, even death on a cross. Therefore God has highly exalted him and bestowed on him the name which is above every name, that at the name of Jesus every knee should bow, in heaven and on earth and under the earth, and every tongue confess that Jesus Christ is Lord, to the glory of God the Father.[4]

The epic dimensions of this pre-Pauline hymn, appropriated by the apostle Paul in correspondence with the Philippians, comprehends a divine openness to the finite other that is an embrace of the personal, human, and mundane. In almost two millennia of theological speculation, the mysterious self-emptying or *kenosis* from the heavenly realm was given no specific content or definition.[5] It was simply the inscrutable humiliation by which a gracious God unaccountably partook of the human enigma. When, in response to Enlightenment concerns, certain nineteenth-century German and British theologians sought to define "what" exactly had been "emptied" in the deity's incarnational descent, a repudiation of this apparent tendency to substantiate and quantify the deity quickly followed. What alarmed was the assumption that "by kenosis *must* be meant . . . a loss of divine power in the act of incarnation."[6] Dismissing "kenotic Christology," mainstream theologians adhered to the classic position that, whatever kenosis entailed, becoming human did not render the deity less divine.[7] Challenging all to a response, this is precisely the great paradox that Kierkegaard insists is, and must remain, scandalously absurd.

If the arena of dogmatic theology could experience conflict, the exegetical venue suffered a chaotic and chronic free-for-all. "[T]here is, more or less," Schillebeeckx notes, "no biblical pericope on the interpretation of which the experts on exegesis do not disagree among themselves."[8] A. B. Bruce's comment that "the diversity of opinion prevailing among interpreters in regard to the meaning of the principle passage [of Phil. 2:5–11] . . . is enough to fill the student with despair"[9] has been immortalized by M. D. Hooker's observation that the situation was not in any measure improved one hundred years later. In fact, she was forced to note, "the cause of the despair has increased out of all proportion . . . !"[10] Sanders, Hammerton-Kelly, and Wright have each contributed ingredients of clarity at various moments in the debate. The bibliographies of Martin and O'Brien provide a surfeit of literature.[11]

Apart from issues concerning the hymn's background, exegetes have tortured over whether the subject of the kenosis was a preexistent being (the divine Logos) or an already mundane figure.[12] Scholars have puzzled as well over whether it is the divine form or the divine equality that was relinquished and whether these are identical. At issue, too, is the relinquished prize: was it a present possession or a potential attribute and, thus, did the grasping—or not grasping—refer to the possibility of usurping something that is not one's own or refer, instead, to the refusal to clutch what, justifiably, might be construed as one's own?

Since this study does not concern theology or Christology but focuses instead on anthropological and psychological insight—that is, understanding the dynamics or "how," to use Kierkegaard's concern, of being human—these exegetical subtleties can be put aside. Nevertheless, one milestone of exegesis should be highlighted since it underscores—more through its contrariety—vital concerns of this chapter.

Ernst Käsemann, in a study of the hymn that exerted incomparable influence for more than three decades, argued—contrary to the tradition that included, by his own admission, the Reformation perspective—that the Philippians hymn held no *paraenetic* value, or appeal to personal application, since it celebrates the objective drama of redemption, with the enthronement of its protagonist as cosmic lord—none of which could be replicated by simple mortals. "Have this mind among yourselves" simply appealed to the fact that, by reason of religious conversion, the Philippians were now "in the realm of Christ." This is to say both too much and too little, although Ralph Martin eventually honed Käsemann's position to a fault: "The Apostolic summons is not: Follow Jesus by *doing* as He did—an impossible feat in any case, for who can be a 'second Christ' who quits His heavenly glory and dies in shame and is taken up into the throne of the universe?"[13]

John Macquarrie's remark about Karl Barth, in another context, applies with equal force to Käsemann's position: "[H]e really destroys the humanity of those whom he is so anxious to save, because he makes salvation a purely objective and external matter. . . ."[14] What is eclipsed in Käsemann's exclusively objective orientation, trivializing if not blaspheming the toil of living, is the human being, itself, being human. As one playwright has said, placing the words on the lips of wise King Solomon, "Being human's the hardest thing / whether you're a beggar or a king."[15] However much one may find oneself objectively "within the realm of Christ," the transition of the "new birth" is not a magic one, as in a shaman's circle. However much one is justified solely through faith in the redemptive act, to highlight the Reformation concern, human beings are never overwhelmed by graced action and reduced to automatons or zombies. Neither existence nor the individual human being—in whom, Kierkegaard would maintain, this graced and objective salvific potential must be concretely realized—is obliterated by the divine dispensation.

Undoubtedly, as a faithful Protestant, Käsemann excitedly inveighed at some other forum against the depravity of human nature, the consequence of an original transgression. This only begs the question—all the more crucially—of Kierkegaard's "how." How is one to live the graced existence; how is the transformed being, or for that matter, human being—although perhaps the two are identical—to be realized?

As many exegetes in the years following Käsemann's study emphasize, he was unduly preoccupied—in a era prior to redaction criticism when form criticism held sway—with the original pre-Pauline hymn and its background. This monopolized his attention to the detriment of the hymn's place within Paul's letter.[16] Consequently, context was ignored for the conjectured original meaning, drawing Käsemann to the conclusion that "the hymn is concerned with eschatology and soteriology and not with ethics."[17] Nevertheless, there is a growing consensus that Paul's use of the hymn—with the appeal to "have this mind among yourselves"—is intended by the letter's author to inform and orient one's conduct and life, a paradigm for the newly transformed existence.

In another important essay,[18] Käsemann at least tacitly acknowledges this necessary impact. In this later study, a recurring theme is that, for primitive Christianity, there was no separation of the earthly history of Jesus of Nazareth from its faith in him as Lord. The early Church "identifies the humiliated with the exalted Lord."[19] From this convergence the gospel genre arose, with its presentation to the faithful of a *life* of Jesus, refusing to allow the story of this concrete existence to evaporate in the glories of the Easter proclamation.[20]

Käsemann's Philippians study, on the other hand, abstracts the "experience" of the self-emptying and humiliated one in service of an objective soteriological proclamation about the exaltation of a cosmic lord. As if the subsequent essay were offering a corrective, Käsemann writes that the evangelists refused to "allow myth to take the place of history [or] a heavenly being to take the place of the Man of Nazareth."[21] The telos of Käsemann's leitmotiv is precisely that of paraenesis: "the story as presented by them [the Synoptists] is not 'once for all' in the sense that it excludes the experiences of those who come after. On the contrary, these people are expressly told that they can have the same experiences of Jesus."[22] Implicit in this later admission is the twofold insight that, on the one hand, it is not enough for one to be objectively "in the realm of Christ"—flesh and blood beings need some guidance for their new life—and, on the other hand, human existence is integral to salvation.

Human existence, Kierkegaard would underscore, "involves a tremendous contradiction, from which [one] does not have to abstract," but the task of remaining in existence so as "to understand the greatest oppositions together, and to understand oneself existing in them, is very difficult."[23] Kenosis, or incarnational self-emptying, is a paradigm that can acknowledge and descriptively explicate this challenge of the concrete human situation. What Käsemann presents in his Philippians study constitutes a partial and docetic anthropology, eclipsing the human ingredient. However objective, salvation is not exclusively, nor first and foremost, an extraterrestrial, otherworldly, or even eschatological occurrence. To the contrary, it is a here-and-now *being* on *earth*, and the how of that existence is crucial. "Humanity in the abstract," especially a redeemed humanity, "is a subject soon disposed of" (it took Käsemann the space of a few paragraphs) but "more forbidding seems the transition to becoming a particular existing human being."[24] To some degree, Käsemann acknowledges this when he says that the "heart of [humanity] should become pure and free, *this* is the salvation of the world."[25] Nevertheless, it was Kierkegaard who saw and said it best.

For Kierkegaard, whatever else Christianity may be—and he believed it to be the absolute—it is an "existence-communication";

that is, it radically orients one toward the *how* of living authentically, subject to the Truth. To Käsemann and Martin he would respond:

> The objective faith, what does that mean? It means a sum of doctrinal propositions. But suppose Christianity were nothing of the kind. . . . Christianity is not a doctrine but an existential communication. . . . Christianity has to do with existence, with the act of existing. . . . Precisely because Christianity is not a doctrine . . . there is a tremendous difference between knowing what Christianity is and being a Christian. In this way Christianity protests every form of objectivity. . . . It is subjectivity that Christianity is concerned with, and it is only in subjectivity that its truth exists, if it exists at all; objectively, Christianity has absolutely no existence.[26]

An irony to be acknowledged is that both Kierkegaard and Käsemann were responding to what each perceived as alarming developments inspired by the Enlightenment and, specifically, to accommodations by ecclesiastical Hegelians.[27]

In the present context, issues of faith and the divine sciences will be bracketed since, as Kierkegaard would insist, faith is realized only through an individual leap, for which "one does not prepare . . . by reading books . . . but by immersing oneself deeper in existence."[28] The focus, instead and in consequence, will concentrate on the essential existence-communication that can be harvested from the Philippians hymn.[29]

Here it is possible to be far more radical than theologians and exegetes in adopting a kenotic paradigm. We do not have to quibble or quiver about how—or whether—there can be change in the deity through kenotic incarnation. Neither must we anguish over whether or not there is a limitation of the divine in its embrace of finitude. Nor is there need to debate if the hymn's kenosis involves a preexisting being. One must only look at Freud and Heidegger to ascertain the appropriateness of the kenotic metaphor. From Heidegger we have glimpsed a preexistent state prior to authentically finite human being that, for the most part, perdures. Freud confirms this by discerning a primordial repression at the brink of conscious life that devolves into the "divine form" of omnipotent, immortal identifications (in Searles's description) of an Eros-driven narcissism that resists amelioration. This "preexistent" antithesis to the mortality of being human is underscored by Searles when he says, on the basis of his psychiatric practice, that an *individual* and *human* identity is a precarious, never definitively established, and deeply resisted phenomenon.[30] Consequently, the psychoanthropological model proposed here can assert that human beings do, and must, change drastically in the conscious embrace or appropriation of primordial, latent finite integrity, voiding an illusory and ethereal ontological denial. Thus, the insights that have marshaled themselves through the investigation of Freud and Heidegger converge toward the conclusion that the key and heart of being genuinely human is the ultimate exodus of kenotic incarnation.

Kenosis and incarnation are concomitant aspects of one dynamism. Kenosis is the relinquishing, emptying of or "dying to" the fraudulent apotheosis of omnipotent defensive structures that subject one to a less than fully human existence in their resistance to contingent, vulnerable humanity. Incarnation is the coincident embrace of finitude and one's concrete, embodied existence. As an integral dynamism, kenosis and incarnation is at once individuating and social, clearing space for relationships grounded in reality, beyond self-distorting illusions.

Let us explore Kierkegaard's use of the kenotic paradigm to understand more richly his psychology of transformation and ascertain what is revealed of the human situation. Kierkegaard employs neither the word "kenosis" nor "self-emptying," but it is clear from *Philosophical Fragments, Practice in Christianity,* and *For Self-Examination/ Judge for Yourselves* that he has the Philippians hymn in mind as he writes about the lowly, humble, and abased one.[31]

As proposed in the "thought experiment" of the *Fragments*, becoming human on the part of one who is absolutely different and unlike humanity—"the god"—is realized through a descent from royal privilege to the place of the lowliest in undiscriminating and

all-inclusive equality.[32] Relinquishing the glories of heaven, Kierkegaard says elsewhere, "it pleases God to walk here on earth."[33] This
exalted one was just like others, "an unimpressive human being."[34]
Since the yawning chasm between God and humanity is the greatest
possible, being God and being human is the "infinitely qualitative
contradiction," and every moment of life tempted him with the
possibility of taking his task in vain.[35] The power was his to manifest the reality of a divine status.[36] Instead, in self-abasement and
"the most profound incognito," he choose to be "truly human."[37]
Possessing all the riches in the world, he "gave up all that he possessed and lived in poverty" as a defenseless, vulnerable human
being.[38] The one who held "all possibilities in his hand," dwelled in
abasement on the earth.[39]

"Look, there he stands. . . . Where? *There.* Can you see him?" asks
the *Fragments'* thought experiment.[40] Recalling Heidegger, one is
alert to the significance of the *there* and of anyone *who* is there.

Lest one fails to comprehend, Kierkegaard underscores the
point: "Thus does the god stand upon the earth, like unto the lowliest. . . ."[41] For Kierkegaard this utterance is key, and the whole of
his authorship revolves around—in his terminology—this absurd
and absolute paradox.

Implicitly, here is a phenomenology and psychology of place,
with the suggestion (made explicit in Heidegger's concern for inauthentic Dasein) that human beings are out of place and not
"there."[42] In other words, something is askew and less than human
about human beings because we are not down to earth; somehow
we defy gravity, resisting our finite sphere. There is the further intimation that the way to be "there," standing humanly in place, is
through an analogous kenotic descent.

This hermeneutic of misplacement is ratified in the *Concluding
Unscientific Postscript.* In the *Postscript,* Kierkegaard asserts that we
"have forgotten to exist" and "forgotten what it means to exist as
human beings."[43] Amid exultation and self-importance, we betray
"a sense of despair over being human."[44] Few are "contemporary"
with themselves; most are "absentees" and a hundred thousand
miles removed, defying gravity, indeed.[45] One's terrestrial self is the

problem.[46] Reflection about existence may effortlessly carry one to the "seventh heaven," but "when one begins to do any of it, one becomes a poor existing individual human being who stumbles again and again, and from year to year makes very little progress."[47] Consequently, "no one wants to be an individual human being."[48] It is Kierkegaard's hope, nevertheless, that we might learn how to be human and how to live humanly.[49]

This learning is no easy task or once-and-for-all endeavor. For an "existing individual," the whole of existence is a steady striving; one is, oneself, "constantly in the process of becoming."[50] One "strives infinitely," challenged by the "strenuous difficulties" in the simplest of propositions about existing as a human being.[51] The seeming insignificance of becoming "what one already is" wars against the individual, rendering the task "infinitely difficult."[52] The death of the "exalted one," as Kierkegaard notes in his journal, betrays the "eternal strenuousness" of what it means to be human.[53]

Inspired by the Philippians hymn, Kierkegaard places the definitive and thus defining incarnational act in the event of death. Death is the consummation of becoming and being human: it is *there*—the ultimate and absolute pathos of finitude—that we "behold the man!"[54] Nevertheless, it is not the biophysical death closing a life-story that Kierkegaard contemplates; rather, the psychology of returning to oneself and being in place comprehends a suffering that is ingredient to the whole of one's life. "The suffering of death is not his suffering, but his whole life is a story of suffering" because, from the beginning, his life was "akin to dying."[55]

This is the kenosis or self-emptying that is a "dying away" from everything that resists, represses, or evades the finite earth of simple and uncontested human being, opening more and more beyond immediate self-interest to the otherness of all that relativizes and voids a privileged, lordly life—the "exalted" domination of omnipotent narcissism.

This "preexistent" or prior state, voided throughout life in suffering the humanizing birth, is a condition of unfreedom resulting from one's reaction to the traumatizing lesion of mortality. Evoking Freud's notion of repression, Kierkegaard says that "no captivity is so impossible to break out of as that in which the individual holds [it]self captive!"[56]

The apparently privileged life, thus, is no real life at all. Kierkegaard says it is analogous to a state of nonexistence. Like a transition from nonbeing to being, a change takes place in the finitizing act of kenotic incarnation that can only be called a birth, or rebirth, in light of the miscarriage of primordial repression—or, as Kierkegaard broached the same crisis, putting it in question form: "is not everyone stillborn in infancy?"[57]

Not surprisingly, recoiling from the foundational threat of one's own finitude places a person defensively at the center of reality. As the "midpoint" or axis, everything focuses upon or revolves around one's ceaseless self-concern. Constituting what Kierkegaard might call a "bad infinity," this, of course, is the Erotic self-centering that strives to make the tenuous organism ever greater at the expense of everything and anyone. The whole world is "forgotten" and others are eclipsed in the symbiotic merger that Kierkegaard calls immediacy.[58] As Harold Searles, on the strength of his psychoanalytic practice, corroborated a century later, this situation generally lasts a lifetime.[59] As both Searles and Kierkegaard recognize, this symbiotic identity is undifferentiated from, and coextensive with, the environmental totality to which the infantile psyche clings in the stupor of its amniotic bond: "Too closely attached to the world" and "dreaming . . . itself sensuously at one with everything," the immediate self is confounded and confused; its identity evaporates in fantasy.[60] In truth, the self is nonexistent; one's "inmost being . . . is as dead."[61] Despairingly, Eros compulsively fills this black hole of insatiable nonbeing.

With a "strong bent and passion to become something more and different" than indigently human, the "child" of immediacy refuses to remain in the "existential training school."[62] It labors inhumanly to preemptively distinguish itself.[63] In its "absolute relationship to the relative," engrossed in a phantom power to coerce and commandeer, it struggles to be secured against the "uncertainty of the earthly life."[64] Inflexible and domineering, immediate consciousness demands its way with everyone, insisting that all conform to its whims and wishes to possess everything and to do anything.[65] Advantage over others is anxiously won.[66] Distinctions invidiously accrue. Fortune and prestige as well as honors, position, power, and rank inspire avaricious pursuit.[67] Befriending whoever might assist in securing what is coveted, others are subjected to power or held in venal servitude.[68] All are used shrewdly to their disadvantage, even as success confines and diminishes, reducing one to the objects of selfish aspiration.[69] Craving vainly, one is consumed by the acquisitive life, even as it consumes others.

The kenotic death to self-immediacy demands a complete breach with this destructive, self-inflicted inexistence. Seduced by immediacy's fatuous promise and clinging to its illusion as though to life, one tenaciously resists the apparent impotence of a transformed existence.

Nevertheless, Kierkegaard insists, however painful the process may be, the Philippians hymn prescribes the task. If the transcendent one came down to earth, so can we. "He managed . . . what we should learn to do": from paramount heavens of superiority and clouds of unconsciousness to get down to earth and begin the "immense detour" of kenotic dying, which alone issues in life and depth—fully and unconditionally present, open to reality, to others, and to all.[70] His footprints mark the way.

Existence is always something of an embarrassment, Kierkegaard admits.[71] In lieu of the whole world, one gains only oneself.[72] Instead of abstracting from obstacles and misfortune, one sets aside the "wishful imaginative order of things" and the "bourgeois sugarcoating" in which one habitually is wrapped.[73] Penetrating all delusions, one becomes more and more concrete.[74] The process of concretion or of becoming oneself, willing to exist as a particular, individual being, persists as long as one remains in the "medium of existence."[75] This requires "the most complete separation" from the tranquilizing immediacy of the collective that Kierkegaard variously refers to as the public, world, or crowd.[76] We are wrested from the cohesion to which we cling, "cut . . . off in this way from what we animals regard as the true well-being, from coalescing with the herd."[77]

Consciously penetrating the suffering of this breach, one realizes that the destruction of the symbiotic world and hegemonic, acquisitive life is pregnant with the possibilities of "coming into existence" and being truly and completely oneself.[78] Dedicated more and more to the task of existing, one is profoundly *there*—where one needs to stand—"loving the human."[79]

If kenotic self-emptying is entering into the vulnerability and trauma of existence, incarnating is holding fast to "what it means to be a human being" in the "frailest expression of the finite," no longer seeking emancipation from "telluric conditions."[80] Being in place and simply down to earth, no longer an absentee soaring above the suffering of reality, one has entered the domain of the lowly and frail.[81] It is soon discovered that everyone shares in the equality of suffering.[82] In this all-inclusive fellowship of the indigent, sharing the plain earth of simple and vulnerable humanity that is the birthright of all, one no longer regards oneself as better than or superior to another.[83] In the fact of being human, whatever one's station or status, no one is above or beneath another, however much fantasies and dreams might campaign to the contrary.[84] The datum of the earth makes this inexhaustibly clear as one transcends oneself, emerging from the protective stupor of illusions, in an increasing assent to the finite.[85] Exhausting the suffering of being human, this is a place to share.[86]

Heretofore, as one apprehended danger everywhere, guarding against others and securing oneself in every way, interpersonal relations betrayed a narcissism struggling to enhance itself and playing out the self-deceiving wish "to be the only I in the world."[87] "Dreamily the spirit projects its own actuality," Kierkegaard discerned in a manner anticipating core aspects of C. G. Jung's understanding of the contrasexual.[88] From the viewpoint of Jung's archetypal psychology, a male projects his psychic feminine upon members of the opposite sex, while a female projects her psychic masculine in like manner, with the consequence that one does not actually relate to an other. To the contrary, one is enamored with aspects of one's own self that have remained unconscious until the projection makes them accessible, reflected in appropriate persons and events. "In erotic love and friendship," Kierkegaard warns, "the two can selfishly become one self."[89] Speaking of what today would be called narcissism, Kierkegaard notes that this is the "very height of self-feeling, the I intoxicated in the other-I."[90] The presence of intoxication indicates that one is not yet dealing with the reality of a concrete other. The relationship is "highflying" fantasy, "always about to fly after or fly away with the beloved's perfections."[91] We "vault into heaven" seeking the perfect object to mirror a flawless narcissism. Although known by the mass as "love," this is only self-ishness. "[W]hat we extol under the name of love is self-love," Kierkegaard writes.[92] Indeed, the other is not loved or perceived at all, but only "the first I once again, but more intensely."[93] The drama ensues, and "the more securely the two I's come together to become one I, the more this united I selfishly cuts itself off from others. At the peak of love and friendship the two really become one self, one I . . . a new selfish self."[94] In consequence—and not surprisingly—it is said that "[n]either one of them has yet the spiritual qualifications of a *self*."[95]

Authentic relationships and love, Kierkegaard proposes, are genuinely open to an *other* and genuinely *relate* to the other; identities are not fused, bonded, or merged. The relationship of profoundest regard for another person as other "is love between two *individual* beings . . . ; two spirits are never able to become a single self in a selfish way."[96] There is no symbiosis of immature psyches desperate for embellishment and security. Incarnational love descends from archetypal heavens to the actualities of earth. "[L]oving the person [one] sees" throughout all changes, the other becomes the "first-Thou."[97]

This constitutes a fundamental revolution, Kierkegaard says. "There are a *you* and *I* and yet no *mine* and *yours*! For without *you* and *I* there is no love, and with *mine* and *yours* there is no love. . . ."[98] This is relationship *between* two individual beings, each open to and recognizing the other, each sharing the space of life where, heretofore, Eros's possessive narcissism usurped the field. The drive to be ever greater—at others' expense—is voided as one's finitude, once embraced, liberates an individual to engage the concrete particularities of shared existence, standing forth from the tyranny of repressed humanity, which issues more and more in the vicious circle of inhumanity, to exist "on an essentially equal basis" with every person.[99] "[T]o descend from heaven means limitlessly to love the person[s] you see just as you see [them] . . . with all [their] imperfections and weaknesses. . . ."[100] Dedicated to sober reality, kenotic love is not eclipsed when love is unreciprocated.[101]

Prior to the incarnational transformation, Erotic being crushed the individuality of others, "inhumanly" subjecting them to oneself or otherwise demanding conformity, implacably insisting that everyone be molded in one's own image.[102] Although quaint to modern ears, the quality that most auspiciously characterizes the relational strength of transformed being is, Kierkegaard says, servanthood: voiding the polarizing distinction "mine"—emptying "narcissism" in today's parlance and "selfishness" in Kierkegaard's—"the I is no longer itself primary but the you."[103]

One is now approachable, no longer dwelling in Olympian security, untouched by the vicissitudes of earthly specificity and untroubled by others, with little time and less thought for anything but oneself.[104] In emptying narcissism more and more, or as Kierkegaard phrases it, self-love's "self-deification," one becomes able to share, no longer seeking exclusively for oneself as the only "I."[105] Equally important, freed from the need to press everything into ego-syntonic conformity, others are liberated from one's painful tyranny. Released from the deluding apotheosis of Eros, one can acknowledge "the given independence in every [person] and . . . do all that can in truth be done to help someone preserve it."[106] Moreover, laboring on behalf of others, assisting them to realize their unique potential and come into their own, one is now capable of being a peer.[107] This genuine care "does not seek its own" but "loves each human being according to the other's individuality."[108]

This recognition and ratification of others through self-transcending incarnation ushers in a celebration of difference that was first glimpsed in the *spielraum* of *Being and Time* and, in Heidegger's mature vision, the four-dimensional interplay of *Ereignis*. Above all else, Kierkegaard says, no distinctions are made in the community of shared humanity.[109] The boundaries of the earth are all-inclusive.

In its regard for all, however, the open, transformed existence "makes infinite distinctions in loving the differences."[110] All are embraced, each "in particular but no one in partiality."[111] Everyone is a delight to be celebrated. If being human signifies anything, it signifies equality in the kinship of all.[112]

Kierkegaard grants that existing is an ordeal, racking us with ever greater intensity. He acknowledges as well the hazards of the task and the repelling valence of kenotic incarnation. The cure of transformation, not untypically, may appear far worse than the disease.[113] However, no one other than Lacan has emphasized that the imperial, Eros-driven ego is "the human symptom *par excellence*, the mental illness of [humanity]," remarking that the "fundamental absurdity of interhuman behaviour can only be comprehended in the light of this *system* . . . called the human ego. . . ."[114] The crisis of this dilemma is a real one—pathological processes or the exodus of Kierkegaard's sober vision: "First death—then life."[115]

No less than Freud and Heidegger, Kierkegaard believed that "being purely and simply a human being,"[116] although a rare phenomenon, bore a significance beyond the anxiety of becoming. While he insisted that no one could warrant the path another must travel, he did believe that, if the risk is ventured and the trauma endured, one discovers "how glorious it is to be a human being."[117] Then, no longer fearful or in flight, an individual opens ever more faithfully to reality. Always incrementally, one "embraces the whole world," delighting in the "splendor of the earth."[118]

10

Beginning Anew

Envoi & Cross-Cultural Entrée

> . . . led by the vision of a new humanism: of
> authentic universality, of psychic integrity!
> —St.-John Perse, Nobel Address

Throughout his career, Freud was concerned with the therapeutic challenge of bringing to memory that which is forgotten. In his philosophical mode, Heidegger was similarly concerned with a healing retrieval. What has been eclipsed or forgotten, Heidegger would say, and what must be reappropriated to re-member a scattered self is the gift of authentic Being, *being* authentically and concretely finite. Only this is human existence; only this initiates a shared and human world. Freud would make explicit that authentic life, whatever else it might be, is a life that is lived consciously. Both would concur, although only Freud is truly explicit, that this life is a life of embodiment. Freud's well-known focus on sexuality and its traumas articulates his sensitivity to the incarnational demands of authentic existing.

The deepest significance of this sexual focus, drawing Freud toward consensus with Heidegger, lies in the latent implications of the primal scene—Freud's designation for parental coition and, specifically, its happenchance discovery by a youthful (usually preoedipal) child. However disconcerting the discovery may be, as a source of trauma and a foundation for neurosis, the primal scene remains incomprehensible at the manifest level of apprehension. As Freud emphasized, the deeper layers of the psyche, by which he meant the unconscious, must be involved for the production of pathology.

What is overwhelmingly at issue in the primal scene, especially for an infant psyche already primed by a primordial repression at the threshold of consciousness, is one's very self. The primal scene is not something we view; it is something we are. The witness we bear to this originating nexus is the burden of finite existence. The erotic bond of our realization is the primeval unconscious memory, inscribed in our blood and bones, of incomplete, imperfect, impoverished creating. We are the failure of Eros; at the summit of its power, its creation is insecure.

As Heidegger has said, we are the beings whose being is in issue. This is the onus of Freud's ruminations in *Beyond the Pleasure Principle*. What we suffer from is life, the peculiar and vexatious poverty of finite being, vulnerable equally to embodied excitations and to impingements from a threatening world. If, as Freud confesses, the instincts are his mythology, then *Beyond*—with its innovative death instinct—is Freud's mythological fantasy of wish-fulfillment. Revealing a yearning to be anything other than finite, subject to the tension and turmoil of a hostile environment, Freud's fantasy struggles to reverse the insult of defective origins. Whatever Freud may have imagined of its instinctual aim, "inanimate," "inorganic," and "nirvana" betray the essential ambiguity of his mythological drive, searching for a prior state beyond the temporality of outrageous fortune.

Harold Searles helps us to recognize the true ambition of such a richly overdetermined death instinct. Articulating the most secret of desires, our deepest fantasies, his clinical experience tells us, disclose a fascination with the inanimate, inorganic nonhuman environment. Identification with the technological sphere exempt from death and wonderously powerful although inanimate bespeaks a longing to be similarly constituted. Our greatest fantasy, Searles reports, aspires to the impervious quality of this indestructible realm. Such a transformation magically transmutes us into the immortal: absolute, all-powerful, limitless, undying, the catastrophic primal nexus is annulled, restoring the illusory prior state of omnipotent impassibility. The desire of desires is fulfilled. Thus, as Freud recognized, *Beyond's* death instinct operates as a pleasure principle, converging with Eros and collapsing his dual instinct theory and conflict model of the psyche.

Ultimately, as we recognized, *Beyond the Pleasure Principle* must be construed as a dream whose latent content divulges a profound understanding of the humanizing task. In the return of the repressed, relentlessly driving to transcend ego resistances and restore the divided being to original integrity, we discover that the only solution to the crisis of finitude is its willing and conscious embrace. Opening to the threatening otherness of incarnate vulnerability—and emancipating ourselves as incipiently whole persons—opens us as well to the greater otherness of a shared world, liberating all from subjection to our narcissistic, often aggressive, imperialism. Kierkegaard would call this incarnational dynamic kenosis: emptying ourselves of all that impedes, blocks, represses, divides, or defends us from the earth of our humanity.

Within the context of *Beyond's* failed conflict model, we have recognized this resurgent integration as a counterforce to Eros that restores the collapsed structure of dual instincts, regarded by Freud as essential for psychoanalysis. While Eros, reinforcing a primordial evasion, strives to secure the organism as ever greater, unconscious of and untouched by impoverished human actuality, the Exodus dynamic strives to transcend repression and revive all that had been obliterated in the initial trauma of embodied self-awareness. With emancipating consequences for both self and others, this trajectory of emergence from an enclosed system of entrenched narcissism into a relational world of authentic engagement bestows the name "Exodus" upon this drive and reality principle.

The Exodus principle unites the function of *Beyond's* death instinct with the dynamism of the return of the repressed, proportionately extinguishing the life of tension to the measure inner divisions and resultant divisiveness are eliminated through the integration of repressed material. Although the term is novel, the Exodus drive—dying into reality, beyond the pleasure principle—can be glimpsed in contemporary analysis.

Rebeca and Leon Grinberg's exploration of migration and exile, endorsed by Otto Kernberg as an extraordinary, comprehensive study, reaches the insightful conclusion that human development bears the character of an inexhaustible, lifelong migration.[1] The crises and traumas of geographic transitions are analogous to the transformations of individual psychic life. On the one hand, a human being reveals a profound desire to transcend or "migrate" beyond fixed borders, venturing forth to realize (as W. R. Bion conceives it) what one *is,* "embodying one's own truth," in absolute responsibility.[2] On the other hand, a conflicting tendency actively opposes this dynamism while clinging to all that is safe and familiar. This reluctance to abandon the secure and the certain, risking the unknown and the new, compounded by a fear of growth and change, militates against transformation as various defenses conspire with the resistance to obstruct one's path.

Migration—or Exodus—may be a change of such magnitude, the Grinbergs report, that one's identity is put in question and placed in jeopardy. As an upheaval, migration possesses the power to shake one's psychic foundations. At the very least, confounded by the loss or transmutation of established structures, the migrant is exposed to a state of disorganization. More critically, one may suffer a wholesale deprivation of the most meaningful relations, both external and internal, severely damaging the ego or otherwise endangering the self.

A migrant's incursion into the unpredictable often produces a weakened sense of belonging as prescribed rules of group behavior and social conduct dissipate in the transition. Anguish, depression, and ever-present anxiety in the face of change greet anyone who departs from the personal or communal status quo. To venture beyond the threshold elicits periods of inscrutable pain as one inhabits emotional and mental states that are difficult to endure. Intense sorrow is sustained for all that must be left behind: a former world and a former self, or parts of a self, that are irretrievably lost.

In truth, one is undergoing a sort of death, dying to a dependable, settled life and to the identity it helped to fashion. This contains a potential for catastrophe; nevertheless, the migrant embarks upon an exodus that can prove to be a journey into self-discovery and renewal.

Although the crisis provoked by the series of traumas constituting migration is instinctively avoided, "throughout [one's] life, an individual lives through the vicissitudes, pain, and losses of various migratory experiences."[3] Thus, one's attitude may largely determine whether the experience culminates in the liberty of homecoming or the expulsion of exile. If one can unceasingly work through the numerous disjunctions, assimilating the losses of each stage by going through a process of mourning, one will emerge personally enriched. The deconstruction and dissolution that threaten instability and the therapeutic mourning for lost aspects of the self are part of a larger process that consolidates a renovated identity that is equivalent to a new birth or a succession of births. In sum, working through proves to be the challenge of self-integration, with each successive and complementary step undertaken only through the ability to grieve. Integration is a gradual and difficult travail. Reorganization, insight and growth, increased ability to live fully in the present, enriched creative potential, and a deepened capacity for individuation redound for those who persist.

"One might be inclined to think that upon reaching maturity," the Grinbergs conclude, "the individual achieves stability and permanently maintains the sense of identity [one] has acquired, having no need of further migrations. However, each important new situation unsettles [one] and foments new crises. . . ."[4] Development and integration are a never-ending task. Continuously working through a lifetime of changes, "individuals must repeatedly suffer and accept the loss of previous stages of life" as they surpass themselves, moving forward into regions "where new realities reign."[5] Overcoming nostalgia, one eventually realizes that "one never goes back, one always goes forward."[6]

Prior to the Grinbergs' significant study, and uniting the psychoanalytic perspectives of Fairbairn and Winnicott with his own clinical experience, Harry Guntrip highlighted a similar dynamic.[7] Guntrip is in agreement with Searles and so many other psychotherapists that all of us, even the putatively healthy, suffer some measure of immaturity, self-hate, repression, regression, and fragmented or split ego-structure. One may be a hearty extrovert, an accomplished professional, a successful corporate climber, yet a profound sense of inadequacy hides beneath a pseudo-adult veneer of convention and social conformity. Forced into life, although divided against oneself and threatened by overwhelming others, each copes as a defensively vigilant personality. In spite of desperate struggle and a simulation of strength by the "everyday self," most remain frightened children, unable to realize a basic psychic unity or integration. After strenuous efforts, even the most mature feel at some unconscious depth that they are merely nobodies.

Although a matter of degree, this psychological situation is virtually inescapable, with the vital personality and its truest potential remaining buried, lost, unevoked, and unborn. The foundational distress, Guntrip says, is the innate and traumatizing vulnerability of the human infant.

So long dependent upon caretakers for the simplest of needs, the infant is defined by a steadily increasing awareness of helplessness, weakness, and penury. "Gradually the child must grow to feel . . . that it is too frightening to be weak in an unfriendly and menacing world, and also that one cannot afford to have needs that one cannot get satisfied."[8] Ultimately this recognition turns to hate for one's embodied indigence, with the infant seeking to "disown, split off, hide, and repress" what it construes to be an aspect or mere part of itself.[9] The result is a desperate child struggling to deny and crush its needs, with inferiority and intolerance structured into its psychic organization.

In striving to overcome its debilitating weakness, the infant or child ensures its continuation, "creating an endopsychic situation in which natural development is impossible."[10] The original needy, but now rejected, psyche remains the basis of all subsequent function-ing. One's needfulness is never overcome, and the helplessly weak ego with its infantile fear is never totally outgrown.

The endangered, repudiating psyche despairingly flees its hostile environment, retreating from both traumatic world and traumatizing self in search of a protective haven, while abandoning to a caretaking "false self" the everyday world of conformity and compliance. The terrified withdrawal does not cease until one is ensconced in a secure inner citadel. However, security is contingent upon the impossi-ble—eradicating the source of one's vulnerability—and the closed system of an impregnable stronghold turns into a prison of self-persecution. Not only is the wounded but potentially real self, with all its possibilities for spontaneous and creative living, locked away and abandoned, but its impoverished nature is subjected to a frenzy of inner hostility.

As much in panic as from rage, the frustrated but divided, self-destructive psyche directs all of its aggression at the perceived weakness. Inadequate and needy to the core, one suffers an abyss of inner violence to extinguish or master primary fears and criminal contingency. One is a virtual slave, Guntrip tells us, to the cruel tyrant of self-suppression.

For intermittent relief, aggressive self-hate is directed toward others. While rigid self-control allows no weakness to be otherwise revealed, a mask of defenses "against the entire outer world" main-tains a "power cult" of domination in relations with others.[11]

However intolerable the closely guarded citadel of tortured exist-ence, it is extremely intractable. The suffering "child" trapped within seems unable to relinquish the internal persecutor. "[T]oo insecure to venture and therefore too attached to break away," one is simply too afraid to reemerge.[12] In truth, an emergence of the infantile, fear-ridden self is an inconceivable ordeal, but most cling to the depleted self because it is the only self they know: locked into a closed system of self-traumatizing defenses, it is impossible to comprehend what a "true self" might be.

In fact, one resists amelioration because the status quo is infi-nitely "preferable to opening up devastating conflicts" that reach uncertain solutions at the price of major disturbances and severe anxiety.[13] This conflict, of course, is the psychic division over accepting, or even recognizing, the repudiated and repressed natural vulnerability dwelling deep within.

One instinctively recoils from the return of the repressed; thus, the most virulent defenses are mobilized to keep awareness of the self's indigence from breaching consciousness. If the repressed does approach awareness, it is not perceived "as the starting point of new growth" but as a threat, promising to undermine the stability of one's "adult" personality.[14] Breakdown feels imminent; one fears collapse. It seems appallingly like a death, and few will brave extinction.

The risk may be resisted but there is, nevertheless, the secondary fear of not escaping this self-imprisonment. Although the initial flight to security proved to be a brutal retreat, it was an attempt to salvage an endangered personal core. Amid one's ordeal persists a longing for return as well as a powerful need for recuperation and "a sense of reality." United with the hope that one's fragmented, lost core might suffer a healing reemergence, deep in the unconscious there is the secret wish that "death should prove to be a pathway to rebirth."[15]

This is precisely the issue for psychoanalytic therapy, Guntrip maintains. An invitation to become "an open system in touch with outer reality," psychotherapy is an "opportunity to grow out of deep down fears . . . and start . . . on the road to rebirth and regrowth."[16] This comprehends the emancipation of all one's potentialities. Whether inside or outside of therapy, the process will not be radical enough unless it penetrates the inner redoubt to liberate the devitalized heart of the total personality for healthy and vigorous growth. If the "core of reality in the person," the "primary natural self," is released "from the internal persecutor, it is capable of rapid development and integration with all that is valuable and realistic" in one's everyday self.[17] Restored to incipient wholeness, the "total psyche" can regain its "sense of being" and "capacity to feel real."[18]

There is a "basic need to find a real self," Guntrip tells us.[19] To become a "person," he discovered, is "the primary drive in every human being."[20] An emergence of a "whole personal self," this "total life-drive" of the "dynamic urge to be" is the Exodus principle driving us beyond our defensive citadels. Freeing us from the pharaohs of self-captivity, opening us to the greater world of interpersonal involvement and concern, its legacy is the endowment of a human world.

Reading Guntrip and Winnicott, it is impossible not to note that the language of their clinical papers often suggests the vocabulary of Martin Heidegger. *True self, real self,* and *false self* evoke *authentic* and *inauthentic* Dasein; *everyday ego* and *compliant self* bring to mind *das Man*. Concerns about *being, on-going being,* and *ontological insecurity*, as well as *openness* and *death* are equally evocative. Both Guntrip and Heidegger speak of our *flight* from existence or from life, while Winnicott's hallmark *holding* is midway between Heidegger's *falling* and *self-standing constancy*. What is startling about this convergence is that, unlike others who deliberately appropriated Heidegger's philosophy for their psychological theory, these mainline analysts did not.[21]

Guntrip's *sense of being* paralleling Heidegger's *sense* or *meaning of being* also arrests the eye, for both Guntrip and Heidegger are concerned with uncovering eclipsed human foundations. For Guntrip, no less than for Heidegger, this is primordial finitude. Not unlike Aristophanes of the *Symposium,* Guntrip is in pursuit of a split or cut off primary nature without which one cannot be genuinely human. What must be recovered, accepted, and reunited to conscious life is the long-repressed but primordial contingency of a weak, needy, psychosomatic self. Only gradually and quietly, over a relatively long period of time, is a person able to abandon defenses and inadequate solutions through the process of internal self-discovery. If one persists with the challenge of embracing all that is uncovered, the formerly repressed emerges as a dynamic nucleus of new growth. As discovered in chapter 6 of this study, the terrible but humanizing paradox is that psychic totality necessitates a reappropriation of unconscious finitude.

While evolving discourse may unite Freud and Heidegger to a degree, Heidegger remains problematic due to his befuddling association with Nazi Germany. In 1933 he became a controversial figure when he accepted, under the auspices of National Socialism, the rectorship of Freiburg University. Believing that the goals enunciated by the recently elected party "provided the inevitable way for the self-assertion of German scholarship," Heidegger advocated "alignment" with the "new revolutionary reality" in his public addresses. "As Karl Löwith remarked," James Collins reports in a 1952 study, "people who listened to Heidegger's official speeches were never quite sure whether to resume their study of the Pre-Socratics or to don the uniform of the Storm Troopers, so close a connection did he make between learning and political life."[22]

Not surprisingly, the basic concepts of Heidegger's fundamental ontology suffered a frightening transvaluation; "with one stroke," Habermas writes, "they change[d] their very meaning." The significance of authentic Dasein is displaced from the existing individual to the historical *volk,* "yolked together by the Führer into a collective will."[23] Although disenchantment swiftly succeeded his initial fervor, leading Heidegger to relinquish the appointment within a year, his "hellish endorsement"[24] imposed an indelible blight upon both his life and work.

It was not Heidegger's "profession of faith" in the nascent reich that Habermas finds revolting and subject to condemnation, since all who dwell at a greater or safer distance, he sagely observes, "cannot know whether in a similar situation they, too, would not have failed. What is irritating is the unwillingness and the inability of this philosopher, after the end of the Nazi regime, to admit his error with so much as *one* sentence. . . ."[25]

Habermas acknowledges that Heidegger's rude encounter with National Socialism precipitated the famous reversal or *Kehre* in his philosophizing that inevitably distanced him from anything the Third Reich could envision or embrace. Thus, it might be asserted cogently that this consequential shift in thinking articulates Heidegger's awareness of and responsibility for his various wrongs. Two elements nuance and compound the original grievance while undermining this rationale. Most egregious, Heidegger appears to be guilty of blaming the victim, Habermas reports. While acknowledging his failure of vision, in postwar years the ex-rector chastised the "prophetically gifted": "Is there not also a guilt of essential omission? . . . Why didn't those who thought they knew in 1933, why didn't they rise up then to turn everything toward the good, from the ground up?"[26] Perhaps more alarming for human and philosophical integrity, Heidegger transmuted subjective culpability into objective and ontological epiphany. He "detache[d] his actions and statements altogether from himself as an empirical person and attribute[d] them to a fate for which one cannot be held responsible. . . . That the eyes of the most resolute philosopher were only gradually opened up to the nature of the regime . . . the course of the world itself is supposed to assume authorship, not concrete history, indeed, but a sublimated history promoted to the lofty heights of ontology. Thus was born the concept of the history of Being."[27]

To some extent, the latter-day controversy surrounding Heidegger is a rehashing, perhaps toward political or academic profit, of matters confronted decades ago. As early as 1941, Heidegger's "demonic personality" was denounced in philosophical journals that assailed his politics in lieu of professionally scrutinizing his thought. Nevertheless, Collins concluded in 1952, "it is no longer possible to evade the philosophical task." Heidegger's work, antedating the rise of Nazism, merited serious study: "He has raised a number of significant issues which must be faced for their own sake."[28]

Paul Shih-yi Hsiao reached a similar conclusion. Groping with the same sense of bewilderment as many others, but reluctant to abandon a teacher who had so profoundly influenced him, Hsiao met with Heidegger in 1946 and found his gravest concerns assuaged. A thoughtful appraisal resulted: "in the future one must study [Heidegger's] philosophy more assiduously and carefully. If it is understood properly, it will have great relevance for the future."[29]

In spite of his own revisionary statements, it is impossible to know what Heidegger thought he was doing in 1933—or imagined he could effect—but Rorty intimates that there may be room for construing something less than a demon at work: "the sort of leader Heidegger had in mind in his constantly repeated invocation of 'the leaders and protectors of the destiny of the German people' was not Hitler, but himself. The rectorial address puts forward, in entire seriousness, the claim that only Heideggerian philosophy can bring the universities into the service of this destiny. One cannot exaggerate the degree to which Heidegger took philosophy, and himself, seriously."[30]

Once all the evidence from that sordid epoch is marshaled, nuanced, and assessed, one may be forced to concur with Rorty's judgment that "one of the century's most original thinkers happened to be a pretty nasty character"; but one may conclude with Thiele that it is possible "to derive from a philosophy sensibilities that its author has not earned, and might perhaps disown." One may even "think through Heidegger's politics to arrive at sober philosophical insights . . . [and] to derive worthy theoretical lessons from unworthy practices."[31]

Whatever the outcome of this particular and grave appraisal, former colleagues attest to an inexplicable richness even as they highlight the essential paradox of this scurrilous enigma. Writing to Karl Jaspers in 1949, Hannah Arendt was especially vexed at the reported complicity of Heidegger in the humiliating dismissal of Edmund Husserl, his former mentor, from academic life. After clarifying those circumstances, Jaspers nevertheless laments to Arendt: "Can someone with an impure soul . . . perceive what is purest? . . . What is strange is that he has knowledge of something that hardly anyone notices these days. . . ."[32]

Arendt's response is a somewhat humble and humorous, if surprising, corrective. "Heidegger: because human beings are not consistent, not I at any rate, I was pleased," she tells Jaspers. "You are right a thousand times over in each of your sentences. What you call impurity I would call lack of character—but in the sense that he literally has none and certainly not a particularly bad one." Concluding, she acknowledges the correctness of his assessment that Heidegger is in touch with uncommon profundities: "At the same time, he lives in depths and with a passionateness that one can't easily forget."[33]

It must be noted that there is a frequent accusation of which Heidegger stands acquitted. Dallmayr highlights the charge: "In the reading of some of his detractors, Heidegger was unable to transgress the traditional limits of subjectivity; in the terminology of *Being and Time,* authentic *Dasein* is claimed to be synonymous with a private fortress immune from the inroads of world and other human beings."[34] In an otherwise superb study, Webb is emblematic of this misreading when he writes:

> Heidegger talks at length of the "call" of conscience, but what that is a call to is strictly a relation to oneself—that is, to authentic consciousness of one's "ownmost" possibility, which is simply the possibility of choosing to face with open eyes one's own mortality. Not only is there no real place in Heidegger's thought for the alterity of a genuinely "other" person, but when he does speak of others it is either as potential sources of temptation to inauthenticity ("the 'they'") or else as examples to be used as instruments in one's own quest for authenticity. Even when he speaks explicitly of otherness, it has nothing to do with the possibility of a relation to a personal other, a "thou." . . .[35]

This misunderstanding is easily attained. While Webb is correct about the decision to face mortality (resoluteness), he is otherwise mistaken. As chapter 7 of this study indicates, authentic Dasein, Being-in-the-world, is inescapably Being-with or Dasein-with. To quote Heidegger anew: "Dasein in itself is essentially Being-with . . . Dasein-with remains existentially constitutive for Being-in-the-world."[36] With equal pertinence, he subsequently says, "[Authentic] Dasein's *resoluteness* towards itself is what *first* makes it possible to let the Others who are with it 'be' in *their* ownmost potentiality-for-Being, and to co-disclose this potentiality in the *solicitude* which leaps forth and liberates."[37] That Heidegger does not employ the conventional language of love, relationship, or bonding may or may not be a strength, but it does not diminish the reality of the ontological and relational valence that concerns him.

The difficulty arises, Heidegger has underscored, when ontological statements concerning Dasein are misunderstood as ontical characteristics of a specific, solipsistic subject and its ethical egoism. Attempting a definitive clarification, he has emphasized that "In choosing itself Dasein really chooses precisely its being-with others. . . . As a result of this commitment, Dasein commits itself to a capability of being toward-itself *as* able-to-be-with others. . . ."[38]

A shared existence is at the heart of the praxis implicit in *Being and Time*. This authentic quality of Dasein is unmistakable to Scott and to Theunissen, for instance. Theunissen's very title, *The Other: Studies in the Social Ontology of Husserl, Heidegger, Sartre and Buber* spells an emphatic refutation of the common misinterpretation.[39] Nevertheless, Scott offers a summarizing word: "The question of ethics in the context of *Being and Time* is a way of being that is concerned in the world and with other people. Heidegger's analysis in Part I of *Being and Time* has made it clear that dasein is constituted in world relations. . . . Solipsism is an ontological impossibility for dasein since dasein occurs only in disclosive relations . . . hence the emphasis on continuously twisting free of cultural domination *in* cultural life, never outside of it."[40]

Of additional note is the interest in Heidegger beyond Western boundaries. "Whether in America or the Far East, whether in India, Africa, or in Latin America," Gadamer writes, "the impetus for thinking that emanated from him is to be found everywhere."[41] This signals a possibly broader relevance for issues that have emerged in this dialogue than ostensible Western concepts might generally anticipate. In fact, a schema of cross-cultural corroboration of key elements can be sketched.

If some of the key elements that emerge from this dialogue are the interlocking notions of (a) self-emptying (b) death (or "dying away from") issuing in a deeper, (c) more integrated self that concurrently (d) opens to the broader world of others and otherness, the work of Ananda Coomaraswamy offers a pithy overview. Thirty years the curator of Asiatic art at the Boston Museum of Fine Arts, this son of Ceylon and progeny of East and West[42] spent his adult life exegeting the scriptures of Hinduism and Buddhism, synthesizing his findings in superb and sapiential writings.

Through "a succession of deaths and rebirths," writes Coomaraswamy, we penetrate from the outer court of our existence to the inner center of our being. "Every step of this way has been marked by a death to a former 'self' and a consequent and immediate 'rebirth' as 'another man'"—or as we would say today with our inclusive awareness, "another person." This "transmigration" is a regeneration that may take place "in part or in its entirety" before one's natural death, "as well here and now" as in the act of dying.[43]

The venture—a progressive self-naughting—is inspired by a sensitivity to the unreality that "self" and "I" ordinarily signify: "The Ego is 'not my Self'." One intuits that "the whole complex of 'I' and 'mine'" is not one's truest or deepest being.[44] Indeed, such is precisely an "elemental" or "petty" self, absorbed in self-reference and the seeking of one's exclusive ends, that must be naughted. Nevertheless, self-naughting is not a process of annihilation.[45]

In the context of the ancient scriptures, the reference of self-naughting, "naught of mine," indicates a dynamic of dis-possessing.[46] Evoking Heidegger, the understanding of this traditional psychology emphasizes that what is "emptied" or dis-possessed in the relinquishment of an "appetitive," "greedy" mind and soul is precisely an identification with "things" and "whats" and the confusion of oneself—and perforce others—with "*what* is not-Self." One's truest Self is "not any 'what'."[47] Detaching or emptying "one thing after another," one enters the "Station of no-what-ness," coming into one's own in the remembering of *who* one is.[48]

Thus, the praxis of dis-possession or self-naughting is the path of self-realization as one is "emptied out" of self to enter into one's "whole self." "This dying is to self" as "my real Self," "true Person," or "real Person" comes into being.[49] The empty, self-naughted person is a happy person.[50] No longer plagued by internal conflict, one is unified and at peace. At peace with oneself, devoid of incessant craving, released from the shackles of self-destruction, one is no longer hostile and inclined "to wage war on others." Indeed, one now fosters "offspring" in recognizing and valuing the manifesta-tion of "the many."[51]

"[T]he greater part of these symbols are of prehistoric, at any rate neolithic, if not greater antiquity," Coomaraswamy concludes, emphasizing that this perennial wisdom "is then, the art of dying. . . . Assuming that we are now 'true philosophers', we shall inevitably begin to make a practice of dying."[52]

Coomaraswamy, sums up his biographer and editor Roger Lip-sey, "was not prepared to say that 'death in life' is just a literary anal-ogy to the real and final death of the psychophysical vehicle. Something indeed dies, just as it [does] later, but the peculiar human opportunity seems to be that to die in life permits a birth of still more life."[53]

It is this insight into the vivifying power of death that we find struggling for articulation in the communal awareness of the Dinka, as reported by anthropologist Mary Douglas.[54] A herding people living on the margins of subsistence, the Dinka dwell in a vast arc of savanna withn the central Nile basin of southern Sudan. The burial ceremony of their old, yet living, Masters of the Fishing Spear, a clan of hereditary priests, is the crucial and most efficacious rite of Dinka life. It is a rite, Douglas tells us, "by which the Dinka face and triumph over death itself."[55] The generative principle is that their leader must not undergo the common fate of mortals, exhausting his life—"the life of his people which is in his keep-ing"—by suffering involuntary death.[56] To die of such necessity, a last breath escaping his dying body, would squander the people's life, imperiling the Dinka's very existence. This ultimate service on behalf of the people, transcending the Spearmaster's individual and personal existence, secures continuing viability for the Dinka community.

This special form of death, celebrated and bestowed by the peo-ple, is requested by the aged Spearmaster at a moment of his choos-ing. Entering deliberately and consciously into his own dying, the Spearmaster ensures that his people's life is safeguarded and renewed as his spirit is publicly bequeathed to a successor through the communally executed ritual.

Before his naturally anticipated death, the ancient Spearmaster is "reverently carried to his grave" and lowered into the earth. Lying therein, he "says his last words to his grieving sons," before all—male and female, young and old—cover the grave.[57] "By confronting death and grasping it firmly he has said something to his people about the nature of life."[58] By a free decision, the people live, triumphant through death.

"Here," Douglas observes, "we can discern primitive existentialists. . . . When someone embraces freely the symbols of death, or death itself, . . . a great release of power for good should be expected to follow." The community "should rejoice, because on this occasion there is a social triumph over death."[59] More accurately, through a voluntary dying—a life-giving embrace of the earth—the community is preserved, vitalized, and renewed.

Relying on his own African fieldwork with the Ndembu of Zambia as well as that of other anthropologists among the Nuer of Sudan, Bemba of Zambia, Tallensi and Ashanti of Ghana, and Swazi of southeastern Africa, Victor Turner has employed a broad spectrum of ethnographies to illustrate a phenomenon he calls "communitas."[60] Although discernible throughout history in rare and frequently offbeat circumstances within societies, communitas is best highlighted in contrast to everyday social structure by the various initiations or rites of passage that punctuate primitive and early agrarian life—among others, circumcision rights for boys, puberty rites for girls, installation rites for chiefs.

Such are periods of disengagement from the accoutrements of culture as participants are withdrawn to the margins of social interaction and set apart, "secluded from the spheres of everyday life."[61] Here nothing is allowed to distinguish one from another. The structures of tribal society—status, rank, class, position, and power—separated, divided, and distanced one from another, while reducing all to a corporate subservience. The oppositions of stratification, hegemonies of we/they, in-group/out-group, and higher/lower exclusions, as well as competition for office, participation in feuds, factions, and coalitions, and all other "structural attributes" must be stripped away.[62]

Dissolving the governing norms of structural or institutional relationships is the task of initiation. Indigence is the attribute of these marginal beings; they *have* nothing: no status, property, insignia, authority, position, clothing, or ought else that would demarcate them from other neophytes. "All attributes that distinguish categories and groups in the structured social order are here in abeyance. . . ."[63]

The social world produced only relationships between segmented and partial personas—social masks; individuals did not meet person to person but role to role, persona to persona, based on the artifice of categorization and hierarchy. Suffering the ordeal of marginal existence, a participant is ground down to a human *prima materia* that all share in common. Identified with the earth, returned to a naked or near-naked condition, often covered with earth, clay, or dust, initiates discover a nakedness or "honesty of being" that is a "basic, even primordial mode of human interlinkage."[64]

Writing prior to Turner's data, Mary Douglas has underscored that "to go out of the formal structure and to enter the margins is to be exposed to power that is enough to kill [the neophytes] or make their manhood. The theme of death and rebirth, of course, has other symbolic functions: the initiates die to their old life and are reborn to the new."[65]

Turner concurs, pointing out that the nakedness of the neophytes indexes both corpse and neonate, both tomb and womb. "One dies *into* nature to be reborn *from* it."[66] This vulnerable hiatus of weakness and poverty is a passage of growth and transformation. The entire process is felt to "effect an ontological transformation, . . . to change the inmost nature of the neophyte[s], . . . transform[ing] them from one kind of human being into another."[67] It is a transformative dynamic "that goes to the root of each person's being and finds in that root something profoundly communal and shared."[68] Camaraderie and communion flourish. This is communitas. Individual equality and egalitarian cooperation within a homogeneous, unstructured, seemless whole is its characteristic spirit.[69] Mutuality, spontaneity, peace, the common weal, comity, and recognition of a shared humanity are some of its values.[70] Thus, a vital sentiment of "humankindness" emerges, with a strong sense of a "generic human bond, without which there could be no society.[71] Potentially transcending tribe or nation, communitas is inclusive and ideally embraces all, coterminous with the human species. As an "open society," universal and boundless, it is "extensible to the limits of humanity."[72]

One's "full human capacity," Turner notes, is rarely evoked and generally inhibited, "locked out" by the constraint and regimented procession of normative social routine.[73] Released to discover oneself as initiation emancipates from the "segmental status" and "partial persona" of everyday tribal affairs, initiates are liberated for "direct, immediate, and total confrontations of human identities."[74]

"People can 'be themselves'," Turner remarks, "when they are not acting institutionalized roles."[75] Since communitas preserves unique, idiosyncratic human distinctiveness, and since it liberates capacities for cognition, affect, volition, and creativity, one can grow into a "total," or complete, person. No longer a "master" but an equal, one is free to enter into authentic interpersonal engagement as a whole person in vital relations with other whole persons. Individuals encounter one another, not in conditioned roles or "transactional" relations of self-interest, but as concrete, integral persons, "in their wholeness wholly attending."[76] Turner appeals to Kierkegaard to describe this transformed person as a "qualitative individual" who may be outwardly indistinguishable from others within the social structure but who is "henceforth free from its despotic authority [and] an autonomous source of creative behavior."[77]

It may be noted that the foundational dis-possession of stripping and divestment, suffered in marginal experience and conducing to transformation, recalls kenotic self-emptying—all the more because Turner likens communitas to the emptiness of a wheel's nave, which unites all the spokes. "Communitas," he says, "might well be represented by the 'emptiness at the center'."[78] Perhaps more arresting is the remarkable dynamism that evokes Heidegger: a movement beyond inauthentic—or not fully authentic—collectivity into a space or "clearing" of ontological realization that opens one to a broader horizon. Communitas, creating a "total rather than a partial perspective on the life of society," results in an order that "transcends the contradictions and conflicts inherent in the mundane social system."[79] Turner does not hesitate to call this a "cosmic order" that might intimate "the unused evolutionary potential" of our species.[80]

Another glimpse of a clearing or opening that quells conflict and cleavage and, in Turner's words, regenerates torn social tissue is gleaned from a glance at Samoa. Jeannette Mageo has noted the dual and disparate ethos by which Samoan life is conducted.[81] A public norm and ideology, a face of decorum, dictates respect for other *'aiga* (families)—that is, the putting of other families first in this highly communal society. Coincidently, loyalty to one's kin demands that the concerns of one's own family are championed above those of the other *'aiga*. Since the Samoan polis is constituted by manipulation and competition among *'aiga* for dominance, a "perpetual struggle for ascendancy . . . is endemic to the Samoan social cosmos." The gravity of this ongoing and potentially disruptive friction is indicated by the literal meaning of *tauva*, or competition, as a "war between."[82]

Bradd Shore has written cogently of the conflicting cultural models that inform, govern, and sometime devastate the Samoan world.[83] This dichotomy of competing models comprehends values that emphasize "cooperation, harmony, deference to authority, and the subordination of antisocial impulses to the needs of the group," as well as contradictory values emphasizing "boldness, competitiveness, fierce loyalty to one's own group at the expense of social harmony, and personal touchiness at perceived attacks on personal or family honor."[84]

During his fieldwork in Western Somoa, Shore sadly witnessed an imminent chaos overwhelm his village when a senior chief was murdered by the son of another ranking chief over drunken absurdities, allegations of cheating at poker. The mortal deed was the horrific fruit of an ancient and bitter rivalry between aristocratic families. Twice more the placid demeanor of village harmony was riven: first, when a local pastor publicly implored forgiveness and forbearance, only to assert privately to the eldest son that faithfulness to his father demanded retribution; and second, when the distraught survivor struck the apprehended murderer with a nonlethal machete blow to the neck.[85]

Fearful that escalating violence and a chain of revenge would unravel the consensual village accord releasing deeper substratums of aggression, both Christian and Somoan ideals were invoked to urge restraint and calm. Once the dead chief's body was returned to his home for mourning, elders of the slayer's family approached the house. Sitting utterly still upon the ground, heads bowed in ritual humiliation throughout the night, they sought "to avoid war by publicly apologizing on behalf of one of their own."[86]

Throughout the following week the village tried to comprehend the tragedy. A state funeral ensued with a period of mourning prescribed. Sermons and oratory struggled "to refocus attention on harmony rather than division."[87] The village chiefs, representing every political faction, gathered in a lengthy, emotionally charged meeting; instead of recalling the principals, they focused on village political structure and its contribution to the crime.

Ultimately, the entire village was convened for a gathering on the *malae*, the circular or elliptical village green and communal center. Shore had not witnessed such an exceptional measure heretofore. The *malae*, Shore says, "may be compared to a radiant source of dignity and power."[88] It was to this sacred (*sa*) center (*moa*) that every member of the community was summoned to restore the village peace and rededicate the sacred *va*.

The *va*, Mageo tells us, is both the space of relationship and the heart or center of the encircling, unifying bond.[89] As the open expanse marking a village center, the *malae* might be identified as the manifest or geographical symbol of the ontological *va*. To step within the *malae*, to enter the village center, is to dispense with rivalry and strife and to become, beyond divisions, integrally related to all.

It might be said that by entering the sacred clearing, what Turner calls the "emptiness at the center," that is, by *becoming open*, we kenoticly transcend ourselves to create a human, interpersonal, and shared world.

Beyond Samoa, an interest in such self-emptying kenosis is evident, as well as explicit, at the farthest reaches of the Pacific. The Kyoto School of Philosophy in Japan has long brought the insights of Zen Buddhism into dialogue with Western thought. Martin Heidegger has been a particular focus of attention, while in his *Last Writings* the initiator of this dialogue, Nishida Kitaro, first appealed to the kenosis of Paul's Letter to the Philippians.[90] As self-emptying, its convergence with Buddhist *sunyata*—emptiness, nothingness, void—is evident. Nevertheless, sunyata is not to be construed negatively; it is an affirmative standpoint: it is the ground of liberation and spontaneity by which each being is precisely what or who it is.

Following Nishida, Nishitani Keiji and Abe Masao continued to interface kenosis and sunyata in their considerations of both ultimate reality and our temporal selves. In the English translation of one of his major works, Nishitani noted that Buddhist life and thought "are permeated with *kenosis* and *ekkenosis* [making oneself empty]," while Abe has stressed, under the impact of kenosis, that sunyata is not static but dynamic and should be perceived as a verb, not a noun.[91] Whether comprehended as kenosis or sunyata, all that is said about emptiness is meaningless "if it is taken apart from the problem of the human ego, or our own existential problem of the self."[92] Real emptiness is lived; anyone and everyone must undergo a self-emptying to awaken or realize the "individual non-ego" that, transcending both nirvana and samsara, opens one to realities beyond oneself.[93] Indeed, positively articulated, sunyata is compassionate and boundless openness.[94]

The true—or authentic—self, Ueda Shizuteru remarks in a wonderfully engaging essay, emerges as "a selfless dynamic" disclosing, or "laying bare," an "infinite openness." Thus the self opens or "unfolds," and within the liberated space "the other in its otherness belongs to the selflessness of the self."[95] This emancipated horizon is unrestricted and unconditional, so that all may celebrate within what Heidegger calls the ontological "playroom" (*spielraum*) and Ueda calls the inner "playground."[96] One becomes "boundlessly open to universal relationships."[97] As Abe has emphasized, echoing Kierkegaard, "boundless interdependence between everything can take place . . . without eradicating the particularity of [any]thing."[98] "I" *am* beyond myself opening to others. Evoking Heidegger, Ueda calls this *ex-sistence*; such is an awakening to the subjectivity of "one's true egoless Self."[99] As Nishitani has underscored in his own context, "in speaking of subjectivity here I do not mean the subjectivity of the ego. Quite to the contrary, it is the subjectivity that comes about from the absolute death of ego . . . [of the] narcissistic mode . . . wherein the self gets caught up in itself."[100] This ontological transformation, this inner revolution or realization, "means denying *eros*" and "making oneself empty"—empty of one's "self-being . . . as a self-centered ego."[101] Again and again, an "outburst of altogether fresh vitality" is released as kenosis, or dynamic sunyata, penetrates "to that innermost depth of personality that has been closed off since the very beginning."[102]

For the Kyoto School, this true and vital self is empty or nothing or void because, as *living*, it is *unobjectifiable*. "The Ground of our existence is nothingness, Sunyata, because it can never be objectified"; and as the ground of our existence, sunyata *"expands endlessly into all directions."*[103] "True Emptiness" is "the dynamic whole."[104]

In an echo of the Dinka, Nishitani has pungently summed up the experiential profundity of this self-emptying dynamic: "life is always interfused with death, or rather, death is the spring—or at least the springboard—of life."[105]

It might be noted that as a form of Buddhism, Zen and its wisdom are anchored by ancient roots that reach to earliest Hinduism and perhaps to antecedents beyond in the yogis and forest dwellers of 3000 BCE or earlier. It would demand exhausting detail or frivolous conjecture to trace the ancient lineage inherited by the Kyoto School, but as we turn our gaze toward Sumer and the first consolidations of civilization, we can pause between the sixth century BCE and the second century CE to glimpse a surprising discovery from Early Taoism.

At the threshold of chapter 9, we saw that Isaac Luria's *zimzum* had adumbrated the creative withdrawal of Heidegger's latter writings. In Luria's sixteenth-century cosmogony, the divine All withdrew power and presence to create a primordial space that made room for finite being. N. J. Girardot tells us in a marvelous study of Early Taoism:

> The closest parallel to the Taoist cosmogony . . . is found in the tradition of the Lurianic Kabbala of the sixteenth century. . . . [In] its doctrine of *zimzum* [as] . . . the primordial empty "place" . . . we can see the amazingly close approximation of the Taoist theory. Based on the discussion and analysis of Scholem and Jürgen von Kempski, it can even be said that the Lurianic doctrine of *zimzum* reads almost like a commentary on the Taoist theory of creation.[106]

While acknowledging a "strong congruence in mythological structure as well as a convergence in religious-mystical intentionality," Girardot discounts a historical connection "for this curious semantic and phonetic similarity."[107]

Proceeding toward the cradle of civilization, we might pause anew at dynastic Egypt to remind ourselves that this was a civilization in awesome and overarching dialogue with death. The Egyptian Book of the Dead is justly famous and has only recently taken a supporting role to its cousin from Tibet. It is often said that these two classics are as much about how to live as how to die. A similarly intriguing if scantier text from Egypt sketches a dialogue between an individual, weary with life, and his soul.[108] The intent of the piece is ambiguous. Even if the translator's caption—"A Dispute over Suicide"—is correct, it is clear that in the Egyptian mentality death is the passage to a genuine and liberated life.

However, what the text suggests is that the protagonist, on the verge of what the Kyoto philosophers call "the Great Death . . . which springs from the bottomless depth of Sunyata,"[109] trembles hesitatingly on the threshold of the transforming plunge. Satiated with insipid, vexatious life, the protagonist is nevertheless challenged to overcome the inertia that restrains the transcending breakthrough that he instinctively intuits will resolve his torment in a vapid world. In this perspective, the document captures the liminal hiatus of psychic vacillation.

Although the sketch remains inscrutable, the images of the new life that is initiated though death evoke the non-ego or selfless self of the Koyto philosophers: Death "is like going out into the open after a confinement," like being under "the clearing of the sky." Above all, and assuaging a terrible longing, death would be like returning home after a long absence or (bringing to mind Guntrip as well) like coming home after "many years held in captivity."[110]

Pressing on to Sumer, we discover the marvelous cuneiform account of "Inanna's Descent to the Nether World."[111] The excavated tablets that have preserved the myth were inscribed during the first half of the second millennium BCE, although the story may well have a more ancient pedigree because the Sumerians had been a presence in the vicinity since the second half of the fourth millennium BCE, while the region, the Tigris-Euphrates valley of southern Mesopotamia, had seen inhabitants as early as the fifth millennium BCE.[112]

The tale opens with Inanna, queen of heaven and goddess of love, inspired to enter the underworld, realm of her elder sister Ereshkigal.

> From the "great above" she set her mind toward the "great below,"
>   The goddess, from the "great above," she set her mind towards the "great below,"
>   Inanna, from the "great above," she set her mind towards the "great below."

Bedecking herself with the splendor of her station, Inanna placed a crown upon her head, lapis stones around her neck, and sparkling stones about her breast; a gold ring and a breastplate completed her accessories. She then arrayed herself with the garment of ladyship, assumed measuring rod and line, and departed:

> My lady abandoned heaven, abandoned earth, to the nether world she descended,
>   Inanna abandoned heaven, abandoned earth, to the nether world she descended,
>   Abandoned lordship, abandoned ladyship, to the nether world she descended.

At the gate of the underworld she demanded admittance. Neti, chief gatekeeper of this "land of no return," consults with Ereshki- gal and, following his queen's command, unlocks the gates for Inanna's entrance.

> Upon her entering the first gate,
>> The sugurra, the crown of the plain of her head was removed.

"What, pray, is this?" a startled Inanna protests. "Be silent," she hears, "the ordinances of the nether world are perfect; O Inanna, do not question the rites of the nether world."

> Upon her entering the second gate,
>> The measuring rod (and) line of lapis lazuli [were] removed.
>> "What, pray, is this?"

"Be silent," she hears again, ". . . do not question the rites of the nether world." At each of five remaining gates, as she relinquishes more and more, she will receive the same reply to her increasingly desperate questioning.

> Upon her entering the third gate,
>> The small lapis lazuli stones of her neck were removed.
>> "What, pray, is this?"
>> . . . .
>> "O Inanna, do not question the rites of the nether world."

> Upon her entering the fourth gate,
>> The sparkling stones of her breast were removed.
>> "What, pray, is this?"
>> . . . .
>> "O Inanna, do not question the rites of the nether world."

Upon her entering the fifth gate,
    The gold ring of her hand was removed.
    "What, pray, is this?"
    . . . .
    "O Inanna, do not question the rites of the nether
world."

Upon her entering the sixth gate,
    The breastplate . . . of her breast was removed.
    "What, pray, is this?
    . . . .
    "O Inanna, do not question the rites of the nether
world."

Upon her entering the seventh gate,
    The pala-garment, the garment of ladyship of her body,
was removed.

Naked and bowed low, she now submits to the throne of Ereshkigal
as the seven Anunnaki impose judgment, fixing their eyes of death
upon her:

At their word, the word which tortures the spirit,
    The sick "woman" was turned into a corpse, [and]
    The corpse was hung from a stake.

After three days and nights of anxious waiting at the threshold of
the nether world, Inanna's faithful messenger, recalling the cautions
of his mistress, flees to a triad of gods and successively implores
them to aid their daughter. Only Enki, god of wisdom, responds.
Fashioning two creaturely emissaries, he commissions them to
revive Inanna with the food and water of life, which he entrusts to
them. Sixty times they sprinkle the food of life upon the corpse
hanging from the stake; and sixty times they sprinkle the water of
life. Thus revived, Inanna ascends from the neither world.

Although Jacobsen provides a compelling explanation for this remarkable tale that focuses on the seasonal fluctuations of the Sumerian agricultural year,[113] it is clear that the insight and power of the myth exceed such agrarian intent. No simple katabasis, Inanna's descent evokes the self-emptying kenosis of Paul's Letter to the Philippians that we viewed at the beginning of chapter 9:

> though he was in the form of God, [he] did not count equality with God a thing to be grasped, but emptied himself, taking the form of a servant, . . . [a]nd being found in human form he humbled himself and became obedient unto death, even death on a cross.[114]

A remarkable parallel whatever the poem's intent, the manifest richness of the myth signals a significance beyond the agriculturally obvious. Why the plunge into the underworld and what this tale might have signified to these ancient people may be gleaned from consulting their creation epic, the Enuma elish.[115]

There we discover that the cosmos was created following a rift between the gods. Heaven and earth were created by sundering the vanquished Tiamet. This first division was compounded by a second as the imputed instigator of the godly strife was severed to produce man and woman. Already we recognize an intimation of the motif most famously associated with Plato's Aristophanes: the longing to rediscover a primordial unity. Thus Inanna, queen of heaven, plunges into the earth to encounter the elderly presence of her sister, queen of the nether world and the depths of the earth.

A disconcerting element within the myth helps to nuance and enrich the initial insight. Inanna's ascent is not without a price: an exchange is exacted. The Anunnaki demand a substitute, and demons follow Inanna to secure the necessary corpse. Thrice they are about to snatch their prey when Inanna protects the victim—each having fallen to the dust at her feet, grateful their mourned queen has returned. Only Dumuzi, Inanna's regal spouse, has ignored her plight, triumphant on his throne. It is to Dumuzi that Inanna directs the demons—inscrutably cruel and appalling behavior for the goddess of love, far from the familial or connubial piety we would anticipate. The condemnation is ultimately mitigated by allowing Geshtinanna, Dumuzi's faithful and loving sister, to substitute for her brother during half the year; but such alternation only compounds the myth's perplexity.

With the presence of Dumuzi and Geshtinanna, however, the (divided) genders are finally manifested, although the myth continues to underscore, through the sibling relationship, that the unity it comprehends lies beyond the realm of compulsive eros, beyond impulsion or instinct.

The key to understanding the myth resides in discerning that the rationality and ratiocination of our day, which Jaspers attributes to a shift in consciousness during the "axial period" between the eighth and second centuries BCE, are not operating in this more ancient poem.[116] Rather, the myth articulates its insight through the logic of a pictorial, iconic idiom, as is appropriate for cuniform writing founded upon pictographs. It is a logic through images.

We see via Inanna that the realms of heavenly vitality and earthly mortality must unite; original divisions must be overcome. Moreover, and most importantly, the myth explains through the to and fro of the siblings that there must be an ongoing commerce and communication between what is experienced as sundered or opposing realms. A dialogue with reality is needed, a dialogue between the various dimensions of (our) existence. Like the kenotic and vulnerable Inanna, we can only encounter the otherness of life in dispossessing openness. If we cannot radically or nakedly open to opposing sides or split-off parts, we remain ever divided (whether between poles or impaled upon a single pole), estranged from ourselves and from our human kin.

This union of incommensurable or ostensibly opposing poles is precisely how Kierkegaard, surprisingly uniting ancient Sumer and the Kyoto Buddhists, understands the self. "The self is a relation," Kierkegaard tells us, and the incommensurables to be united in a prodigious synthesis are the infinite and the finite, the temporal and the eternal, freedom and necessity, psyche and body.[117] The synthesis takes place, ironically, only when a person realizes that he or she does not constitute themselves, that in fact they, themselves, are powerless and nothing. Such is the paradoxical key: it is only by "becoming a nothing"[118]—as the Buddhists enter into sunyata, discovering the true self, or, for that matter, as Inanna came to nothing in uniting with her sister—and by dwelling within this realization, conscious of our finitude, that one rests transparently in a unified being.

Returning to a more recent moment, the concluding word of cross-cultural corroboration is heard in a dialogue between two monks, one Tibetan and one American, one Buddhist, the other Christian. On November 16, 1968, Thomas Merton and Chatral Rimpoche met near Darjeeling in Ghoom, India, to explore numerous concerns. "We started talking about dzogchen and Nyingmapa meditation and 'direct realization'," Merton notes in his journal,

> and soon saw that we agreed very well. We must have talked for two hours or more, covering all sorts of ground . . . but all leading back to dzogchen, the ultimate emptiness, the unity of sunyata and karuna. . . . He said he had meditated in solitude for thirty years or more and had not attained to perfect emptiness and I said I hadn't either.
>
> The unspoken or half-spoken message of the talk was our complete understanding of each other as people who were somehow on the edge of great realization and knew it and were trying, somehow or other, to go out and get lost in it—and that it was a grace for us to meet one another.[119]

The "great realization" of shared existence that incarnational self-emptying promises to open may seem like a remote and unfathomable blessing. If it hinges on the humanizing embrace of one's own finite and fallible earth, the question begs to be asked how this might come to be. What gives pause to the seemingly irreversible flight that estranges us more and more aggressively from both ourselves and others?

What might reverse the irreversible, Hannah Arendt asks, realizing that no human life is otherwise viable. "The possible redemption from the predicament of irreversibility—or being unable to undo what one has done though one did not, and could not, have known what [one] was doing—is the faculty of forgiving," she reflects.[120] Since who we are, in part, is a product of the actions of (many) others, and since who we are both grounds our acts and reflects our activities, there is an intricate interrelation between being and action. Forgiveness may "make it possible for life to go on"[121] but, more profoundly, forgiveness can alter who we are and how we shall become.

In an interesting convergence, it may be recognized that in some sense forgiveness is the tacit analytic attitude. The fundamental rule of psychoanalysis is that the analysand speaks whatever may come to mind, withholding no word (and whatever history it masks, embodies, or threatens). If one is willing to speak it, one is free to speak it, and because one speaks it—before the forgiving acceptance of the analyst—one may be free of it forever. We need not be shackled; our destiny is to be liberated from the irreversible.

With forgiveness something new is possible because forgiveness creates (and is) the gift of beginnings, a moment of birth that is miraculously unexpected and, thus, pregnant with impossibilities—all that, heretofore, we were powerless to conceive. This is the inexhaustible fecundity of our own emancipating exodus. If our being is in issue, it is because, as a poet muses, "we can never be born enough."[122] In our irrepressible opening to all that lies beyond, we are ever expectant of the other, the unknown, and the new.

Through forgiveness humanity becomes possible. With forgiveness being human can begin. One must forgive oneself; one must forgive one's parents for their genes of imperfection; above all, one must forgive one's God for the cruel contingency that constitutes our numbered and onerous days. Irreversibly finite, tenuous, and incomplete, being human is challenging indeed. Nevertheless, as Kierkegaard anxiously alerted us, we suffer the potential of that glorious and many-splendored thing.

Notes

Notes to Fore-Sight

1. Freud's remark to Binswanger during a stroll, from Binswanger, *Sigmund Freud*, 81.
2. Hegel, *Phenomenology of Spirit*, 19.
3. Kierkegaard, *Journals and Papers*, vol. 1, 339.
4. Cummings, *Complete Poems*, 461.
5. Quoted by Freud at the conclusion of *Beyond the Pleasure Principle* (p. 64); this is from the *Maqâmât* of al-Hariri.

Notes to Prologue

1. Sartre, *Being and Nothingness*, 615.
2. Turner, *The Ritual Process*.
3. Mahler et al., *Psychological Birth of the Human Infant*.

Notes to Chapter 1

1. This invitation is gleaned from two statements. In the middle of chapter 6, Freud says that, in view of the "obscurity that reigns at present in the theory of the instincts, it would be unwise to reject any idea that promises to throw light on it" (*Beyond the Pleasure Principle*, 53). While it is true that he was probably thinking of his own explorations, when united with an opening comment that psychoanalysts would "readily express our gratitude to any philosophical and

psychological theory which was able to inform us of the meaning of the feelings of pleasure and unpleasure which act so imperatively upon us" (7), the invitation seems a just extrapolation, faithful to the spirit of his inquiry. See note 3 below as well.

2. Freud, *New Introductory Lectures,* 95.

3. In fact, after acknowledging in correspondence that much of *Beyond* "is pretty obscure," Freud concluded: "the reader must make what he can of it" (Jones, *Life and Work of Freud,* vol. 3, 40).

4. See Derrida, *Postcard,* for his own reading of *Beyond the Pleasure Principle.*

5. Freud, "Psycho-Analysis," 266.

6. Freud, "Two Encyclopedia Articles," 253.

7. For example, hypothetical: *Beyond the Pleasure Principle,* 7, 8, 23; figurative: *Beyond,* 60; fictional: *Interpretation of Dreams,* 598; and mythological: *New Introductory Lectures,* 95; "Why War?" 211, 212; and see Spence, *Freudian Metaphor.*

8. *Beyond the Pleasure Principle,* 59, 24.

9. While hypothesis might conceivably prejudice one's empirical perception, speculation after the fact might justifiably warrant a greater integrity.

10. *Beyond the Pleasure Principle,* 59.

11. Jones, *Life and Work of Freud,* vol. 3, 266–80; Brenner, *Elementary Textbook,* 16–32; Meissner, *Freud and Psychoanalysis,* 141.

12. Fenichel, *Collected Papers,* 363–72; Guntrip, *Personality Structure,* 129–32.

13. In this and the following statement, I am thinking, especially, of such matters as desexualized libido, fusion and defusion of instincts, the conflict over whether the ego or the id is the reservoir of libido, the confusion over whether the source of aggression is the object instincts or the death instincts.

14. Derrida, "Of an Apocalyptic Tone," 61. See Ricoeur, *Freud and Philosophy;* Schur, *Freud: Living and Dying;* Sulloway, *Freud, Biologist of the Mind;* and Krell, *Intimations of Mortality,* in dialogue with Heidegger, for diverse perspectives on *Beyond.*

15. *Beyond the Pleasure Principle,* 53.

16. James Strachey, the general editor of Freud's *Standard Edition* translated *Trieb* as instinct, although Freud rarely used the German *Instinkt,* as is generally recognized today. Since "drive" is acknowledged to be a more faithful rendering of *Trieb,* "instinct" and "drive" will be used interchangeably in this study. For a discussion of the

differences between instinct and drive and of Freud's use of both, see Brenner, *Elementary Textbook,* 17–18, and Nagera, *Basic Psychoanalytic Concepts,* 19–22.

17. Freud, *Ego and Id,* 42.
18. *Beyond the Pleasure Principle,* 50–52.
19. Ibid., 50.
20. Ibid., 52.
21. Ibid.
22. Nagera, *Basic Psychoanalytic Concepts,* 26–43, documents a four-phase developmental history.
23. *Beyond the Pleasure Principle,* 52.
24. Ibid.
25. Ibid., 53.
26. Ibid., 52–53; "Two Encyclopedia Articles," 255–56, 257.
27. *Beyond the Pleasure Principle,* 53. In the context, *The Standard Edition* inserts a redundant interpolation: "to point to any [ego-] instincts other than the libidinal ones." Three years later the situation had not altered: "Nevertheless," Freud stated, "it has to be borne in mind that the fact that the self-preservative instincts of the ego are recognized as libidinal does not necessarily prove that there are no other instincts operating in the ego" ("Two Encyclopedia Articles," 257).
28. *Beyond the Pleasure Principle,* 56. The dilemma that Freud perceived was that, in spite of the pleasure principle's strong intimations of a death instinct, the sexual instinct—and, thus, its successor, Eros—did not admit of the very dynamic (the compulsion to repeat) upon which he had projected the instinct of death and predicated the conservative or retrograde character of instincts in general. "If, therefore, we are not to abandon the hypothesis of death instincts," Freud concluded, "we must suppose them to be associated from the very first with life instincts. But it must be admitted that in that case we shall be working upon an equation with two unknown quantities" (57).
29. Jones (*Life and Work of Freud,* vol. 3, 266) concurs with this characterization of the book, saying: "It is somewhat discursively written, almost as if by free associations. . . ."
30. The pleasure principle operates in three possible ways: "to free the mental apparatus entirely from excitation or to keep the amount of excitation in it constant or to keep it as low as possible. We cannot yet decide with certainty in favour of any of these ways of putting it . . ."

(*Beyond,* 62). In short, it reduces, removes, or keeps excitations constant (55).

31. Ibid., 16–17.

32. Ibid., 10.

33. Under the influence of the pleasure principle, desires, thoughts, or needs were initially fulfilled through purely mental or imaginary responses. Since this means of satisfaction was bound to disappoint expectations, "the psychical apparatus had to decide to form a conception of the real circumstances in the external world and to endeavour to make a real alteration in them. A new principle of mental functioning was thus introduced; what was presented in the mind was no longer what was agreeable, but what was real, even if it happened to be disagreeable. This setting-up of the *reality principle* proved a momentous step" ("Formulations on Two Principles," 219 [Freud's emphasis]).

34. *Beyond the Pleasure Principle,* 10, 11.

35. Ibid., 10.

36. Ibid., 20–21, 36. In chapter 2, Freud first considers traumatic neuroses, then a single child's play in the face of his mother's absence as manifestations of unpleasure. Neither are satisfactory for his purposes. Child's play is rejected since Freud found that no certain decision could be made, in part because children "repeat everything" (16–17). A consideration of war and peacetime traumatic neuroses was abandoned rather hurriedly when it became evident that the dreams of such neurotics threatened "our belief in the wish-fulfilling tenor of dreams" (13).

37. Ibid., 20–21. In Freud's considerations, the first love object is one's mother.

38. Ibid., 21, 36.

39. Ibid., 36.

40. Ibid., 38 (Freud's emphasis). This perspective of Freud's begs several questions, most prominent of which is whether or not the *inertia* of matter constitutes an instinct, that is, a drive, force, or power or is, instead and quite simply, *inertia*—resistance to being driven. Additionally, is the initial state of the *organism* rest? That is, is matter an organism prior to being alive; by definition, can matter be an organism if it is not alive?

41. Ibid., 27.

42. Ibid., 29.
43. Ibid., 20.
44. Ibid., 23.
45. Ibid., 20.
46. "Metapsychology" is the term that comprehends all of the perspectives with which psychoanalysis views mental phenomena:

> We see how we have gradually been led into adopting a third point of view into our account of psychical phenomena. Besides the dynamic and the topographical points of view, we have adopted the *economic* one. This endeavors to follow out the vicissitudes of amounts of excitation and to arrive at least at some *relative* estimate of their magnitude.
>
> It will not be unreasonable to give a special name to this whole way of regarding our subject-matter for it is the consummation of psycho-analytic research. I propose that when we have succeeded in describing a psychical process in its dynamic, topographic, and economic aspects, we should speak of it as a *metapsychological* presentation. ("The Unconscious," 181 [Freud's emphasis]; and cf. *Beyond,* 7)

Dealing with the processes of excitation and their rise and fall, *Beyond* is principally concerned with the economic perspective. The topographic model, focusing on "locations" such as unconscious, preconscious, and conscious realms of the psyche, hails from *The Interpretation of Dreams.* The dynamic viewpoint is chiefly concerned with mental forces and counterforces that control the inclusion and exclusion of ideas into or from consciousness through the processes of repression and resistance ("Note on the Unconscious," 261–64; *Ego and Id,* 14). To these three, *The Ego and the Id* added the structural perspective that deals with the interrelated systems of ego, id, and superego. Thus, the comprehensive theoretical—or metapsychological—optic of psychoanalysis perceives topographic, dynamic, economic, and structural aspects of any psychic datum, although the topographic model is sometimes construed as the first structural articulation. Since Freud, analysts are likely to speak of genetic and adaptive components of metapsychology as well (Rapaport and Gill, "Points of View"; Meissner, *Freud and Psychoanalysis,* 187–90).

47. Freud, "On Narcissism," 76–77.

48. Ibid., 100.
49. Ibid., 73–74, 75; concerning "cathexis," see n. 77 below.
50. Ibid., 75, 76, 87.
51. Ibid., 77.
52. *Ego and Id,* 17.
53. "On Narcissism," 75, 85.
54. See ibid., 91, 98, 100; "Instincts and Their Vicissitudes," 134–36.
55. "On Narcissism," 93–94.
56. Ibid., 93, 99–100.
57. Ibid., 99–100, 93–94.
58. The correlation between the sexual and relational (instincts) is Freud's own; cf. "Short Account," 198, 208; *Ego and Id,* 42, 43; *Autobiographical Study,* 37.
59. "On Narcissism," 87.
60. Ibid., 87–89. Object choice of "anaclitic" or "attachment" love, attributed by Freud to men, reflects dependency (upon another), while narcissistic object choice, attributed principally to women, reflects the fact that one seeks oneself as a love object. However, one's self, albeit under different aspects, is at the heart of each, as is tacitly acknowledged when Freud says: "object-love of the attachment [anaclitic] type . . . displays the marked sexual overvaluation which is doubtless derived from the child's original narcissism and thus corresponds to a transference of that narcissism to the sexual object" (88).
61. Ibid., 99. One indication of this has already been viewed through the transference (*Beyond,* 20). As a reaction to the failure of love (and loss of position and security) in the oedipal transition, love thereafter appears as possessive or clinging in an attempt to avoid the possibility of further and future loss. In other words, it is Erotic, binding and bonding the object to oneself, mimicking the secure merger of the preoedipal period. Nevertheless, this action cannot secure love at all; at best the object is a captive, servant to insecurity and need.
62. "On Narcissism," 93, 100.
63. An example of this in *Beyond* comes in response to the transference. Freud attempts to procure the client's "toleration of that unpleasure [caused by the return of the repressed] by an appeal to the reality principle" (20). In spite of his best efforts, he notes that resistance and repression often win out.

64. "On Narcissism," 79.
65. *Beyond the Pleasure Principle,* 52, 55–56, 50.
66. Ibid., 50.
67. *Ego and Id,* 46.
68. "Instincts and Their Vicissitudes," 134–36.
69. *Beyond the Pleasure Principle,* 50.
70. "Instincts and Their Vicissitudes," 135–37.
71. Ibid., 136.
72. Ibid., 139.
73. Ibid., 135, 136, 137.
74. Ibid., 137.
75. *Beyond* itself will note that "object-love itself presents us with a second example of a similar polarity—that between love (or affection) and hate (or aggressiveness)" (53).
76. *Beyond* footnotes (p. 60) that the bonding and binding of Eros is sought through *force*, making explicit the violence that is otherwise and obviously implicit in the text.
77. *The Standard Edition* translates *Besetzung* as "cathexis." Brenner (*Elementary Textbook,* 19) remarks: "The accurate definition of 'cathexis' is the amount of psychic energy which is directed toward or attached to the mental representative of a person or thing. That is to say cathexis refers to a purely mental phenomenon. It is a psychological, not a physical concept. Psychic energy cannot flow out through space and cathect or attach itself to the external object directly. . . . The greater the cathexis, the more 'important' the object is, psychologically speaking, and vice versa." Granted that psychic energy does not physically flow "out" to "external" objects, Brenner nevertheless speaks with a sophistication and nuance that did not preoccupy Freud, who speaks readily of the outer and external world (in a vital and important distinction to the inner or internal world) and of objects therein that are cathected. See, generally, "On Narcissism," and "Instincts and Their Vicissitudes." As late as the *Outline* (150, emphasis added) Freud wrote, "libidinal cathexes are *sent out* to objects," while at the same time speaking of "cathect[ing] the *ideas* of objects," anticipating the perspective Brenner would insist upon. Regarding the translation of *Besetzung* by "cathexis," Jones (*Life and Work of Freud,* vol. 2, 323) remarks that " 'cathexis' (Besetzung) . . . roughly means a 'charge of energy'," and Freud, corresponding in

English with Jones, makes this correlation: "withdrawal of *interest* ('Besetzung')" (ibid., 63, emphasis added). Converging with Freud's indication, Brennan comments that employing "cathexis" to translate *Besetzung* "loses the connotation of occupation, of being occupied, being engaged, also conveyed by the German term. *Besetzung* connotes both the act of becoming occupied or attached to an idea, object, etc., and the quantity of energy or quota of affect involved in that attachment" (*Interpretation of the Flesh,* 67, n. 40).

78. Freud, "Formulations on Two Principles," 219.
79. See Freud, *Interpretation of Dreams,* 488–508, for a discussion of secondary revision. After presenting the myth of Aristophanes (*Beyond,* 57–58), Freud breaks off with a "few words of critical reflection" for a page and a half. His chapter 7, a recap and overview, extends this secondary revision of the primary process associations.
80. *Beyond the Pleasure Principle,* 57 (Freud's emphasis).
81. Ibid., 57–58.
82. Ibid., 20–21.
83. Freud, *Autobiographical Study,* 42.
84. Perse, *Collected Poems,* 587.

NOTES TO CHAPTER 2

1. Kierkegaard, *Either/Or,* 331, 344.
2. Ibid., 363, 416, 380.
3. Ibid., 356.
4. Ibid., 304.
5. Coles, *Walker Percy,* 84.
6. Levinas, *Totality and Infinity,* 43.
7. Ibid., 46.
8. Ibid., 47.
9. *Either/Or,* 308.
10. Ibid., 356.
11. Kierkegaard, *Stages on Life's Way,* 103.
12. *Either/Or,* 356, 380.
13. Ibid., 380, 356 (emphasis added).
14. Ibid., 372, 380 (emphasis added).
15. Ibid., 420, 337 (emphasis added).
16. Ibid., 363 (emphasis added).
17. Ibid., 380.

18. Ibid., 436.
19. Ibid., 320, 347.
20. Ibid., 388, 347.
21. Ibid., 337, 356, 380.
22. Ibid., 406, 435.
23. Ibid., 435, 380 (emphasis added).
24. Ibid., 380.
25. Ibid., 415.
26. Ibid., 367.
27. Ibid., 399 (emphasis added).
28. Ibid.
29. Ibid., 364.
30. Ibid., 337.
31. Ibid., 331.
32. Ibid., 380.
33. Ibid., 344.
34. Ibid., 304.
35. Ibid., 426.
36. Ibid., 380.
37. Ibid., 440, 380.
38. Ibid., 356.
39. Ibid., 372.
40. Ibid., 364.
41. Ibid., 437, 439.
42. Ibid., 438.
43. Ibid.
44. Kierkegaard, *Sickness unto Death,* 51.
45. Ibid., 63, 57–58; Kierkegaard, *Eighteen Upbuilding Discourses,* 265. Guntrip would concur about the perdurability of this fundamental characteristic as a residue from earliest infancy. He says that people "have resisted recognition of the truth that we . . . struggle to suppress the fact that deep within our makeup we retain a weak, fear-ridden infantile ego that we never completely outgrow" (*Schizoid Phenomena,* 125). "What keeps the child alive inside so long? Why is he not normally and naturally outgrown as the years go by, along with increasing physical and intellectual maturity?" Guntrip asks (185). Evoking Fairbairn, Guntrip elsewhere says: "He traces trouble deeper [than the Oedipus complex], to a failure to outgrow *infantile dependence*" (54, Guntrip's emphasis).

46. Kierkegaard, *Concept of Anxiety,* 41, 43, 48–49.
47. Kierkegaard, *Sickness unto Death,* 51.
48. Ibid., 27, 46.
49. Contemporary psychoanalysis agrees: "Our need for object-relation-ships [relations with others] lies in the fact that without them it is impossible to develop an ego that is sound, strong, and stable. . . . The primary drive in every human being is to become a 'person'. . . . This can only be done in the medium of personal object-relation-ships" (Guntrip, *Schizoid Phenomena,* 174, original emphasis deleted). Kierkegaard understands the self to be relational in a threefold sense. Beyond the question of interaction with others, the self is a relation that cannot be constituted apart from a relation to another, *the* other—the deity or power—who establishes the self:

    > The self is a relation that relates itself to itself. . . . If the relation that relates itself to itself has been established by another, then . . . this relation, the third, is yet again a relation and relates itself to that which established the entire relation.
    > The human self is such a derived, established relation, a relation that relates itself to itself and in relating itself to itself, relates itself to another. (*Sickness unto Death,* 13–14)

    Thus, by definition, the self cannot be constituted without the pres-ence of the other. And see Dunning, *Kierkegaard's Dialectic of Inwardness,* 246–49) on the relational self in Kierkegaard.
50. *Sickness unto Death,* 51, 53.
51. Kierkegaard, *Concept of Anxiety,* 99, 101.
52. *Sickness unto Death,* 27.
53. Ibid., 54. The metaphor of awakening has roots in the West as remote as Heraclitus. Interestingly, the notion of an individuating separation anticipates such diverse theorists as Carl Jung and Marga-ret Mahler. According to Mahler and her associates, following a period of normal intrapsychic symbiosis, the infant, around four or five months, embarks upon a separation-individuation phase that will continue through the thirtieth to thirty-sixth month. "Separation consists of the child's emergence from a symbiotic fusion with the mother," while the complementary process of individuation, pro-ceeding through four subphases, "consists of those achievements marking the child's assumption of his own individual characteristics.

These are intertwined, but not identical, developmental processes. . ." (*Psychological Birth of the Human Infant,* 4). For an alternative to the infant's development that is critical of Mahler's schema, see Stern, *Interpersonal World of the Infant.* S. Johnson, *Symbiotic Character,* takes both Mahler and Stern into account.

54. Kierkegaard, *Concept of Anxiety,* 41.
55. *Sickness unto Death,* 50, 57.
56. Ibid., 58, 56, 52.
57. Kierkegaard, *Concluding Unscientific Postscript,* 412; *Sickness unto Death,* 59.
58. *Sickness unto Death,* 59, 13.
59. Ibid., 57.
60. Ibid., 101.
61. Ibid., 43.
62. Ibid., 53.
63. *Concept of Anxiety,* 44.
64. *Sickness unto Death,* 35.
65. *Concluding Unscientific Postscript,* 412.
66. *Sickness unto Death,* 43.
67. *Concluding Unscientific Postscript,* 388–89.
68. *Sickness unto Death,* 52.
69. Winnicott, *Maturational Processes,* 102. See Koenigsberg, *Symbiosis and Separation,* for a psychology of culture from the perspective of symbiosis and separation.
70. In the context of gender enculturation, Schafer speaks of the "societal seduction" of youth, which is sufficiently elemental that it can represent the whole of social and cultural induction:

[I]t will be necessary to overcome or mitigate the societal seduction of boys into uneasy representatives of pure masculine force and of girls into demoralized representatives of pure feminine milieu. Here is a start on a social psychological theory of seduction of children that can replace the theory which Freud once entertained and then mostly rejected, that is, the theory of physical seduction of children who later became neurotic. The psychological theory would, however, have to take account of what psychoanalysis has established, namely, the eagerness with which children participate in these categorical seductions owing to the thrilling and terrifying features of their infantile fantasy life.

In light of this new seduction theory, we may hope to reclaim many disclaimed actions in the interest of helping people be whole, responsible, reciprocally related persons. (*Language and Insight,* 170–71)

71. Winnicott, *Maturational Processes,* 146.
72. What follows is a synthesis of a portion of "The Present Age" in Kierkegaard, *Two Ages,* 68–112. And see Perkins, ed, *International Kierkegaard Commentary,* and Westphal, *Kierkegaard's Critique.*
73. *Two Ages,* 92.
74. Ibid., 88.
75. Ibid., 84.
76. Ibid., 91, 93.
77. Ibid., 93.
78. Ibid., 88, 85, 90.
79. Ibid., 101.
80. Ibid., 85, 93.
81. Ibid., 94, 93.
82. Ibid., 107, 93.
83. Ibid., 93.
84. Ibid., 106, 86; Kierkegaard, *Practice in Christianity,* 42.
85. *Two Ages,* 87, 106.
86. Ibid., 96, 101, 86.
87. Searles, *Countertransference,* 506.
88. Searles, *Nonhuman Environment,* 55, 56 103, 269. Guntrip, *Schizoid Phenomena,* concurs.
89. Searles, *Countertransference,* 176. The hazard of the peerless work of Mahler et al., *Psychological Birth of the Human Infant,* is to see symbiosis and individuation as stage specific or once and for all. Searles's remarks concerning Jacobson's classic, *The Self and the Object World,* are an appropriate caution for those concentrating too narrowly on the focus of Mahler's work, viz., infants: "She greatly underestimates the role of symbiosis, ceaselessly returned to more or less overtly, and ever-present at a subterranean level in human relatedness. Similarly, instead of her seeing . . . identity formation to be going on throughout life, she describes all these as though in some developmental era they were finally achieved, with a relatively static structure existing thereafter. . ." (*Countertransference,* 41).

While Mahler (4) says that the principle psychological achievements of separation-individuation take place within the first three years, underscoring the focus of her study as intrapsychic processes of early childhood and cautioning that "[w]e do not mean to imply, as is sometimes loosely done, that every new separation or step toward a revised or expanded feeling of self at any age is part of the separation-individuation process," she also comments: "Like any intrapsychic process, this one reverberates throughout the life cycle. It is never finished; it remains always active; new phases of the life cycle see new derivatives of the earliest processes still at work" (3). S. Johnson (*Symbiotic Character,* 79) observes: "Like all other characterological issues, the symbiotic one is existential and lifelong. . . . The strategies found successful in liberating the 'symbiotic character' can be of nearly universal significance. Becoming optimally integrated with others, yet remaining autonomous, is an accomplishment of only the wisest and most fortunate."

90. Searles, *Countertransference,* 177.
91. Ibid., 50.
92. Searles, *Nonhuman Environment,* 102, 103.
93. Ibid., 104; *Countertransference,* 41. Winnicott concurs: "Adults must be expected to be continuing the process of growing and of growing up, since they do but seldom reach to full maturity" (*Maturational Processes,* 92).
94. Searles, *Countertransference,* 140; cf. 163.
95. Searles, *Nonhuman Environment,* 405.
96. Ibid., 103.
97. Searles, *Countertransference,* 176, 44. Elsewhere, clarifying the possibly offensive "over against," Searles remarks that without experiencing the environment as something "meaningful and real 'over against'" oneself, one can neither distinguish between oneself and the environment, nor feel a sense of profound kinship with it (*Nonhuman Environment,* 396). "Over against" does not indicate opposition but differentiation, leading, as the ensuing paragraph makes clear, to harmonious and healthy relationship.
98. Searles, *Nonhuman Environment,* 107, 101.
99. Ibid., 107.
100. Searles, *Countertransference,* 44.
101. Ibid., 70.

102. Ibid., 42.
103. Ibid., 58–59.
104. Ibid., 42.
105. "Collectivity" is not Heidegger's term, but it is a convenient, more felicitous way to refer to what he indicates with other terms. Thus, it is necessary to emphasize, in accord with Heidegger's meaning, that *das Man,* the "they," is not a sum of all its elements as if a certain quantity or number were needed before "they" existed. Each is *das Man,* although the "they" is an aggregate in the sense of being thrown or fallen together without qualitative relationship, without intentionality or decision. (Similarly, "the multitude" has been suggested by Philipse, *Heidegger's Philosophy of Being,* 349.) In part, "collectivity" is suggested by Jung's use of the term. Both Heidegger's and Jung's "collectivity" represent a proximal structure or condition of unconscious embeddedness from which—though not necessarily—one must be individuated to wholeness (Jung) or individualized to authenticity (Heidegger). It does not appear that Heidegger was conversant with Jung's work, although he may have known of it through hearsay via his association with Medard Boss, a onetime colleague of Jung. For Jung's hostile and affect-laden reactions to Heidegger, see Jung, *Letters: 1906–1950,* 331 and *Letters, 1951–1961,* xliv, 121; and see Kaufmann's response, *Discovering the Mind,* 289–90. I am indebted to Kegan, *Evolving Self,* 31, 78) and his acknowledged source for bringing the notion of embeddedness to my attention.
106. This discussion of the "they" is a synthesis of Heidegger, *Being and Time,* 163–68, 219–24, 312–13. W. Richardson, *Heidegger,* 71, translates *das Man* as "people," noting: "'People' seems to be the closest equivalent of *Man,* for colloquial English has nothing so flexible as the French *on.* . . . Other possibilities: 'everybody', 'they'." "They" is the translation employed by Macquarrie and Robinson, the English translators of *Being and Time.*
107. *Being and Time,* 167.
108. Ibid., 163–64.
109. Ibid., 164.
110. Ibid., 167.
111. Ibid., 165.
112. Ibid., 164.
113. Ibid., 167.

114. Ibid., 164.
115. Ibid., 154 (Heidegger's emphasis).
116. Ibid., 165.
117. Ibid., 220, 167, 166.
118. Ibid., 165, 164, 166, 162.
119. Ibid., 313.
120. Ibid., 312, 313, 443.
121. Ibid., 312: Selfhood is identical with "ways of Being."
122. Ibid., 164, 312.
123. Ibid., 165, 222.
124. Ibid., 219–24 and 396–400. In lieu of "falling," Stambaugh translates *verfallen* as "entanglement" or "falling prey" in her translation of *Being and Time*. While this is felicitous and comprehends the implication of an "ineluctable drag toward comportment with beings" (W. Richardson, *Heidegger,* 38) and the "absorption in" and "Being-lost in" the "they" that Heidegger ascribes to *verfallen* (*Being and Time,* 220), both terms may misplace the descriptive valence from Dasein to *das Man* or the world. As Heidegger elucidates, *verfallen* indicates that Dasein "'lives' *away from itself*" (*Being and Time,* 223, Heidegger's emphasis). For the difficult translation, Mehta, *Martin Heidegger,* employs "forfeiture," but this may be too penal for Heidegger's usage. W. Richardson, *Heidegger,* 37, 70–71) opts for "fallen-ness."
125. *Being and Time,* 165; cf. 166.
126. Ibid., 222, 223.
127. Ibid., 223.
128. Ibid., 167.
129. Searles, *Nonhuman Environment,* 399, 396.
130. Ibid., 395.
131. Ibid., 224, 236.
132. Searles, *Countertransference,* 237.
133. Ibid., 240, 234, 236. Becker, *Escape from Evil,* 140–41, has written in a similar vein of a cultural type "who earns his immortality from identification with the powers of machines. . . . The mechanical man may scorn and fear living things, but I think it is precisely because he feels that they do not have the power over life and death that machines have; his eternity symbol is then the machine which transcends both life and death."
134. Searles, *Countertransference,* 240.

135. Ibid., 239. Again, Becker, *Escape from Evil,* 141, articulates pertinently: "Mass destruction committed under the reign of God the Machine is a tribute to the expansion of an implacable, efficient force with which modern men can identify. . . ."

136. Searles, *Countertransference,* 241.

137. Ibid., 241 (emphasis added). And cf. Arendt, *The Human Condition,* 1, who reports that on the successful launch of the first artificial satellite the "immediate reaction, expressed on the spur of the moment, was relief about the first 'step toward escape from men's imprisonment to the earth'." Cf. also, Mumford, *Transformations of Man,* 135–36.

138. Searles, *Countertransference,* 241–42.

Notes to Chapter 3

1. *Being and Time,* 294. And see Demske, *Being, Man, and Death.*

2. *Being and Time,* 306–7.

3. Ibid., 307–8.

4. Ibid., 311.

5. Ibid., 310 (Heidegger's emphasis). Anxiety fades from view in Heidegger's later work, and see Langan, *The Meaning of Heidegger,* 38, for an emphasis on the positive aspect of *angst* in *Being and Time.*

6. *Being and Time,* 21.

7. While *What is Called Thinking?* 99–101, indicates that Aristotle laid the foundation for all subsequent Western misconceptions, *Being and Time* is somewhat ambivalent since Heidegger acknowledges that the question of Being "provided a stimulus for the researches of Plato and Aristotle, only to subside from then on," while complaining that initial Greek contributions provided a foundation for the dogmatized neglect of Being (21, and cf. 256–57). Cf. Heidegger, *Early Greek Thinking,* 13–58; "Letter on Humanism," 240; and see Langan, *The Meaning of Heidegger,* 152–61.

8. Although "Being" is a gerund in form, Campbell, *Truth and Historicity,* 319, among others, alerts us that the substantive attribute should not mislead because "Being" *(Sein)* maintains the verbal force of the infinitive: to be (and see p. 42 at n. 19). Nevertheless, for the convenience of both reader and writer alike the hyphenated form stressing the active and dynamic infinitive will not be employed.

9. Heidegger writes: "Being-disclosive" (*Being and Time,* 300).

10. John Caputo, *Heidegger and Aquinas,* superbly demonstrates amid a lucid discussion of Heidegger's later period how the great synthesis of medieval Scholasticism—principally through its architect, Thomas Aquinas—failed also to recognize the ontological difference despite its emphasis on *esse.* See Heidegger, *Basic Problems of Phenomenology,* as well as Vail, *Heidegger and Ontological Difference,* on the ontological difference.

11. *Being and Time,* 32 (Heidegger's emphasis). Cf. "[W]e of today, despite our interest in metaphysics and ontology, are scarcely able any longer properly to raise even the *question* of the Being of beings—to raise it in a way which will put in question our own being so that it becomes questionable in its relatedness to Being, and thereby open to Being" (Heidegger, *What Is Called Thinking?* 78, his emphasis). Cf. "The Being of beings is the most apparent; and yet, we normally do not see it—and if we do, only with difficulty" (ibid., 110). And see Heidegger, *Kant and the Problem of Metaphysics,* especially 149–66. See Mehta, *Martin Heidegger;* Kockelmans, *Heidegger's "Being and Time";* Dreyfus, *Being-in-the-World;* and King, *Guide to Heidegger's* Being and Time, for some studies of *Being and Time.* Biemel, *Martin Heidegger;* Elliston, *Heidegger's Existential Analytic;* Pöggeler, *Martin Heidegger's Path of Thinking;* Philipse, *Heidegger's Philosophy of Being,* and Polt, *Heidegger: An Introduction,* comprehend both *Being and Time* and the later authorship. Amid a study of authenticity, Zimmerman, *Eclipse of Self,* provides a lucid entrée to *Being and Time.*

12. See *Being and Time,* 245, 351, 381, for indications of "Reality," "substance," and "subject," and cf. 32–33, 67–68 with regard to Dasein's distinctiveness. With regard to being human, Heidegger has written ("Letter on Humanism," 243–44): "Where else does 'care' tend but in the direction of bringing the human being back to his essence? What else does that in turn betoken but that man *(homo)* become human *(humanus)*?" Also: "Metaphysics thinks of the human being on the basis of *animalitas* and does not think in the direction of his *humanitas*" ("Letter on Humanism," 246–47). Elsewhere, he has said: "Metaphysics remains what comes first in philosophy. What comes first in thinking, however, it does not reach. . . . But if our thinking should succeed in its efforts to go back into the ground of metaphysics, it might well help to bring about a *change in the human essence,* a change accompanied by a transformation of metaphysics" (Heidegger,

Introduction to *What Is Metaphysics?* 279, emphasis added). And see Scott, *Language of Difference,* 53–88.

13. An irony must be noted. In his introduction to Adorno, *Jargon of Authenticity,* xvii, Trent Schroyer summarizes: "For Adorno, Heidegger's existentialism is a new Platonism which implies that authenticity comes in the complete disposal of the person over himself—as if there were no determination emerging from the objectivity of history." See Rosen, *The Question of Being,* on Heidegger and Plato, and see Wolz's study of selfhood in *Plato and Heidegger.*

14. From an expansive literature see, with regard to Kant: Sherover, *Heidegger, Kant, and Time;* Schalow, *Renewal of the Heidegger-Kant Dialogue;* with regard to Hegel: Kolb, *Critique of Pure Modernity;* Schmidt, *Ubiquity of the Finite;* Taminiaux, *Dialectic and Difference;* with regard to Kierkegaard: Schrag, *Existence and Freedom;* M. Wyschogrod, *Kierkegaard and Heidegger;* Dreyfus, *Being-in-the-World,* Hoberman, "Kierkegaard's *Two Ages*"; Magurshak, "Concept of Anxiety" and "Despair and Everydayness"; Caputo, "Kierkegaard, Heidegger, and the Foundering of Metaphysics"; Spanos, *Heidegger and Criticism;* and Weston, *Kierkegaard and Modern Continental Philosophy* .

15. And see Olafson, *Heidegger and the Philosophy of Mind,* and J. Richardson, *Existential Epistemology.* Taminiaux's study of Heidegger's sources, *Heidegger and the Project of Fundamental Ontology,* includes Descartes and, minus Kierkegaard, all of the above figures (see n. 14), plus Nietzsche and Aristotle. With regard to the latter, see also Kisiel, *Genesis of Heidegger's* Being and Time.

16. *Being and Time,* 251.

17. See ibid., section 18, 114–23.

18. Ibid., 80. See Hemming, *Heidegger's Atheism,* 53, on Heidegger's "reversal of the Cartesian order."

19. *Being and Time,* 67. And see Haar, *Heidegger and the Essence of Man.*

20. *Being and Time,* 71.

21. Ibid., and see n. 22.

22. Ibid., 32–33.

23. Ibid., 32–33, 67–68, 91–92, 245, 255; but see 82.

24. Ibid., 121, 154.

25. Ibid., 33, 183.

26. Ibid., 287 (Heidegger's emphasis), 370; cf. 292.

27. Ibid., 280 (Heidegger's emphasis).

28. Ibid., 67–68, 78, 162–63.
29. Ibid., 33.
30. Ibid., 152 (Heidegger's emphasis).
31. Ibid., 255 (Heidegger's emphasis); cf. 32 and 67.
32. Ibid., 32, 78.
33. Ibid., 308.
34. Ibid., 152.
35. Heidegger notes a "double meaning of the term *'cura'* according to which it signifies not only 'anxious exertion' but also 'carefulness' and 'devotedness'," adding: "In the 'double meaning' of 'care', what we have in view is a *single* basic state in its essentially twofold structure of thrown projection" (ibid., 243, Heidegger's emphasis).
36. Ibid., 368.
37. Ibid., 230–31, cf. 22.
38. Ibid., 232–34.
39. Ibid., 233, 322.
40. Ibid., 224.
41. Ibid., 69, 276, 381, 166, 153.
42. Here "reality" is used in distinction to Heidegger's "Reality" (ibid., 245, 351, the present-at-hand) and in the sense of Being authentic, beyond the illusion of *das Man's* (inauthentic) collectivity (311, 358, 443).
43. Ibid., 234, 321.
44. See ibid., 229, 359, 235, 301.
45. Ibid., 301. Note the issues Zimmerman raises (*Eclipse of Self,* 44–47), but see Thiele's remarks in *Timely Meditations,* 235 n. 20.
46. *Being and Time,* 229.
47. This clarification of the argument and structure of II.1 and II.2 is perhaps necessary since W. Richardson (*Heidegger,* 77–84) may inadvertently mislead by proposing that two "answers," which must be correlated, are given to the issue of authenticity.
48. *Being and Time,* 226. The [self-]disclosure of Dasein's Being takes place through understanding, mood or state of mind, and discourse. Understanding has a state of mind while each state of mind has an integral understanding. *Da* can have an *understanding* of its Being, a *sense* or feel or mood [*befindlichkeit*] about "how it is" (233) and can deduce how it is by the indication of its *discourse*—whether a silent comprehension of that Being or the evasive distraction of idle talk.

49. Ibid., 226.
50. The Macquarrie-Robinson footnote bears replication: "While the terms 'ontisch' ('ontical') and 'ontologisch' ('ontological') are not explicitly defined, their meanings will emerge rather clearly. Ontological inquiry is concerned primarily with *Being;* ontical inquiry is concerned primarily with *entities* and the facts about them" (*Being and Time,* 31 n. 3).
51. Ibid., 33 (emphasis in original).
52. Ibid., 226.
53. Ibid., 226, 277.
54. Ibid., 227.
55. Ibid.
56. Ibid., 235–38, 274, 293.
57. See W. Richardson, "Place of the Unconscious," on the unconscious in Heidegger.
58. *Being and Time,* 488, 376, 374, 377, 277.
59. Ibid., 273.
60. Ibid., 276 (Heidegger's emphasis).
61. Ibid.
62. Ibid., 277.
63. Ibid., 311 (emphasis added and original emphasis deleted).
64. Ibid. At this point Heidegger overlooks his earlier statement that "holding death for true does not demand just *one* definite kind of behaviour in Dasein, but demands Dasein itself in the full authenticity of its existence" (309–10, Heidegger's emphasis). He had also spoken of Dasein, in light of the anticipation of death, as "[f]ree for its ownmost possibilities, which are determined by the *end* [death] and so are understood as *finite* [*endliche*]" (308, Heidegger's emphasis).
65. Ibid., 277.
66. Ibid., 311 (Heidegger's emphasis).
67. Ibid., 322, 336.
68. Ibid., 335–41.
69. Ibid., 314, 340–41.
70. Ibid., 219–24, 229–30, 264.
71. Ibid., 318–19, 320–21.
72. Ibid., 321, 322, 332.
73. Ibid., 174.

74. While Adorno comments upon existentialism in the figures of Kierkegaard, Buber, and Jaspers, the apex of this mendacious development is attributed to Heidegger: "The physiognomy of the vulgar jargon leads into what discloses itself in Heidegger" (Adorno, *Jargon of Authenticity,* xxi).

75. *Being and Time,* 321, 330, 356.

76. Ibid., 329 (Heidegger's emphasis).

77. Ibid., 330.

78. Ibid., 330. There is somewhat conflicting language. Heidegger says (his emphasis) that Dasein "has *not* laid that basis *itself*" while speaking of the "Self, which as such has to lay the basis for itself. . . ." Nevertheless, this second statement continues: "[the Self] can *never* get that basis into its power."

79. Ibid., 329.

80. Ibid., 330.

81. Ibid., 331 (Heidegger's emphasis).

82. Ibid., 330 (Heidegger's emphasis).

83. Ibid., 330, 332.

84. Ibid., 329.

85. Ibid., 330.

86. Ibid., 274, 342, 353–54, 372, cf. 33, 331.

87. Ibid., 353 (original emphasis deleted), and cf. 343, 346–47.

88. Ibid., 340–41, 347.

89. Ibid., 322.

90. Ibid., 321, 325–26.

91. Ibid., 320 (Heidegger's emphasis). 'It' is capitalized only as the initial word of the sentence. See p. 111 at n. 6 below.

92. Ibid., 321.

93. Ibid., 322.

94. Ibid., 323.

95. Ibid., 322.

96. W. Richardson, *Heidegger,* 84.

97. *Being and Time,* 313 (Heidegger's emphasis).

98. Ibid., 343 (Heidegger's emphasis).

99. Ibid., 349, 353, 343.

100. Ibid., 350.

101. Ibid., 353 (Heidegger's emphasis).

102. Ibid., 354 (Heidegger's emphasis), and see 356–57.

103. Ibid., 357 (Heidegger's emphasis).

104. Ibid., 353, 357.

105. Ibid., 354 (emphasis added and original emphasis deleted).

106. Ibid., 355, 364.

107. Ibid., 354 (original emphasis deleted).

108. Heidegger distinguishes between factuality and Dasein's facticity (ibid., 82, 174). "The primary existential meaning of facticity lies in the character of 'having been'" (376). Facticity is Dasein's "thrownness," its "that-it-is" (174).

109. Ibid., 355 (original emphasis deleted), and cf. "'*Self-constancy*' signifies nothing other than anticipatory resoluteness" (369, Heidegger's emphasis).

110. Ibid., 357.

111. Temporality is not to be confused with time (ibid., 374), and Heidegger is at great pains to distinguish temporality from the ordinary, common sense, and everyday conception of time, which is comprehended as a pure or infinite sequence of nows (377, 477) that come into being, then pass away (373).

112. Heidegger distinguishes "having been" from the past or being past. "'As long as' Dasein factically exists, it is never past, but it always is indeed as already having *been*. . . . On the other hand, we call an entity 'past', when it is no longer present-at-hand. Therefore Dasein, in existing, can never establish itself as a fact which is present-at-hand, arising and passing away 'in the course of time', with a bit of it past already" (ibid., 376, Heidegger's emphasis).

113. A sense of what Heidegger is attempting to convey by "moment of vision" (*Augenblick*) as Dasein's authentic present can be gleaned through a consideration of the following texts (all emphasis is Heidegger's): "Thus the 'they' covers up [that] . . . death . . . *is possible at any moment*" (ibid., 302). "In its projective character, understanding goes to make up existentially what we call Dasein's 'sight'. . . . The sight which is related primarily and on the whole to existence we call '*transparency*' . . . to designate 'knowledge of the Self . . .'" (186). "[T]his authentic potentiality-for-Being also opens our eyes for the *constancy of the Self* . . . [which is the] counter-possibility to the non-Self-constancy . . . of irresolute falling. Existentially, '*Self-constancy*' signifies nothing other than anticipatory resoluteness [of death]" (369). "The moment *of vision* . . . brings existence into the Situation and

discloses the authentic 'there'" (398). A reader for the press was good enough to underscore that *Augenblick* is the very word Kierkegaard (*Attack upon Christendom;* The Moment *and Late Writings*) uses for the moment or instant of transformation; "the moment of decision and newness when time and eternity meet" (The Moment *and Late Writings,* 630 n. 1).

114. *Being and Time,* 373 (Heidegger's emphasis).

115. Ibid., 351, 374.

116. *"Temporality is the primordial 'outside-of-itself' in and for itself.* We therefore call the phenomena of the future, the character of having been, and the Present, the *'ecstases'* of temporality" (ibid., 377, Heidegger's emphasis).

117. Inauthentic care, it will be recalled, is falling.

118. Cf. *Being and Time,* 308, 443–44.

119. Ibid., 311, 369.

Notes to Chapter 4

1. "Being" will not be capitalized outside of the context of *Being and Time.*

2. Freud and Breuer, *Studies on Hysteria,* 103, 133–34, 164, 217.

3. Cf. Breger, *Freud: Darkness in the Midst of Vision,* 116–17, on the greater prominence of death and loss than sexual disturbance: "as early as the *Studies,* Freud was ignoring his own case material."

4. "Symbolic" is Freud's term: *Studies on Hysteria,* 5. And cf. Lear, *Open Minded,* 86–89.

5. *Studies on Hysteria,* 157.

6. Freud, "Fragment of an Analysis," 7–122. See Lakoff and Coyne, *Father Knows Best,* on the exercise of power in the analysis of Dora, and see Rieff, *Freud: Mind of the Moralist,* 173–85, for Freud's anti-feminist preconceptions.

7. Freud, "On Beginning the Treatment," 139–40.

8. *Studies on Hysteria,* 156.

9. Ibid., 156.

10. Ibid., 149.

11. Ibid., 174.

12. Ibid., 150.

13. Ibid., 135.

14. Veith, *Hysteria*, 1–15; Drinka, *Birth of Neurosis*, 30–31; Ellenberger, *Discovery of the Unconscious*, 142, 337; Clark, *Freud: The Man and the Cause*, 72.
15. *Studies on Hysteria*, 143.
16. Ibid.
17. Ibid., 140.
18. Ibid., 151.
19. Ibid., 156.
20. Ibid., 142.
21. Ibid., 156.
22. Ibid., 151.
23. Ibid., 156.
24. Cf. ibid., 6.
25. Elisabeth was the youngest of three sisters. The three families referred to are the households constituted by Elisabeth and her mother, the eldest sister's family, and the elder sister's family. Freud refers to the eldest sister as the elder and to the elder sister as the second or the younger (of the two elder sisters).
26. *Studies on Hysteria*, 151.
27. Ibid.
28. Ibid., 156.
29. Ibid., 140.
30. Ibid., 141.
31. A. Freud, *The Ego and the Mechanisms of Defense*, 117–31.
32. *Studies on Hysteria*, 153, and see 135.
33. Ibid., 143.
34. Ibid., 142.
35. Dunne, *A Search for God*, 223.
36. Dreaming or stupor, to use Kierkegaard's specific language; and cf. "The self is the conscious synthesis of infinitude and finitude . . ." (*Sickness unto Death*, 29); "however, a synthesis is unthinkable if the two are not united in a third. This third is spirit. . . . So spirit is present, but as immediate, as dreaming" (*Concept of Anxiety*, 43).
37. "[A]nxiety is the dizziness of freedom, which emerges when the spirit wants to posit the synthesis and freedom looks down into its own possibility. . . . Freedom succumbs in this dizziness" (*Concept of Anxiety*, 61). "Synthesis" refers to the integration and emergence of one's self (see *Sickness unto Death*, 13); and cf. "The self is freedom" (*Sickness unto Death*, 29).

38. *Studies on Hysteria,* 159.

39. Kierkegaard, *Upbuilding Discourses in Various Spirits,* 289, adjusting the Hong translation (road) to read *Vei* as "way" (and cf. Kierkegaard, *Gospel of Our Sufferings,* 93 and *Edifying Discourses,* 209). In view of Kierkegaard's parallel use of the same pericope from Matthew's gospel (7:14) that provides the theme and caption of this discourse in another and earlier discourse (*Upbuilding Discourses in Various Spirits,* 152–53) from the same collection—and the Hongs' translation of *Vei* as "way" in that setting— "road" is a curious choice in the present context. To modern ears, "road" can evoke images of vehicular traffic, and it is clear from both this discourse and Kierkegaard's prior usage that he is indicating an individual and *pedestrian* dynamic and metaphor. However, when employed in an explicit pedestrian context, "road" can be effective: "they are all walking along the road of life and are all walking along the same road" (291; but see n. 42 below).

40. The pertinent stanza comes, of course, from his "Elegy Written in a Country Churchyard," discovered in any anthology of classic English poetry:

The boast of heraldry, the pomp of pow'r,
And all that beauty, all that wealth e're gave,
Awaits alike th' inevitable hour:
The paths of glory lead but to the grave.

41. Dunne, *A Search for God,* 223.

42. Kierkegaard, *Upbuilding Discourses in Various Spirits,* 291. The Hong translation reads: "How . . . walk the right road on the road of life?" "Right road" suggests that the issue is one of selecting *which* road is to be traveled, while "right way" more accurately captures the metaphor and meaning of Kierkegaard's *how* (and cf. note 39 above).

43. Dunne, *Reasons of the Heart,* 91.

44. Ibid.; and see the latter part of chapter 6 below on Plato and need.

45. Kierkegaard, *Eighteen Upbuilding Discourses,* 314.

46. Ibid., 313.

47. Ibid., 315.

48. Ibid., 315, 316.
49. Ibid., 314.
50. Ibid., 315.
51. Ibid., 314. If the first self does yield to the deeper, authentic self, a reconciliation takes place, and the two, now united and companions on the way, "walk on together" (316). Challenges remain because, if one is really to know oneself, "there are new struggles and new dangers," but the engagement is now that of an integral, if incipiently whole, being (317).
52. The case of Anna O. merits a collaborating presence because Freud attributed the beginnings of psychoanalysis to it in the "Five Lectures" delivered at Clark University ("Five Lectures on Psycho-Analysis," 9; cf. also, "Short Account of Psycho-Analysis," 193). And see Breger, *Freud: Darkness in the Midst of Vision,* 99–110. To disciples who urged that a distinction be made between the cathartic treatment of Breuer and Freud's *Studies on Hysteria* and the psychoanalysis of free association, Freud was dismissive ("On the History of the Psycho-Analytic Movement," 8). A happy resolution to the dispute appears in an article Freud prepared for the first presentation of psychoanalysis in the *Encyclopaedia Britannica.* There Freud recognized two originating events: "The beginnings of psycho-analysis may be marked by two dates: 1895, which saw the publication of Breuer and Freud's *Studies on Hysteria,* and 1900, which saw that of Freud's *Interpretation of Dreams*" ("Psycho-Analysis," 269).
53. Freud never wholly subscribed to Breuer's theory ("On the History of the Psycho-Analytic Movement," 11; *An Autobiographical Study,* 23). Although Freud suggests that he distanced himself from Breuer's view from the beginning, he did not fail to employ its rationale (*Studies on Hysteria,* 128). Freud was inclined to understand conversion neurosis as the result of resistance and repression—a neurosis of defense ("On the History of the Psycho-Analytic Movement," 11). For a period he attempted to allow the two theories to coexist, but eventually it became clear that "repression is the cornerstone on which the whole structure of psycho-analysis rests" (ibid., 16).
54. "Five Lectures on Psycho-Analysis," 19.
55. *Studies on Hysteria,* 115.
56. Ibid., 116.
57. Ibid., 117.

58. Ibid., 116.
59. Ibid., 120–21.
60. Ibid., 115.
61. Ibid., 117.
62. Ibid., 115.
63. Ibid., 121.
64. Ibid., 125.
65. Ibid., 126.
66. Masson, *Assault on Truth,* 87, proposes that Emma Eckstein was the patient "who provided Freud with the seduction theory" (and see Krüll, *Freud and His Father,* xv). The transition from a seduction theory of neurosis (or external conflict paradigm) to a theory and model of intrapsychic conflict, eventuating in the Oedipus complex, has been well rehearsed by Freud (see, e.g., "On the History of the Psycho-Analytic Movement," 17–18 and *Autobiographical Study,* 33–34) and expositors (see, e.g., Wollheim, *Sigmund Freud,* 23–29 and Sulloway, *Freud, Biologist of the Mind,* 110, 204–7). Without entering the controversy or politics generated by Masson's book about the "renunciation of the theory of seduction" (but cf. Krüll, xv–xvi), it must be noted that in his final accounting Freud (*An Outline of Psycho-Analysis,* 187) lists seduction and child abuse among "certain influences which do not apply to all children, though they are common enough," in the production of neuroses. For a discussion of the losses that accompany the gains in this move to depth psychology, see Napier and Whitaker, *Family Crucible,* 40–44. For a consideration of the "received" and "revisionist" views of Freud and the seduction theory, see Blass and Simon, "Freud on His Own Mistake(s)." See Ludwig, *How Do We Know Who We Are?* 151–55, for a discussion of Freud's unconscious motivations in this shift.
67. *Studies on Hysteria,* 130.
68. Ibid., 128. Identifying Franziska as a sister (Breger, *Freud: Darkness in the Midst of Vision,* 114), goes beyond Freud's later footnote (*Studies on Hysteria,* 134).
69. *Studies on Hysteria,* 129.
70. Ibid.
71. Ibid., 132.

72. Ibid., 131. Katharina describes her father as "lying on" the girl, with his clothes on (128, 129). "Intercourse" is Freud's interpolation—perhaps a conclusion or a slip, revealing one of his own youthful discoveries. See Krüll, *Freud and His Father*, 124–26, who suggests a possible liaison between Freud's mother and his much older half-brother.
73. *Studies on Hysteria*, 131.
74. Ibid., 128.
75. Ibid., 129.
76. Ibid., 132.
77. Ibid., 126.
78. See *Inhibitions, Symptoms, and Anxiety* for Freud's second, mature view of anxiety. Via the idiom of unpleasure, this was adumbrated in *Beyond:* "Most of the unpleasure that we experience is perceptual unpleasure. It may be perception of pressure by unsatisfied instincts [first theory of anxiety]; or it may be external perception which is either distressing in itself or which excites unpleasurable expectations in the mental apparatus—that is, which is recognized by it as a 'danger' [second theory of anxiety]" (*Beyond the Pleasure Principle*, 11, original emphasis deleted).
79. *Studies on Hysteria*, 126.
80. Ibid., 125.
81. Ibid., 132. The face is the last memory and recognition to surface, indicating the deepest and key repression. Note that it represents the father during the cataclysm of the family's disintegration.
82. Ibid.
83. Ibid., 131.
84. Ibid., 105; and see Ellenberger, *Beyond the Unconscious.*
85. *Studies on Hysteria*, 52.
86. Ibid., 53.
87. Ibid., 55.
88. Ibid., 60.
89. Ibid., 49.
90. Ibid., 72.
91. Ibid., 77.
92. Ibid.
93. Ibid., 78.
94. Ibid., 78, 79.

95. Ibid., 80, 82.
96. Ibid., 83.
97. Ibid., 84.
98. Ibid., 102.
99. Ibid., 102–3.
100. Ibid., 88.
101. Ibid., 103.
102. These pictures (53), which Emmy saw "with all the vividness of reality," were the "animal scenes and pictures of corpses" issuing from the numerous deaths that were ingredient to her childhood and that Freud had called the "traumatic precipitating causes" of Emmy's illness (52).
103. Ibid., 53.
104. Ibid., 77.
105. Ibid., 101.
106. Ibid., 48 (emphasis added).
107. Ibid., 84. In fact, it was during his work with Frau Emmy that Freud "began for the first time to have grave doubts about the validity of Bernheim's assertion *'tout est dans la suggestion'* ['suggestion is everything']" (101, *Standard Edition*'s brackets). Such an admission indicates that suggestion must have played a sufficiently important (and, by implication, dominant) role to necessitate such grave doubts. Freud not only studied with Bemheim in Paris, he was also the German translator of Bernheim's work (77).
108. Ibid., 97, 102. This seems to qualify Freud's statement that "only those symptoms of which I carried out a psychical analysis [compared to the cathartic procedure] were really permanently removed" (101).
109. Ibid., 50.
110. Ibid., 63.
111. Ibid., 99.
112. Ibid., 56.
113. Ibid., 96.
114. On the issue of Freud and death, see Becker, *Denial of Death,* and Yalom, *Existential Psychotherapy.*

NOTES TO CHAPTER 5

1. Freud, *Inhibitions, Symptoms, and Anxiety,* 129.
2. Ibid.

3. Ibid.
4. Ibid.
5. Ibid., 130.
6. *Interpretation of Dreams,* 254.
7. *Inhibitions, Symptoms, and Anxiety,* 93.
8. Ibid., 94.
9. Ibid., 93–94.
10. Ibid., 136. See Guntrip (*Schizoid Phenomena,* 51–54) for a discussion of Rank's thesis at a profounder conceptual level than earliest psycho-analysis could entertain.
11. *Inhibitions, Symptoms, and Anxiety,* 135.
12. Ibid.
13. Ibid., 130.
14. Ibid., 135.
15. Ibid., 137.
16. Ibid. (Freud's emphasis).
17. Ibid., 137.
18. Freud, *Outline of Psycho-Analysis,* 185.
19. Schafer's remark (*Language and Insight,* 196–97) that "Too often, psycho-analysts confuse the subjective experience of the body with biology" may be pertinent here.
20. In fact, Freud comments that "there is much more continuity between intra-uterine life and earliest infancy than the impressive caesura of the act of birth would have us believe" (*Inhibitions, Symptoms, and Anxiety,* 138). When Freud continues to speak of "the analogy of birth" or of "anxiety-states as a reproduction of the trauma of birth" (133), it is in large part due to what Heidegger would call a fore-conception, one of three elements of the hermeneutical situation or circle through which a problem or phenomenon is approached for resolution or interpretation. For Heidegger, human understanding is never exacted as "presuppositionless apprehending." To the contrary, whatever is to be understood cannot be interpreted unless a preliminary or tentative understanding is already present. It is this fore-knowing that allows us to proceed on the path of interpretation. Interpretation appeals to "nothing other than the obvious undiscussed assumption of the person who does the interpreting" (*Being and Time,* 192). However, this is simply the initiation of a process of working through or working out the possibilities of

understanding. Thus, the hermeneutical circle begins with a *fore-having* by which a matter or issue comes under the scope of our concern. *Fore-sight* gives a preview or advance glimpse that "takes the first cut" at comprehension and combines with fore-having to present a *fore-conception* that allows an initial grasp of the situation. The circle moves from a preliminary understanding or analysis, through interpretation, to an appropriated—and conceivably transformed—understanding (*Being and Time*, 188–95, 275). Freud's continual birth references manifest the fore-knowing that guided his explorations, chiefly under Rank's influence, and magnetized his language and orientation toward the primal trauma.

21. *Inhibitions, Symptoms, and Anxiety,* 136 (emphasis added).
22. Ibid., 133.
23. Ibid., 97.
24. Like the question of the chicken or the egg, the priority of repression or the ego is a futile issue; it cannot be determined since the two interface. What is primary, therefore, and what instigates each, is the primal trauma and the matrix of unconscious reaction. *Beyond* underscores the relationship between ego-consciousness and (traumatic) excitations: "What consciousness yields consists essentially of perceptions of excitations coming from the external world and of feelings of pleasure and unpleasure [interior excitations] which can only arise from within the mental apparatus" (24). Moreover, the sense of the reciprocal influence of ego and repression and of the ego's scarring or "deformity" by its initial trauma is captured in the following remarks from the *Outline*:

> The neuroses are, as we know, disorders of the ego; and it is not to be wondered at if the ego, so long as it is feeble, immature and incapable of resistance, fails to deal with tasks which it could cope with later on with the utmost ease. In these circumstances instinctual demands from within, no less than excitations from the external world, operate as "traumas.". . . The helpless ego fends them off by means of attempts at flight (*repressions*), which later turn out to be inefficient and which involve permanent restrictions of further development. The damage inflicted on the ego by its first experiences gives us the appearance of being disproportionately great. . . . No human individual is spared such

traumatic experiences; none escapes the repressions to which they give rise. (184–85, Freud's emphasis)

25. *Inhibitions, Symptoms, and Anxiety,* 93, 109–10.
26. Lacan has called the ego a system "of defenses, of denials, of dams, of inhibitions" (*Seminar,* 17).
27. Freud says that the "conscious ego . . . is first and foremost a body-ego" (*Ego and Id,* 27).
28. See Laplanche, *Life and Death,* and cf. Stepansky, *History of Aggression.*
29. *Inhibitions, Symptoms, and Anxiety,* 97.
30. Ibid., 91–92.
31. See p. 26 at n. 45 above, and cf. Kierkegaard, *Without Authority,* 31.
32. See chapter 2 for a discussion of immediacy and chapter 9 for a discussion of dying away from immediacy.

NOTES TO CHAPTER 6

1. *Being and Time,* 295 (original emphasis deleted). In passing, Heidegger has spoken of "suppression" (*Kant and the Problem of Metaphysics,* 160).
2. Freud, *Outline of Psycho-Analysis,* 185. See chapter 5, n. 24 for Freud's text.
3. *Beyond the Pleasure Principle,* 18.
4. Ibid., 19–20.
5. *Being and Time,* 388, 394. Pomedli, "Heidegger and Freud"; Langfur, "Death's Second Self"; Davis, *Inwardness and Existence;* and Hans, *Question of Value,* interface Freud and Heidegger. Nevertheless, it must be emphasized that Heidegger's use of "repetition" bears greater affinity to or similitude with Kierkegaard's "repetition" than with any Freudian use. In fact Stack underscores that Heidegger appropriated the category directly from Kierkegaard (*Kierkegaard's Existential Ethics,* 135–36). For both German and Dane, the term indicates an authentic relation (or ongoing recommitment) to the self of human *existing.*
6. *Being and Time,* 320–21.
7. Ibid., 263.
8. Ibid., 321.
9. Sexuality concretizes one in time and place, imposing the law of mortal necessity with its suffering of earth-bound limitations. Both sexuality and dying are epiphenomena of humanity's fundamental facticity, the great onus of embodied finitude. Both threaten to

unravel and destroy the compromise formation of repression's body of death—the foundational alienation of our selves from the challenges and possibilities of incarnate existence. Although vehicles of embodiment, each seems, proximally and for the most part, to propel one into deeper evasion.

10. On the translation of *das Man* as "one," in the sense of one-like-many, W. Richardson comments: "Correct, but too formal" (*Heidegger,* 71n.). Nevertheless, see Macomber, *Anatomy of Disillusion,* 81–84, for a rich discussion of the "impersonality of the one"; cf. Mehta, *Martin Heidegger,* 142–44; and cf. Philipse, *Heidegger's Philosophy of Being,* 26, 346, who employs both "the They" and "the One."

11. Roth, *Psychotherapy,* 113–25.

12. Freud, *Totem and Taboo,* 159. Although the text is somewhat ambiguous, it appears that Freud's reference to "their narcissistic organization" is not an explicit reference to social organization but to the narcissistic state of the primitive mentality. Nevertheless, it is precisely in consequence of this narcissistic condition that the transition from the "patriarchal horde" to the "fraternal clan" arose. Thus, one is justified in characterizing the consequent social transition, a product of the narcissistic psyche, as being narcissistic, and this converges with Freud's characterization in *Civilization and Its Discontents* of the erotically impelled social union.

13. *Civilization and Its Discontents,* 133.

14. See Rieff, *Freud: The Mind of the Moralist,* 228 and Wallace, *Freud and Anthropology,* but see Paul, "Did the Primal Crime Take Place?" With regard to Freud's sources for *Totem and Taboo,* see Rieff, 191, 193.

15. *Totem and Taboo,* 141.

16. Ibid., 142.

17. Ibid., 143.

18. Freud, "Instincts and Their Vicissitudes," 136–39; see p. 13–14 above.

19. See n. 12 above and cf. Freud, *Civilization and its Discontents,* 133.

20. See, for example, *Beyond the Pleasure Principle,* 28–29.

21. Paul recovers and highlights the quality of intergenerational conflict through a cross-cultural consideration of the Oedipus complex ("Symbolic Interpretation"; *Tibetan Symbolic World*).

22. Freud, *Interpretation of Dreams,* 619.

23. Ibid., 256.

24. Ibid., 257.

25. Freud, "Analysis of a Phobia," 5–149; *Inhibitions, Symptoms, and Anxiety*, 101ff.

26. Schafer, *Language and Insight*, 175–76. Schafer remarks:

> Psychoanalysts should develop no more theory than they need for their method. What is appropriate is not so much an ambitious, all-encompassing theory of mind as a modest empirical theory of how to name and interpret the human activity that is . . . observed and inferred during the psychoanalytic process. Most analysts have, however, followed Freud in attempting to develop psychoanalysis as a general psychology or an all-encompassing theory of personality development. . . . (176–77)

Schafer also comments that

> Freud underestimated and so understated the extent to which his attempts to develop a general psychology of the mind ("the mental apparatus") were philosophical projects. . . . Nothing in the clinical analytic method leads to any conclusions about . . . psychoeconomic closed systems, or overarching regulatory psychobiological principles such as repetition compulsion and life and death instincts. Far from being empirical conclusions, these are philosophical a prioris concerning the age-old mind-body problem, and at best they are dubious. (175, 195–96)

See Holt, *Freud Reappraised*, for a cogent appraisal of Freudian theory, and Spence, *Narrative Truth and Historical Truth*, 293–96, for cautions about general theory interfering with clinical work.

27. Freud, "Family Romances," 237–41. With the Family Romance, discrimination and differentiation are called for, sensitive to the clinical nuances that, as Schafer has suggested (n. 26 above), must direct interpretation and empirical theory. As in the situation of Little Hans's hostility, the matrix of sibling birth provokes the reaction that Freud labels "Family Romance." In the Family Romance syndrome, unlike Hans's situation, hostile attitude or conduct is not manifested toward another. Neither does the phantasy life configure a threatened danger as in the traditional Oedipus complex. Instead, the diminishment of attention that the subject experiences, and the disappointment it occasions, provoke the positive psychic creativity of phantasizing a

more noble lineage than the impoverished conditions of actuality. The fact that the renounced parents are the basis of the imagined world does not, as Freud pointed out from his own perspective, nullify the rejection.

28. See chapter 1, n. 29.

29. Freud, "Why War?" 209; see also Freud, *Group Psychology*, 91.

30. Addressing the difficulty in discerning Plato's perspective, Nussbaum comments: "We do not always so clearly see what choice 'Plato' wants us to make. This makes it dangerous, in such a case, to speak of 'Plato's views', unless we simply mean his view of what the open alternatives are and what the choice of either involves giving up—no trivial view in itself" (*Fragility of Goodness*, 87).

31. The basis for this interpretation is Plato's seventh letter where he asserts:

> One statement at any rate I can make in regard to all who have written or who may write with a claim to knowledge of the subjects to which I devote myself. . . . Such writers can in my opinion have no real acquaintance with the subject. I certainly have composed no work in regard to it, nor shall I ever do so in future, for there is no way of putting it in words like other studies. . . . In a word, it is an inevitable conclusion from this that when anyone sees anywhere the written work of anyone . . . , the subject treated cannot have been his most serious concern—that is, if he is himself a serious man. (Hamilton and Cairns, *Collected Dialogues of Plato*, 1588–1589, 1591)

A similar utterance is found in the second letter (1567).

32. The existence of Diotima remains debated. Guthrie, *History of Greek Philosophy*, 385–86, does not doubt that, whether a historic figure or not, Diotima is to be equated with Socrates in the dialogue and speaks *his* insight, yet the relationship between the two within the structure of the dialogue is still subject to conjecture, if not dispute. Other issues include Diotima's status and, thus, authority as a woman and non-Athenian, the relationship of Diotima's insight to the perspective articulated by Socrates in the *Phaedrus* (and see Nussbaum, *Fragility of Goodness*, 200–3), and, most importantly, the *Meno*'s doctrine of recollection in light of the perspective on forgetting and new knowledge that Diotima conveys.

33. Regarding the *Symposium*, Allen, *The Dialogues of Plato;* Brentlinger, *Symposium of Plato;* Cobb, *Symposium and The Phaedrus;* Dover, *Symposium;* Hamilton and Cairns, *Collected Dialogues of Plato;* Jowett, *Dialogues of Plato;* Plato, *Symposium;* and Rosen, *Plato's Symposium,* have been consulted.

NOTES TO CHAPTER 7

1. *Beyond the Pleasure Principle,* 19–20.
2. Cf. *Being and Time,* 401, 436, 460.
3. Ibid., 436.
4. Ibid., 51ff.
5. Cardinal, *The Words To Say It,* 164.
6. Ibid., 268.
7. Ibid., 164.
8. Ibid.
9. Ibid., 164–65.
10. Ibid., 174.
11. Ibid., 165.
12. Ibid., 293 (Cardinal's emphasis), and see 268.
13. Ibid., 172, and see 166.
14. Ibid., 271.
15. Ibid., 174–75.
16. Ibid., 204.
17. Ibid., 102.
18. Ibid., 175.
19. Ibid., 261.
20. Ibid., 207.
21. Ibid., 268.
22. Ibid., 214.
23. Ibid., 207.
24. Ibid., 215.
25. *Being and Time,* 368.
26. Ibid., 85 (Heidegger's emphasis) and cf. 168.
27. Ibid., 168, 156, 335–36.
28. Ibid., 370, 336.
29. Ibid., 363, cf. 369.
30. Ibid., 186–87 and 321–22. Moreover, the "clearing of Being" is already evident in *Being and Time,* "*as* Being-in-the-world [Dasein] is

cleared in itself, not through any other entity, but in such a way that it *is* itself the clearing" (171, Heidegger's emphasis). And see 401 and 460, as well as notes 33 and 44 below. Cf. also, Marx, *Heidegger and the Tradition,* 219, on the earlier and later clearing.

31. *Being and Time,* 387–88 (Heidegger's emphasis) and cf. 344.
32. King, *Heidegger's Philosophy,* 56–57.
33. *Being and Time,* 438; and cf. "The ecstatical unity of temporality . . . is the condition for the possibility that there can be an entity which exists as its 'there'. . . . *Ecstatical temporality clears the 'there' primordially"* (401, 402, Heidegger's emphasis); and cf. 460.
34. Cf. ibid., 155, 233, 344, 435. See Stambaugh, *Finitude of Being,* on finitude in *Being and Time* and the later authorship.
35. *Being and Time,* 344.
36. Ibid., 155.
37. Ibid., 159.
38. Ibid., 344.
39. Ibid., 318, 344.
40. Ibid., 344.
41. Cf. ibid.
42. Cf. ibid., 158.
43. Cf. ibid., 159, 186.
44. Ibid., 344 (Heidegger's emphasis); cf. "As . . . disclosed, Dasein exists factically in the way of *Being with* Others" (463, Heidegger's emphasis); and cf. 162. Moreover, at 187, the "disclosedness of the 'there'" is correlated to "clearedness" (n. 30 above). And see Theunissen, *The Other,* and E. Wyschogrod, *Spirit in Ashes,* 164–68.
45. *Being and Time,* 434.
46. Ibid., 435, 309 (original emphasis deleted).
47. Ibid., 436 (original emphasis deleted), 309, and cf. 186, 354.
48. Ibid., 436, 443, cf. 311.
49. Ibid., 344, 435.
50. Cardinal, *The Words To Say It,* 172.
51. Ibid., 270.
52. Ibid.
53. *Being and Time,* 344.
54. Ibid., 388.
55. Ibid., 443 (emphasis added).
56. Ibid. (emphasis added).

57. Ibid., 435 (emphasis added).
58. Ibid., 355 (original emphasis deleted).

Notes to Chapter 8

1. This is an essay extracted from introductory portions of a lecture series published under the title *What Is Called Thinking?* A concise and powerful essay, its considerable strength deserves to be encountered on its own terms. For that reason and because it is readily accessible in a standard collection of Heidegger's work, *Basic Writings,* it will be cited primarily in the discussion that follows, supplemented by material from the book. See Mugerauer, *Heidegger's Language and Thinking,* for a study of the work.
2. "What Calls for Thinking?" 347 (original emphasis deleted).
3. Ibid., 345.
4. "[C]apable of doing only what we are inclined to do," it must be the case, since we are still not thinking, that we are *disinclined* from heeding what is essential—especially since "thought is the gift given . . . [whenever] we incline toward it" (ibid., 345).
5. Ibid., 345, 348–49.
6. Ibid., 350.
7. Ibid., 351.
8. Ibid., 346.
9. Ibid., 349, 362, and *What Is Called Thinking?* 165.
10. *What Is Called Thinking?* 165.
11. Ibid., 175 and "What Calls for Thinking?" 362.
12. *What Is Called Thinking?* 169.
13. "What Calls for Thinking?" 353, 349, and see Heidegger, *Discourse on Thinking,* 82, on becoming "more void."
14. We think only in relation to the withdrawing, and since we enter the neighborhood of thinking by a leap, it would appear that it is by a leap as well that one enters the withdrawal.
15. *What Is Called Thinking?* 168.
16. Ibid., 168, 169.
17. "What Calls for Thinking?" 350, 358.
18. Ibid., 357.
19. Ibid., 358.
20. Ibid., 351.
21. Ibid., and *Discourse on Thinking,* 86, 67; cf. "Letter on Humanism," 272.

22. In *Discourse on Thinking,* 58–90.
23. Ibid., 78.
24. "Letter on Humanism," 252, 253.
25. *Discourse on Thinking,* 56.
26. Ibid., 50, 46.
27. Ibid., 54.
28. Ibid., 53–54.
29. *Being and Time,* 336; "Letter on Humanism, 243, 252.
30. *Discourse on Thinking,* 55.
31. Ibid., 78; "Letter on Humanism," 268, 260, 261, 252.
32. "Letter on Humanism," 268.
33. "What Calls for Thinking?" 351 (Heidegger's emphasis).
34. "Letter on Humanism," 268.
35. *Discourse on Thinking,* 82.
36. *What Is Called Thinking?* 169.
37. *Discourse on Thinking,* 66, 82.
38. "Letter on Humanism," 252. See Heidegger and Fink, *Heraclitus Seminar,* 160–61.
39. "Letter on Humanism," 248, 256, 252, 261, 247.
40. Ibid., 247.
41. *What Is Called Thinking?* 148–49, adjusting the translation to read "Dasein" for "man," following W. Richardson, *Heidegger,* 599–605.
42. *What Is Called Thinking?* 149.
43. *Discourse on Thinking,* 46.
44. Ibid., 46, 78–79.
45. "Letter on Humanism," 267.
46. Becker, *Denial of Death,* 23.
47. Ibid., 23, 24.
48. Ibid., 21.
49. Ibid., 59.
50. Ibid., 60.
51. Cardinal, *The Words To Say It,* 175.
52. Becker, *Denial of Death,* 57.
53. "What Calls for Thinking?" 350.
54. See W. Richardson (*Heidegger,* xx–xxi). A footnoted remark by Richardson (614) bears notice: "This conception of *Ereignis* has been discernible since at least 1946. . . . We must overhear also the word *eignen* ('to be adapted to,' 'to be the property of,' etc.) and understand the

process by which Being ap-propriates to man his essence in order to ap-propriate him to itself. . . . Obviously the English 'e-vent' cannot hope to retain all these nuances, but it has certain modest virtues not to be disdained. . . ." See Pöggeler, "Being as Appropriation"; Zimmerman, *Eclipse of Self,* 231–43; Caputo, *Heidegger and Aquinas,* 167–76; Kockelmans, *On the Truth of Being,* 59–65, Bernasconi, *Question of Language,* 81–97; Schürmann, *Heidegger on Being and Acting,* 217–19; Nicholson, *Illustrations of Being,* 118–32; and Hemming, *Heidegger's Atheism,* 103–33. Hemming (69, 155–63) traces the roots of *Ereignia* to pre-*Being and Time* ruminations. Emad and Maly, in their translation of Heidegger (*Contributions to Philosophy*) employ the extravagant neologism "enowning" for *Ereignis.* Whatever its merits (incorporating *eignen* as it does), their suggestion that "event" is incapable of hyphenation to demonstrate movement is gainsaid by Richardson's "e-vent." More alarming is the shortsightedness that asserts "event" (among some other translations) is "totally mute when it comes to the movement that runs through *Ereignis*" (see *Contributions to Philosophy,* xv–xxii). There is nothing more dynamic than the event of e-venting, the event of coming forth, of coming out (from), of coming away (toward). This, in fact, parallels the *ex-sistere* of "existence" in *Being and Time,* while completing and "perfecting" its "standing forth," which might be construed as an isolated or definitive happening, with the clearly never-ending dynamic of an ever new beginning.

55. Heidegger, *On Time and Being,* 24. And see Benjamin, *The Plural Event,* 140–65.

56. *On Time and Being,* 23, cf. 16. See *Discourse on Thinking,* 81 for a reinterpretation of *Being and* Time's "resolve" in light of Heidegger's later thinking.

57. Cf. *Discourse on Thinking,* 83. See Schürmann, *Meister Eckhart;* Zimmerman, *Eclipse of Self;* Caputo, *Mystical Element in Heidegger's Thought;* and Levin, *The Opening of Vision,* 233–50, and *The Listening Self,* 223–35, on releasement (*gelassenheit*).

58. *Discourse on Thinking,* 73 (Heidegger's emphasis), employing "Region" in lieu of the more cumbersome "that-which-regions"; see ibid., 66, n. 1.

59. Cf. ibid., 66–67, 69, 85, 86.

60. Ibid., 55, 48–49.

61. Ibid., 81.
62. "Letter on Humanism," 255.
63. Ibid., 254–55.
64. Ibid., 255. But see Campbell, *Truth and Historicity,* 320, on Heidegger's "semantic insights."
65. *On Time and Being,* 3. And see Campbell, *Truth and Historicity,* 318–21, for a concise look at *On Time and Being.*
66. *On Time and Being,* 5, 8.
67. Ibid., 8, cf. 22.
68. Ibid., 6.
69. Ibid., 10, 5, 3.
70. Ibid., 10.
71. Ibid., 11–12.
72. Ibid., 11.
73. Ibid., 13.
74. Ibid., 14.
75. Ibid., 14, 15.
76. Ibid., 15.
77. Cf. *Discourse on Thinking,* 69, 66, 86, 82, and 84.
78. *On Time and Being,* 23.
79. Ibid., 12, 23.
80. Ibid., 23.
81. Ibid., 8.
82. *Being and Time,* 185, 419 n. 2.
83. Cf. ibid., 358, 155, 159, 344.
84. Ibid., 311, 358, 443.
85. For an enlightening discussion of "clearing" as unburdening, see Krell, *Intimations of Mortality,* 92. And see Levin, *The Body's Recollection of Being,* 322–39, for an exploration of the celebratory clearing.
86. *On Time and Being,* 6.

Notes to Chapter 9

1. See M. Taylor, *Kierkegaard's Pseudonymous Authorship,* 17–18; Stack, *Kierkegaard's Existential Ethics,* 136; Dreyfus, *Being-in-the-World,* 299–336; and Caputo, "Kierkegaard, Heidegger," 224, for assessments of Heidegger's debt to Kierkegaard. Gadamer, *Heidegger's Ways,* 10, underscores that *Being and Time's* "existential engagement" was

"expressed in a vocabulary emulating Kierkegaard's." And see Philipse's interesting hypothesis (*Heidegger's Philosophy of Being*, 350–52).

2. Kierkegaard, *Journals and Papers*, 62.

3. See Scholem, *Major Trends in Jewish Mysticism* and *Kabbala*. *Zimzum* (following Scholem's 1974 spelling) is employed judiciously by theologian Jurgen Moltman (*Trinity and the Kingdom*, 108–21; *God in Creation*, 86–93).

4. Philippians 2:5–11, Revised Standard Version, with the inclusive language of the new RSV taken into account. In addition to the works noted in the text, see Fowl, *The Story of Christ;* Hoover, "The HARPAGMOS Enigma"; Hurst, "Re-Enter the Pre-Existent Christ"; Hurtado, "Jesus as Lordly Example"; Wanamaker, "Philippians 2.6–11"; and Wong, "The Problem of Pre-Existence."

5. See Oden, *The Word of Life*, for a presentation of the tradition. See Pannenberg, *Jesus, God and Man*, 283–323, for the "two natures" impasse and the issues kenotic Christology attempted to resolve.

6. Sykes, "The Strange Persistence of Kenotic Christology," 351 (emphasis in original).

7. See Bruce, *Humiliation of Christ;* Forsyth, *Person and Place of Christ;* V. Taylor, *Person of Christ;* Dawe, *Form of a Servant;* and Welch, *Protestant Thought*, 233–40. Cf. Gorodetzky, *Humiliated Christ.* Richard's *Kenotic Christology* attempts to avoid the hazards of the nineteenth-century genre, as does MacGregor's *He Who Lets Us Be.*

8. Schillebeeckx, *Jesus: An Experiment in Christology*, 36.

9. Bruce, *Humiliation of Christ*, 10–11.

10. Hooker, *From Adam to Christ*, 88.

11. Sanders, *New Testament Christological Hymns;* Hammerton-Kelly, *Pre-Existence, Wisdom;* Wright, "harpagmos"; Martin, *Carmen Christi;* O'Brien, *The Epistle to the Philippians.*

12. In the latter situation, an Adam-Christ topology contrasts an original anthropos (Adam) who inordinately lusted after and sought to usurp divine prerogatives with a second anthropos (Christ) who humbly relinquished inordinate and self-aggrandizing desires.

13. Martin, *Carmen Christi*, 290–91 (emphasis added). One inspiration for Käsemann's study ("A Critical Analysis") was to assert preexistence of the Logos in opposition to Enlightenment and post-Enlightenment predilections. As the following exploration of Kierkegaard

indicates, contra Martin and Käsemann, an individual can empty himself or herself and incarnate, dying away from immediacy.

14. Macquarrie, *Jesus Christ in Modern Thought,* 61.

15. Robert A. Paul (personal communication, re: his unpublished but performed drama, *King Solomon*).

16. Martin would later declare the "hermeneutical assumption" is that one "should isolate the meaning of the terms in the hymn from the use which is made of them by Paul" (*Carmen Christi,* 1983 reprint, xvii).

17. Käsemann, "A Critical Analysis," 87. Here is heard a strong echo of the Lutheran concern for faith and grace in opposition to works and human merit. Kierkegaard would agree that the ethical posture is ultimately inadequate; and his insistence on the leap of faith and standing before God as indispensable for the fullness of selfhood ratifies Käsemann's concerns. Nevertheless, Kierkegaard would insist that one can "follow" and "imitate" the "pattern" or "prototype." See his comments about Luther—"But let us not forget, Luther did not therefore abolish imitation . . ." (*For Self-Examination,* 193, and see 207–9). Note that "imitation" is not an ethics for achieving the graced life, but a paradigm within the already graced existence. Dewey, *New Obedience,* distinguishes facsimile and ascetic imitation from authentic imitation or "following Christ." Also see Dupré, *Kierkegaard as Theologian;* M. Thulstrup, "Kierkegaard's Dialectic of Imitation"; Sponheim, *Kierkegaard on Christ;* Gouwens, *Kierkegaard as Religious Thinker,* 195–97; and Rae, *Kierkegaard's Vision,* 107, 234–36.

18. Käsemann, "The Problem of the Historical Jesus."

19. Ibid., 31, 46, 25.

20. Ibid., 31.

21. Ibid., 25.

22. Ibid., 32.

23. *Concluding Unscientific Postscript,* 313, 316. See R. Johnson, *Concept of Existence,* on existence in the *Postscript;* see also Diem, *Kierkegaard's Dialectic of Existence;* Malantschuk, *Kierkegaard's Thought and Kierkegaard's Concept of Existence;* and Elrod, *Being and Existence.*

24. *Concluding Unscientific Postscript,* 314, 317. And see Perkins, "Kierkegaard's Teleological Humanism."

25. Käsemann, "The Problem of the Historical Jesus," 39 (emphasis added).

26. *Concluding Unscientific Postscript,* 193, 339, 116. See Evans, *Subjectivity and Religious Belief;* Rudd, *Kierkegaard and the Limits of the Ethical,* 54–67; Ferguson, *Melancholy and the Critique of Modernity,* 155–63; and Rae, *Kierkegaard's Vision,* 213–36, on subjectivity; and see Evans, *Kierkegaard's Fragments,* on the religious philosophy of the *Postscript* and *Fragments.*

27. N. Thulstrup, *Kierkegaard's Relation to Hegel.*

28. *Concluding Unscientific Postscript,* 497, and cf. 340 regarding the leap of faith.

29. C. G. Jung validates the possibility of extracting psychological and anthropological insight from religious data since, as he repeatedly points out, whatever else it may represent, the phenomena is not independent of the human psyche. Bergman, *Dialogical Philosophy,* demonstrates that one can have no interest in Kierkegaard's faith and still appropriate his rich existential and dialogical thinking. Cf. M. Wyschogrod, *The Body of Faith,* 145: "It is therefore Kierkegaard who is the philosopher of man."

30. See text, chapter 2 above, at n. 87f and at n. 138.

31. Kierkegaard does cite the Philippians hymn (*Upbuilding Discourses in Various Spirits,* 221). Mackey, *Kierkegaard: A Kind of Poet;* Dunning, *Kierkegaard's Dialectic of Inwardness;* Moseley, *Becoming a Self before God;* and Law, *Kierkegaard as Negative Theologian,* recognize the presence of kenosis.

32. Kierkegaard, *Philosophical Fragments,* 26–31. See Evans, *Passionate Reason,* and Rae, *Kierkegaard's Vision.*

33. *Practice in Christianity,* 170, 25, substituting "walk" (181) for "wander," and cf. Kierkegaard, *Christian Discourses,* 55.

34. *Practice in Christianity,* 126, cf. 65, 192.

35. Ibid., 131; *For Self-Examination,* 59.

36. *Practice in Christianity,* 130.

37. Ibid., 128, 182, and cf. 132.

38. *Christian Discourses,* 35, cf. *Concluding Unscientific Postscript,* 229.

39. *Practice in Christianity,* 34, 182.

40. *Philosophical Fragments.,* 32 (emphasis added).

41. Ibid., 32.

42. In *Christian Discourses,* Kierkegaard makes this concern transparent, asserting that, in spite of appearances, if one were to look closely it could be perceived that "there is no one there" (61). See Webb, *Philosophers of Consciousness,* on incarnate subjectivity.

43. *Concluding Unscientific Postscript,* 235, 223; cf. 216 and *Practice in Christianity,* 134. "The majority of people do not exist at all in the more profound sense," Kierkegaard remarks in *Practice in Christianity,* 129. See n. 57 below.

44. *Concluding Unscientific Postscript,* 317; *Sickness unto Death* is wholly dedicated to cataloging the multiple evasions of oneself and the resulting manifestations of despair.

45. *Christian Discourses,* 77, cf. *Concluding Unscientific Postscript,* 113; and cf. Searles's comments in chapter 2 above, ff n. 135.

46. *Concluding Unscientific Postscript,* 113.

47. Ibid., 229.

48. Ibid., 317.

49. Ibid., 229.

50. Ibid., 469, 79, and cf. 75, 84, 469.

51. Ibid., 84, 79.

52. Ibid., 116.

53. Kierkegaard, *Journals and Papers,* 319.

54. *Philosophical Fragments,* 33. In *Practice in Christianity,* 170, Kierkegaard says that "the passion story of his life" is summed up in the shout: "See what a man!" Käsemann concurs: "Christ's death is the secret goal and the culmination of his incarnation, i.e. that it is not merely a necessary occurrence but participates in the active nature of the incarnation" ("A Critical Analysis," 170).

55. *Philosophical Fragments,* 33; *For Self-Examination,* 61; see *Christian Discourses,* 103; *For Self-Examination,* 76; *Practice in Christianity,* 168, 182; and cf. *Concluding Unscientific Postscript,* 311.

56. *Philosophical Fragments,* 17. For the interface of Kierkegaard and Freud, see Loder, *Religious Pathology and Christian Faith;* Cole, *Problematic Self;* Becker, *Denial of Death;* Nordentoft, *Kierkegaard's Psychology;* Smith, *Kierkegaard's Truth;* Tugendhat, *Self-Consciousness and Self-Determination.*

57. *Concluding Unscientific Postscript,* 311; *Philosophical Fragments,* 18–22, 73–74. Winnicott conceives of the clinically significant "False Self" as one of "nonexistence," although the analysand might be quite successful otherwise (*Maturational Processes,* 134). He tells of a patient, in analysis for many years with others, who said this was all "futile because it had been done on the basis that he existed, whereas he had only existed falsely." When Winnicott "recognized his non-existence [the patient] felt that he had been communicated with for the first

time." The analyst concludes: "we make more headway by recognition of the patient's non-existence than by a long-continued working with the patient on the basis of ego-defence mechanisms" (151, 152).

58. Cf. *Philosophical Fragments,* 19; Kierkegaard, *Works of Love,* 252; *Sickness unto Death,* 51, and see chapter 2, pp. 26–27.

59. For Searles, see chapter 2, at n. 87ff.

60. *Christian Discourses,* 114, 113, *Sickness unto Death,* 53.

61. *Sickness unto Death,* 53, *Christian Discourses,* 60.

62. *Concluding Unscientific Postscript,* 116, 192.

63. *Christian Discourses,* 47–48.

64. *Concluding Unscientific Postscript,* 79, and cf. 360–63, 386–87.

65. *Works of Love,* 252; *Eighteen Upbuilding Discourses,* 265; *Concluding Unscientific Postscript,* 412, 422.

66. Cf. *Christian Discourses,* 47, 120, 124, and cf. *For Self-Examination,* 189.

67. *Christian Discourses,* 285.

68. Ibid., 59.

69. Ibid., 120, 124, 60; cf. *For Self-Examination,* 157.

70. *Christian Discourses,* 79; *Concluding Unscientific Postscript,* 469.

71. *Concluding Unscientific Postscript,* 404.

72. *Eighteen Upbuilding Discourses,* 314; on 313–17 is a marvelous explication of the immediate self, here called the "first self," and the process of being weaned from immediacy.

73. *Concluding Unscientific Postscript,* 412, 397, 431, and cf. 313–14.

74. Ibid., 431, 387.

75. *Sickness unto Death,* 29–30; *Concluding Unscientific Postscript,* 442, 319; cf. 229, 317, 436.

76. Kierkegaard, The Moment *and Late Writings,* 332, 313, with Kierkegaard's influence upon Heidegger's *das Man* readily discerned; see chapter 2 above.

77. Kierkegaard, *Attack upon Christendom,* 221, 167.

78. *Concluding Unscientific Postscript,* 397; *Christian Discourses,* 339–40; and cf. *For Self-Examination,* 82; *Concluding Unscientific Postscript,* 446. Kierkegaard will even say: "The more consciousness, the more self" (*Sickness unto Death,* 29). See Shmuëli, *Kierkegaard and Consciousness,* for a presentation of Kierkegaard's thought in terms of consciousness.

79. *Concluding Unscientific Postscript,* 387, 63; *Christian Discourses,* 339; and cf. *Concluding Unscientific Postscript,* 39.

80. *Concluding Unscientific Postscript,* 177, 422, 113, cf. 432.

81. *Christian Discourses,* 77; *Philosophical Fragments,* 34; cf. *Concluding Unscientific Postscript,* 113, 397, and *Practice in Christianity,* 187.
82. *Concluding Unscientific Postscript,* 392.
83. Ibid., 456, and cf. 77, 142, 319; *Christian Discourses,* 25, 121.
84. *Works of Love,* 92–93; *Christian Discourses,* 29–35, 56–58.
85. *Concluding Unscientific Postscript,* 387, 431, 423.
86. Ibid., 437, and cf. *Christian Discourses,* 121, 127, 362–65.
87. *Christian Discourses,* 60; *Works of Love,* 98; and cf. *For Self-Examination,* 157.
88. *Concept of Anxiety,* 41; Jung, *Two Essays on Analytical Psychology.*
89. *Works of Love,* 69.
90. Ibid., 68.
91. Ibid., 169.
92. *For Self-Examination,* 83, and cf. 78 and *Works of Love,* 123.
93. *Works of Love,* 69.
94. Ibid., 68.
95. Ibid., 69 (Kierkegaard's emphasis).
96. Ibid., 68–69 (emphasis added).
97. Ibid., 169, 69. See Walsh, "Forming the Heart"; Keeley, "Subjectivity and World"; Plekon, "Kierkegaard the Theologian"; and Ferreira, *Love's Grateful Striving,* on *Works of Love.*
98. *Works of Love,* 248.
99. Ibid., 93.
100. Ibid., 170.
101. Ibid. and cf. *For Self-Examination,* 85.
102. *Works of Love,* 252–53, cf. *Christian Discourses,* 124.
103. *Works of Love,* 250, *Philosophical Fragments,* 31–34, 55–56.
104. Cf. *Practice in Christianity,* 42–42, 58–59; *Christian Discourses,* 124.
105. *Works of Love,* 69, 202.
106. *Concluding Unscientific Postscript,* 232–33.
107. *Works of Love,* 260 .
108. Ibid., 252 (original emphasis deleted).
109. Ibid.
110. Ibid.
111. Ibid., 78.
112. Ibid., 78, 80; *Christian Discourses,* 122. And see Hannay, *Kierkegaard,* 276–301.

113. For example, Kierkegaard notes: "Human reason, from its point of view, quite rightly says: What do I want with doctrine or help which makes the matter worse than it was before" (*Journals and Papers,* 192).
114. Lacan, *Seminar,* 16, 17.
115. *For Self-Examination,* 81.
116. *Concluding Unscientific Postscript,* 113.
117. Kierkegaard, *Upbuilding Discourses in Various Spirits,* 194 (original emphasis deleted).
118. *Eighteen Upbuilding Discourses,* 91, 90.

NOTES TO CHAPTER 10

1. Grinberg and Grinberg, *Psychoanalytic Perspectives;* see the foreword for Kernberg's evaluation.
2. Quoted in ibid., 66.
3. Ibid., 191.
4. Ibid., 198.
5. Ibid., 26, 59.
6. Ibid., 216.
7. Guntrip, *Schizoid Phenomena.*
8. Ibid., 186.
9. Ibid., 187.
10. Ibid., 184 (emphasis deleted).
11. Ibid., 238, 196.
12. Ibid., 203.
13. Ibid., 97, 296–97.
14. Ibid., 307.
15. Ibid., 245, 217.
16. Ibid., 213.
17. Ibid., 244 (emphasis deleted), 195.
18. Ibid., 195, cf. 255 (emphasis deleted).
19. Ibid., 285.
20. Ibid., 174 (emphasis deleted). See pp. 317 (emphasis in original) and 182 for the quoted phrases in the following sentence of the text.
21. Binswanger, *Being-in-the-World,* and Boss, *Psychoanalysis and Dasienanalysis.*
22. Collins, *The Existentialists,* 150–51. See Safranski, *Martin Heidegger,* 235, 279, for "alignment" and "new revolutionary realities." Heidegger's inaugural address on his assumption of the rectorate is a matter of

record; see Heidegger, "The Self-Assertion of the German University," and see Wolin, ed., *Heidegger Controversy,* for additional texts.

23. Habermas, *Philosophical Discourse of Modernity,* 157.

24. Caputo, "Heidegger and Theology," 276. See Wolin, ed., *Heidegger Controversy,* on the controversy. See also Ott, *Martin Heidegger.*

25. Habermas, *Philosophical Discourse of Modernity,* 155 (Habermas's emphasis); and see Boss in Hediegger, *Zollikoin Seminars,* xvi.

26. Heidegger, quoted in Habermas, *Philosophical Discourse of Modernity,* 155–56.

27. Ibid., 156, 159. But see Hemming, *Heidegger's Atheism,* 75–133 on the "reversal."

28. Collins, *The Existentialists,* 151. Farías, *Heidegger and Nazism,* initiated the contemporary debate.

29. Hsiao, "Heidegger and Our Translation," 96.

30. Rorty, "Taking Philosophy Seriously," 31.

31. Rorty, *Contingency, Irony, and Solidarity,* 111 n. 11; Thiele, *Timely Meditations,* 7. The whole of Rorty's statement reads as follows: "On the general question of the relation between Heidegger's thought and his Nazism, I am not persuaded that there is much to be said except that one of the century's most original thinkers happened to be a pretty nasty character." For a brief but nuanced assessment, see Hemming, *Heidegger's Atheism,* 236–38.

32. Arendt and Jaspers, *Correspondence,* 141 (Jaspers, Sept. 1, 1949).

33. Ibid., 142 (Arendt, Sept. 29, 1949). See Wolin, *Heidegger's Children,* 31–69.

34. Dallmayr, *The Other Heidegger,* 181.

35. Webb, *The Self Between,* 224.

36. *Being and Time,* 156, 157.

37. Ibid., 344 (emphasis added).

38. Heidegger, *Metaphysical Foundations of Logic,* 190, 192 (emphasis added).

39. Theunissen, *The Other.* Citing Theunissen, Oliver ("The Relational Self," 38–39) proposes, inter alia, that *Being and Time* presents an inadequate social ontology for which Buber's dialogical I-Thou supplies a corrective. Oliver's inexpert reading of the inexact text provided by Theunissen's "renunciation of all that which already corresponds to dialogical thought in *Being and Time*" (*The Other,* 413 n. 9) produces a multiply defective judgment. Nevertheless, granting his questionable

assessment (see Dallmayr, Introduction to *The Other,* xix–xxi), it is in danger of overlooking the fact that *Being and Time* does indeed articulate a social ontology of an intersubjectively shared world. Moreover, it fails to perceive that both of Theunissen's idealized or "extreme reflective positions"—the transcendentalism attributed to Heidegger and Buber's I-Thou—are integral to the dialectic of human emergence. With regard to critiques such as Oliver's and Webb's, Heidegger has responded: "However rich and interesting the analysis of possible I-thou relationships may be, it cannot solve the metaphysical problem of Dasein, because it cannot even pose the problem. . . . There are sociological, theological, political, biological and ethical problems which ascribe a prominence to the I-thou relation; yet the philosophical problems are thereby concealed" (*Metaphysical Foundations of Logic,* 187). And cf. Heidegger, *Nietzsche,* 24–25.

40. Scott, *Question of Ethics,* 108 (Scott's emphasis).
41. Gadamer, *Heidegger's Ways,* 13.
42. Lipsey, *Coomaraswamy,* 1977.
43. Coomaraswamy, *Coomaraswamy,* 17, 18, 19.
44. Ibid., 19, 373, 374.
45. Ibid., 22, 374, cf. 100 n. 25 and 104.
46. Ibid., 98.
47. Ibid., 125, 21, 373–74 (emphasis added), cf. 384.
48. Ibid., 375, 100, 104, 92.
49. Ibid., 33, 121, 93 n. 10, 373, 125 and n. 50, 99. "[T]he death that [one] at last, despite [one]self, desires, is no destruction but a transformation" (32).
50. Ibid., 100.
51. Ibid., 378, 98, 120, cf. 58.
52. Ibid., 378, 373, 374.
53. Lipsey, *Coomaraswamy,* 242.
54. Douglas, *Purity and Danger,* chapter 10 especially.
55. Ibid., 66.
56. Ibid., 68.
57. Ibid., 178; Lienhardt, *Divinity and Experience,* 300.
58. Douglas, *Purity and Danger,* 178.
59. Ibid., 178, 68.
60. Turner, *Forest of Symbols; The Ritual Process; Dramas, Fields, and Metaphors; From Ritual to Theatre.*

61. Turner, *The Ritual Process,* 169.
62. Turner, *From Ritual to Theatre,* 51; *Dramas, Fields, and Metaphors,* 241.
63. Turner, *The Ritual Process,* 103, 128, 95; *Forest of Symbols,* 98.
64. Turner, *Dramas, Fields, and Metaphors,* 266; *Forest of Symbols,* 96, 110; *From Ritual to Theatre,* 26.
65. Douglas, *Purity and Danger,* 96.
66. Turner, *Dramas, Fields, and Metaphors,* 253; *Forest of Symbols,* 99.
67. Turner, *Forest of Symbols,* 102, 108; cf. 94, 99.
68. Turner, *The Ritual Process,* 138.
69. Turner, *Dramas, Fields, and Metaphors,* 259, 238; *The Ritual Process,* 96.
70. Turner, *The Ritual Process,* 177, 134, 136, 140; *Forest of Symbols,* 100, 101.
71. Turner, *The Ritual Process,* 105, 97.
72. Ibid., 112, 116; *From Ritual to Theatre,* 51; *Dramas, Fields, and Metaphors,* 263.
73. Turner, *From Ritual to Theatre,* 46; *Dramas, Fields, and Metaphors,* 241–42.
74. Turner, *From Ritual to Theatre,* 46; *The Ritual Process,* 132, 117; *Dramas, Fields, and Metaphors,* 259 (emphasis deleted).
75. Turner, *Forest of Symbols,* 101.
76. Turner, *The Ritual Process,* 128.
77. Turner, *Dramas, Fields, and Metaphors,* 260.
78. Turner, *The Ritual Process,* 127.
79. Turner, *Dramas, Fields, and Metaphors,* 259, 238.
80. Ibid., 238; *The Ritual Process,* 128.
81. Mageo, "Ferocious Is the Centipede," 411–12.
82. Ibid., 408, 412.
83. Shore, *Culture in Mind,* chapters 11 and 12.
84. Ibid., 288–89.
85. Ibid., 287–88, 374–78.
86. Ibid., 376.
87. Ibid., 377.
88. Ibid., 270.
89. Mageo, "Ferocious Is the Centipede," 404, 407.
90. Nishida, *Last Writings,* 70.
91. Nishitani, *Religion and Nothingness,* 288; Abe, "Kenosis and Emptiness," 24, 22.
92. Abe, "Kenosis and Emptiness," 13.

93. Nishitani, *Religion and Nothingness,* 282; Abe, "Christianity and Buddhism," 62.

94. Abe, "Kenosis and Emptiness," 20.

95. Ueda, "Emptiness and Fullness," 19, 34, 35.

96. Ibid., 19; for Heidegger, see the penultimate paragraph of chapter 8 above.

97. Ibid., 25.

98. Abe, "Christianity and Buddhism," 47.

99. Ueda, "Emptiness and Fullness," 22–23; Abe, "Christianity and Buddhism," 62.

100. Nishitani, *Religion and Nothingness,* 63, 69.

101. Ibid., 58, 59 (Nishitani's emphasis); "Ontology and Utterance," 42.

102. Nishitani, *Religion and Nothingness,* 72.

103. Ueda, "Emptiness and Fullness," 28.

104. Abe, "God, Emptiness, and the True Self," 25, 26.

105. Nishitani, "Ontology and Utterance," 38.

106. Girardot, *Myth and Meaning in Early Taoism,* 299.

107. Ibid.

108. Pritchard, *Ancient Near Eastern Texts,* 405–7, "A Dispute Over Suicide," trans. J. A. Wilson.

109. Abe, "Kenotic God and Dynamic Sunyata," 56.

110. Pritchard, *Ancient Near Eastern Texts,* 407.

111. Ibid., 52–57, "Inanna's Descent to the Nether World," trans. S. N. Kramer; Wolkstein and Kramer, *Inanna,* 52–73; Jacobsen, *Treasures of Darkness,* 55–60.

112. Wolkstein and Kramer, *Inanna,* 115, 116, 127.

113. Jacobsen, *Treasures of Darkness,* 62–63.

114. The convergence is all the more striking when Ephesians 4:9 is taken into account: "In saying 'He ascended', what does it mean but that he had also descended into the lower parts of the earth. . . ."

115. Pritchard, *Ancient Near Eastern Texts,* 60–72, "The Creation Epic [Enuma elish]," trans. E. A. Speiser; and Jacobsen, *Treasures of Darkness,* 167–91. For the interpretation that follows, the text of Inanna's Descent is supplemented by additional texts that amplify the myth. For the supplements, see Jacobsen, 55–61 and Wolkstein and Kramer, *Inanna,* 74–84 and 85–89, as well as Pritchard, 52 n. 6. In the Genesis creation account, humanity is simply and exclusively responsible for its divided or sinful psyche. In the Mesopotamian

perspective, the riven human condition is a native ingredient of the created given. Thus, humanity is sundered by the beneficent creating act of the gods: it is good to be, but to be created is, perforce, to be divided. While the onus for humanity's condition is placed upon the gods, this most ancient of creation myths, through a wedding with the Inanna-Dumuzi stories, also sounds a hopeful note: humanity can seek and find an amelioration—or perhaps a complete healing—of its condition. We are not doomed to division. Christianity would insist that such a boon is impossible without grace, the gratuity of God's saving action, but the Mesopotamian account does not exclude grace. In fact, the epic comprehends grace with the mediated revival of Inanna by Enki, her divine father.

116. Jaspers, *Origin and Goal of History.* Jaspers places the crux of this period "around" 500 BCE (p. 1). As Voegelin has remarked with regard to another Near Eastern myth: "In dealing with its meaning, then, we must distinguish between the content of the mythical story and the experience symbolized by it. For if we select parts of the myth . . . and treat them as if they were propositions in a discourse, carrying their own meaning, we should arrive at dubious conclusions. . . . Interpretations of this kind treat the myth as if it were an empirical study of human behavior, which a myth of gods and demigods obviously is not" (*Order and History,* 20).

117. Kierkegaard, *Sickness unto Death,* 13; *Concept of Anxiety,* 48.

118. *Sickness unto Death,* 71.

119. Merton, *Asian Journal,* 143 (emphasis deleted). "Sunyata" (emptiness) is discussed extensively in the prior explication of Kyoto philosophy; and see Murti, *Central Philosophy of Buddhism,* 271: "Correctly understood, Sunyata is not annihilation, but the negation of negation; it is the conscious correction of an initial unconscious falsification of the real." "Karuna" is the Mahayana Buddhist term for compassion—a quality of those who are enlightened. Of "dzogchen," the glossary of Merton (*Asian Journal,* 373) says that, as the "Great Way of All-inclusiveness" of the Nyingmapa monastic order of Tibetan Buddhism, dzogchen is (the path of) ultimate awakening: "Dzogchen may be defined as the simplest and most beneficial way to rediscover instantly for oneself the transcendental awareness that is within, whose all-inclusive qualities are either presently active or lying latent in human beings. . . ."

120. Arendt, *The Human Condition,* 237.

121. Ibid., 240.

122. Cummings, *Complete Poems,* 461; and cf. Perse, *Collected Poems,* 587: "For many times were we born, in the endless reach of day." In another but related context, Rilke tells a correspondent: "[U]nfortunately that means still more than nine months' gestation and under conditions of the most uneasy and dangerous pregnancy" (*Letters,* 166).

Bibliography

Abe, Masao. "Christianity and Buddhism." *Japanese Religions* 5 (1968): 36–62.

———. "God, Emptiness, and the True Self." *The Eastern Buddhist* 2 (1969): 15–30.

———. "Kenosis and Emptiness." In *Buddhist Emptiness and Christian Trinity*, edited by R. Corless and P. F. Knitter. New York: Paulist Press, 1990.

———. "Kenotic God and Dynamic Sunyata." In *The Emptying God*, edited by J. B. Cobb and C. Ives. Maryknoll, NY: Orbis, 1990.

Adorno, Theodor W. *The Jargon of Authenticity.* Translated by K. Tarnowski and F. Will. Evanston, IL: Northwestern University Press, 1973.

Allen, Reginald E. *The Dialogues of Plato.* Vol. 2, *The Symposium.* New Haven, CT: Yale University Press, 1984.

Arendt, Hannah. *The Human Condition.* Chicago: University of Chicago Press, 1958.

Arendt, Hannah, and Karl Jaspers. *Correspondence, 1926–1969.* Translated by L. Kohler and H. Saner. New York: Harcourt Brace Jovanovich, 1992.

Becker, Ernest. *The Denial of Death.* New York: Free Press, 1973.

———. *Escape from Evil.* New York: Free Press, 1975.

Benjamin, Andrew E. *The Plural Event: Descartes, Hegel, Heidegger.* New York: Routledge, 1993.

Bergman, Shmuel H. *Dialogical Philosophy from Kierkegaard to Buber.* Translated by A. A. Gerstein. Albany: State University of New York Press, 1991.

Bernasconi, Robert. *The Question of Language in Heidegger's History of Being.* Atlantic Highlands, NJ: Humanities Press, 1985.

Biemel, Walter. *Martin Heidegger: An Illustrated Study.* New York: Harcourt Brace Jovanovich, 1976.

Binswanger, Ludwig. *Being-in-the-World: Selected Papers of Ludwig Binswanger.* Translated by J. Needleman. New York: Basic Books, 1963.

———. *Sigmund Freud: Reminiscences of a Friendship.* Translated by N. Guterman. New York: Grune & Stratton, 1957.

Blass, Rachel B., and Bennett Simon. "Freud on His Own Mistake(s): The Role of Seduction in the Etiology of Neurosis." In *Telling Facts: History and Narration in Psychoanalysis,* edited by J. H. Smith and H. Morris, 160–83. Psychiatry and the Humanities 13. Baltimore, MD: Johns Hopkins University Press, 1992.

Boss, Medard. *Psychoanalysis and Dasienanalysis.* Translated by L. Lefebre. New York: Basic Books, 1963.

Breger, Louis. *Freud: Darkness in the Midst of Vision.* New York: John Wiley, 2000.

Brennan, Teresa. *The Interpretation of the Flesh: Freud and Femininity.* London: Routledge, 1992.

Brenner, Charles. *An Elementary Textbook of Psychoanalysis.* Rev. ed. New York: International Universities Press, 1973.

Brentlinger, John A., ed. *The Symposium of Plato.* Translated by S. Q. Groden. Amherst: University of Massachusetts Press, 1970.

Bruce, Alexander B. *The Humiliation of Christ in Its Physical, Ethical, and Official Aspects.* Edinburgh: T. & T. Clark, 1876.

Campbell, Richard. *Truth and Historicity.* Oxford: Clarendon, 1992.

Caputo, John. *Heidegger and Aquinas: An Essay on Overcoming Metaphysics.* New York: Fordham University Press, 1982.

———. "Heidegger and Theology." In *The Cambridge Companion to Heidegger,* edited by C. B. Guignon. Cambridge: Cambridge University Press, 1993.

———. "Kierkegaard, Heidegger, and the Foundering of Metaphysics." In *International Kierkegaard Commentary,* vol. 6, *Fear and Trembling* and *Repetition,* edited by R. L. Perkins, 201–24. Macon, GA: Mercer University Press, 1993.

————. *The Mystical Element in Heidegger's Thought*. New York: Fordham University Press, 1986.

Cardinal, Marie. *The Words To Say It*. Translated by P. Goodheart. Cambridge, MA: Van Vactor & Goodheart, 1983.

Clark, Ronald W. *Freud: The Man and the Cause*. New York: Random House, 1980.

Cobb, William S. *The Symposium and The Phaedrus: Plato's Erotic Dialogues*. Albany: State University of New York Press, 1993.

Cole, J. Preston. *The Problematic Self in Kierkegaard and Freud*. New Haven, CT: Yale University Press, 1971.

Coles, Robert. *Walker Percy: An American Search*. Boston: Little, Brown, 1978.

Collins, James. *The Existentialists*. Chicago: Regnery, 1952.

Coomaraswamy, Ananda K. *Coomaraswamy*. Vol. 2, *Selected Papers: Metaphysics*, edited by R. Lipsey. Bollingen Series 89. Princeton, NJ: Princeton University Press, 1977.

Cummings, E. E. *Complete Poems, 1904–1962*. New York: Liveright, 1991.

Dallmayr, Fred. Introduction to *The Other: Studies in the Social Ontology of Husserl, Heidegger, Sartre and Buber*, by Michael Theunissen. Cambridge, MA: MIT Press, 1984.

————. *The Other Heidegger*. Ithaca, NY: Cornell University Press, 1993.

Davis, Walter A. *Inwardness and Existence: Subjectivity in/and Hegel, Heidegger, Marx, and Freud*. Madison: University of Wisconsin Press, 1989.

Dawe, Donald G. *The Form of a Servant: A Historical Analysis of the Kenotic Motif*. Philadelphia: Westminster, 1963.

Demske, James M. *Being, Man, and Death: A Key to Heidegger*. Lexington: University of Kentucky Press, 1970.

Derrida, Jacques. "Of an Apocalyptic Tone Recently Adopted in Philosophy." Translated by J. P. Leavey. In *Derrida and Biblical Studies*, edited by R. Detweiler. *Semeia* 23 (1982): 63–97.

————. *The Postcard: From Socrates to Freud and Beyond*. Translated by L. Bass. Chicago: University of Chicago Press, 1987.

Dewey, Bradley R. *The New Obedience: Kierkegaard on Imitating Christ*. Washington, DC: Corpus, 1968.

Diem, Hermann. *Kierkegaard's Dialectic of Existence*. Translated by H. Knight. Edinburgh: Oliver and Boyd, 1959.

Douglas, Mary. *Purity and Danger: An Analysis of the Concepts of Pollution and Taboo*. London: Ark, 1966.

Dover, Kenneth J. *Symposium*. Cambridge: Cambridge University Press, 1980.

Dreyfus, Hubert L. *Being-in-the-World: A Commentary on Heidegger's* Being and Time, *Division I*. Cambridge, MA: MIT Press, 1991.

Drinka, George F. *The Birth of Neurosis*. New York: Simon and Schuster, 1984.

Dunne, John S. *The Reasons of the Heart: A Journey into Solitude and Back Again into the Human Circle*. New York: Macmillan, 1978.

————. *A Search for God in Time and Memory*. New York: Macmillan, 1969.

Dunning, Stephen N. *Kierkegaard's Dialectic of Inwardness: A Structural Analysis of the Theory of Stages*. Princeton, NJ: Princeton University Press, 1985.

Dupré, Louis. *Kierkegaard as Theologian: The Dialectic of Christian Existence*. New York: Sheed and Ward, 1963.

Ellenberger, Henri F. *Beyond the Unconscious*. Princeton, NJ: Princeton University Press, 1993.

————. *The Discovery of the Unconscious*. New York: Basic Books, 1970.

Elliston, Frederick, ed. *Heidegger's Existential Analytic*. The Hague: Mouton, 1978.

Elrod, John W. *Being and Existence in Kierkegaard's Pseudonymous Works*. Princeton, NJ: Princeton University Press, 1975.

Evans, C. Stephen. *Kierkegaard's Fragments and Postscript: The Religious Philosophy of Johannes Climacus*. Atlantic Highlands, NJ: Humanities Press, 1983.

————. *Passionate Reason: Making Sense of Kierkegaard's* Philosophical Fragments. Bloomington: Indiana University Press, 1992.

————. *Subjectivity and Religious Belief: An Historical, Critical Study*. Washington, DC: University Press of America, 1978.

Farías, Victor. *Heidegger and Nazism*. Translated by P. Burrell and G. R. Ricci; edited by J. Margolis and T. Rockmore. Philadelphia: Temple University Press, 1989.

Fenichel, Otto. *The Collected Papers of Otto Fenichel, First Series*. New York: Norton, 1953.

Ferguson, Harvie. *Melancholy and the Critique of Modernity: Søren Kierkegaard's Religious Psychology*. London: Routledge, 1995.

Ferreira, M. Jamie. *Love's Grateful Striving: A Commentary on Kierkegaard's* Works of Love. Oxford: Oxford University Press, 2001.

Forsyth, Peter T. *The Person and Place of Christ*. Boston: Pilgrim Press, 1909.

Fowl, Stephen E. *The Story of Christ in the Ethics of Paul. Journal for the Study of the New Testament,* Supplement Series no. 36. Sheffield, England: JSOT Press, 1990.

Freud, Anna.. *The Ego and the Mechanisms of Defense.* New York: International Universities Press, 1946.

Freud, Sigmund. "Analysis of a Phobia in a Five-Year-Old Boy." Vol. 10 of the *Standard Edition,* 5–149. Works below are cited to *The Standard Edition of the Complete Psychological Works of Sigmund Freud,* edited by J. Strachey. London: Hogarth Press, 1953–1974.

———. *An Autobiographical Study.* Vol. 20 of the *Standard Edition,* 3–74.

———. "On Beginning the Treatment (Further Recommendations on the Technique of Psycho-Analysis, I)." Vol. 12 of the *Standard Edition,* 123–44.

———. *Beyond the Pleasure Principle.* Vol. 18 of the *Standard Edition,* 3–64.

———. *Civilization and Its Discontents.* Vol. 21 of the *Standard Edition,* 59–145.

———. *The Complete Letters of Sigmund Freud to Wilhelm Fliess, 1887–1904.* Translated and edited by J. M. Masson. Cambridge, MA: Harvard University Press, 1985.

———. *The Ego and the Id.* Vol. 19 of the *Standard Edition,* 3–66.

———. "Family Romances." Vol. 9 of the *Standard Edition,* 237–41.

———. "Five Lectures on Psycho-Analysis." Vol. 11 of the *Standard Edition,* 3–55.

———. "Formulations on the Two Principles of Mental Functioning." Vol. 12 of the *Standard Edition,* 215–26.

———. "Fragment of an Analysis of a Case of Hysteria." Vol. 7 of the *Standard Edition,* 7–122.

———. *Group Psychology and the Analysis of the Ego.* Vol. 18 of the *Standard Edition,* 67–143.

———. "On the History of the Psycho-Analytic Movement." Vol. 14 of the *Standard Edition,* 3–66.

———. *Inhibitions, Symptoms, and Anxiety.* Vol. 20 of the *Standard Edition,* 77–175.

———. "Instincts and Their Vicissitudes." Vol. 14 of the *Standard Edition,* 111–40.

———. *The Interpretation of Dreams.* Vols. 4–5 of the *Standard Edition.*

———. *Introductory Lectures on Psycho-Analysis.* Vol. 16 of the *Standard Edition.*

————. "On Narcissism: An Introduction." Vol. 14 of the *Standard Edition*, 69–102.

————. *New Introductory Lectures on Psycho-Analysis*. Vol. 22 of the *Standard Edition*, 3–182.

————. "A Note on the Unconscious in Psycho-Analysis." Vol. 12 of the *Standard Edition*, 257–63.

————. *An Outline of Psycho-Analysis*. Vol. 23 of the *Standard Edition*, 141–207.

————. "Psycho-Analysis." Vol. 20 of the *Standard Edition*, 261–70.

————. "A Short Account of Psycho-Analysis." Vol. 19 of the *Standard Edition*, 191–209.

————. *Totem and Taboo*. Vol. 13 of the *Standard Edition*, 1–161.

————. "Two Encyclopedia Articles." Vol. 18 of the *Standard Edition*, 235–59.

————. "The Unconscious." Vol. 14 of the *Standard Edition*, 161–204.

————. "Why War?" Vol. 22 of the *Standard Edition*, 197–215.

Freud, Sigmund, and Josef Breuer. *Studies on Hysteria*. Vol. 2 of the *Standard Edition*.

Gadamer, Hans-Georg. *Heidegger's Ways*. Translated by J. W. Stanley. Albany: State University of New York Press, 1994.

Girardot, N. J. *Myth and Meaning in Early Taoism: The Theme of Chaos (huntun)*. Berkeley: University of California Press, 1983.

Gorodetzky, Nadejda. *The Humiliated Christ in Modern Russian Thought*. London: Society for Promoting Christian Knowledge, 1938.

Gouwens, David J. *Kierkegaard as Religious Thinker*. Cambridge: Cambridge University Press, 1996.

Grinberg, Leon, and Rebeca Grinberg. *Psychoanalytic Perspectives on Migration and Exile*. Translated by N. Festinger. New Haven, CT: Yale University Press, 1989.

Guntrip, Harry. *Personality Structure and Human Interaction: The Developing Synthesis of Psychodynamic Theory*. London: Hogarth Press, 1961.

————. *Schizoid Phenomena, Object-Relations and the Self*. New York: International Universities Press, 1969.

Guthrie, W. K. C. *A History of Greek Philosophy*. Vol. 4, *The Earlier Plato*. Cambridge: Cambridge University Press, 1975.

Haar, Michel. *Heidegger and the Essence of Man*. Translated by W. McNeill. Albany: State University of New York Press, 1993.

Habermas, Jürgen. *The Philosophical Discourse of Modernity.* Translated by F. Lawrence. Cambridge, MA: MIT Press, 1987.

Hamilton, Edith, and Huntington Cairns, eds. *The Collected Dialogues of Plato, Including the Letters.* Translated by L. Cooper et al. Bollingen Series 71. Princeton, NJ: Princeton University Press, 1961.

Hammerton-Kelly, R. G. *Pre-Existence, Wisdom, and the Son of Man.* Cambridge: Cambridge University Press, 1973.

Hannay, Alastair. *Kierkegaard.* London: Routledge & Kegan Paul, 1982.

Hans, James S. *The Question of Value: Thinking through Nietzsche, Heidegger, and Freud.* Carbondale: Southern Illinois University Press, 1989.

Hegel, G. W. F. *Phenomenology of Spirit.* Translated by A. V. Miller. New York: Oxford University Press, 1977.

Heidegger, Martin. *The Basic Problems of Phenomenology.* Translated by A. Hofstadter. Bloomington: Indiana University Press, 1982.

———. *Being and Time.* Translated by E. Robinson and J. Macquarrie. New York: Harper & Row, 1962.

———. *Being and Time.* Translated by J. Stambaugh. Albany: State University of New York Press, 1996.

———. *Contributions to Philosophy (From Enowning).* Translated by P. Emad and K. Maly. Bloomington: Indiana University Press, 1999.

———. *Discourse on Thinking.* Translated by J. M. Anderson and E. H. Freund. New York: Harper & Row, 1966.

———. *Early Greek Thinking: The Dawn of Western Philosophy.* Translated by D. F. Krell and F. A. Capuzzi. San Francisco: Harper & Row, 1975.

———. Introduction to *What is Metaphysics?* Translated by W. Kaufmann. In *Pathmarks,* edited by W. Mc Neill. Cambridge: Cambridge University Press, 1998.

———. *Kant and the Problem of Metaphysics.* 4th ed. Translated by R. Taft. Bloomington: Indiana University Press. 1990.

———. "Letter on Humanism." Translated by F. A. Capuzzi. In *Pathmarks,* edited by W. Mc Neill. Cambridge: Cambridge University Press, 1998.

———. *The Metaphysical Foundations of Logic.* Translated by J. W. Stanley. Bloomington: Indiana University Press, 1984.

———. *Nietzsche.* Vol. 2, *The Eternal Recurrence of the Same.* Translated by D. F. Krell. San Franscisco: Harper & Row, 1984.

———. *On Time and Being.* Translated by J. Stambaugh. New York: Harper & Row, 1972.

———. "The Self-Assertion of the German University." Translated by K. Harries. *Review of Metaphysics* 38 (1985): 467–80.

———. *What Is Called Thinking?* Translated by J. G. Gray and F. Wieck. New York: Harper & Row, 1968.

———. "What Calls for Thinking?" Translated by F. D. Wieck and J. G. Gray. In *Basic Writings,* edited by D. F. Krell. New York: Harper & Row, 1977.

———. *Zollikoin Seminars.* Edited by M. Boss; translated by F. Mayr and R. Askay. Evanston, IL: Northwestern University Press, 2001.

Heidegger, Martin, and Eugen Fink. *Heraclitus Seminar 1966/67.* Translated by C. H. Seibert. University: University of Alabama Press, 1979.

Hemming, Laurence Paul. *Heidegger's Atheism: The Refusal of a Theological Voice.* Notre Dame, IN: University of Notre Dame Press, 2002.

Hoberman, John M. "Kierkegaard's *Two Ages* and Heidegger's Critique of Modernity." In *International Kierkegaard Commentary,* vol. 14, *Two Ages,* edited by R. L. Perkins, 223–58. Macon, GA: Mercer University Press, 1984.

Holt, Robert R. *Freud Reappraised: A Fresh Look at Psychoanalytic Theory.* New York: Guilford Press, 1989.

Hooker, Morna D. *From Adam to Christ: Essays on Paul.* Cambridge: Cambridge University Press, 1990.

Hoover, Roy W. "The HARPAGMOS Enigma: A Philological Solution." *Harvard Theological Review* 64 (1971): 95–119.

Hsiao, Paul Shih-yi. "Heidegger and Our Translation of the *Tao Te Ching.*" In *Heidegger and Asian Thought,* edited by G. Parkes, 93–101. Honolulu: University of Hawaii Press, 1987.

Hurst, L. D. "Re-Enter the Pre-Existent Christ in Philippians 2.5–11?" *New Testament Studies* 32 (1986): 449–57.

Hurtado, L. W. "Jesus as Lordly Example in Philippians 2.5–11?" In *From Jesus to Paul: Studies in Honour of Francis Wright Beare,* edited by P. Richardson and J. C. Hurd, 113–26. Waterloo, Ont.: Wilfrid Laurier University Press, 1984.

Jacobsen, Thorkild. *The Treasures of Darkness: A History of Mesopotamian Religion.* New Haven, CT: Yale University Press, 1976.

Jacobson, Edith. *The Self and the Object World.* New York: International Universities Press, 1964.

Jaspers, Karl. *The Origin and Goal of History.* Translated by M. Bullock. New Haven, CT: Yale University Press, 1953.

Johnson, Ralph H. *The Concept of Existence in the* Concluding Unscientific Postscript. The Hague: Martinus Nijhoff, 1972.

Johnson, Stephen M. *The Symbiotic Character.* New York: Norton, 1991.

Jones, Ernest. *The Life and Work of Sigmund Freud.* Vol. 2, *Years of Maturity, 1901–1919.* New York: Basic Books, 1955.

―――. *The Life and Work of Sigmund Freud.* Vol. 3, *The Last Phase, 1919–1939.* New York: Basic Books, 1957.

Jowett, Benjamin. *The Dialogues of Plato.* 3d ed. New York: Random House, 1937.

Jung, Carl G. *Letters: 1906–1950.* Translated by R. F. C. Hull. Bollingen Series 95:1. Princeton, NJ: Princeton University Press, 1973.

―――. *Letters: 1951–1961.* Translated by R. F. C. Hull. Bollingen Series 95:2. Princeton, NJ: Princeton University Press, 1975.

―――. *Two Essays on Analytical Psychology.* 2d ed. Translated by R. F. C. Hull. Vol. 7 of *The Collected Works of C. G. Jung.* Bollingen Series 20. Princeton, NJ: Princeton University Press, 1966.

Käsemann, Ernst. "A Critical Analysis of Philippians 2:5–11." Translated by A. F. Carse. In *God and Christ: Existence and Province.* Journal for Theology and the Church 5. New York: Harper & Row, 1968.

―――. "The Problem of the Historical Jesus." In *Essays on New Testament Themes,* translated by W. J. Montague. Naperville, IL: Allenson, 1964.

Kaufmann, Walter. *Discovering the Mind.* Vol. 3, *Freud versus Adler and Jung.* New York: McGraw–Hill, 1980.

Keeley, Louise C. "Subjectivity and World in *Works of Love.*" In *Foundations of Kierkegaard's Vision of Community* edited by G. B. Connell and C. S. Evans, 96–108. Atlantic Highlands, NJ: Humanities, 1992.

Kegan, Robert. *The Evolving Self: Problem and Process in Human Development.* Cambridge, MA: Harvard University Press, 1982.

Kernberg, Otto F. Foreword to *Psychoanalytic Perspectives on Migration and Exile,* by Leon Grinberg and Rebeca Grinberg. New Haven, CT: Yale University Press, 1989.

Kierkegaard, Søren. *Attack upon Christendom.* Translated by W. Lowrie. Princeton, NJ: Princeton University Press, 1968.

―――. *Christian Discourses and The Lilies of the Field and the Birds of the Air.* Translated by W. Lowrie. Princeton, NJ: Princeton University Press, 1971.

―――. *The Concept of Anxiety.* Translated by R. Thomte and A. B. Anderson. Princeton, NJ: Princeton University Press, 1980.

————. *Concluding Unscientific Postscript.* Translated by D. F. Swenson and W. Lowrie. Princeton, NJ: Princeton University Press, 1941.

————. *Edifying Discourses: A Selection.* Translated by D. F Swenson and L. M. Swenson; edited by P. L Holmer. New York: Harper & Row, 1958.

————. *Eighteen Upbuilding Discourses.* Translated by H. V. Hong and E. H. Hong. Princeton, NJ: Princeton University Press, 1990.

————. *Either/Or.* Vol. 1, translated by D. F. Swenson, L. H. Swenson , and H. A. Johnson. Princeton, NJ: Princeton University Press, 1944.

————. *For Self-Examination / Judge for Yourself!* Translated by H. V. Hong and E. H. Hong. Princeton, NJ: Princeton University Press, 1990.

————. *The Gospel of Our Sufferings.* Translated by A. S. Aldworth and W. S. Ferrie. Grand Rapids, MI: Eerdmans, 1964.

————. *Journals and Papers.* Vol. 1, translated by H. V. Hong and E. H. Hong. Bloomington: Indiana University Press, 1967.

————. *Journals and Papers.* Vol. 2, translated by H. V. Hong and E. H. Hong. Bloomington: Indiana University Press, 1970.

————. The Moment *and Late Writings.* Translated by H. V. Hong and E. H. Hong. Princeton, NJ: Princeton University Press, 1998.

————. *Practice in Christianity.* Translated by H. V. Hong and E. H. Hong. Princeton, NJ: Princeton University Press, 1991.

————. *Philosophical Fragments/Johannes Climacus.* Translated by H. V. Hong and E. H. Hong. Princeton, NJ: Princeton University Press, 1985.

————. *The Sickness unto Death.* Translated by H. V. Hong and E. H. Hong. Princeton, NJ: Princeton University Press, 1980.

————. *Stages on Life's Way.* Translated by H. V. Hong and E. H. Hong. Princeton, NJ: Princeton University Press, 1988.

————. *Two Ages: The Age of Revolution and the Present Age, A Literary Review* Translated by H. V. Hong and E. H. Hong. Princeton, NJ: Princeton University Press, 1978.

————. *Upbuilding Discourses in Various Spirits.* Translated by H. V. Hong and E. H. Hong. Princeton, NJ: Princeton University Press, 1993.

————. *Without Authority.* Translated by H. V. Hong and E. H. Hong. Princeton, NJ: Princeton University Press, 1997.

————. *Works of Love.* Translated by H. Hong and E. Hong. New York: Harper & Row, 1962.

King, Magda. *A Guide to Heidegger's* Being and Time. Edited by J. Llewelyn. Albany: State University of New York Press, 2001.

————. *Heidegger's Philosophy: A Guide to His Basic Thought*. New York: Macmillan, 1964.

Kisiel, Theodore. *The Genesis of Heidegger's* Being and Time. Berkeley: University of California Press, 1993.

Kockelmans, Joseph J. *Heidegger's "Being and Time": The Analytic of Dasein as Fundamental Ontology*. Pittsburgh: Center for Advanced Research in Phenomenology, 1989.

————. *On the Truth of Being: Reflections on Heidegger's Later Philosophy*. Bloomington: Indiana University Press, 1984.

Koenigsberg, Richard A. *Symbiosis and Separation: Towards A Psychology of Culture*. New York: Library of Art and Social Science, 1989.

Kolb, David. *The Critique of Pure Modernity: Hegel, Heidegger, and After*. Chicago: University of Chicago Press, 1986.

Krell, David F. *Daimon Life: Heidegger and Life-Philosophy*. Bloomington: Indiana University Press, 1992.

————. *Intimations of Mortality: Time, Truth, and Finitude in Heidegger's Thinking of Being*. University Park: Pennsylvania State University Press, 1986.

Krüll, Marianne. *Freud and His Father*. Translated by A. J. Pomerans. New York: Norton, 1986.

Lacan, Jacques. *The Seminar of Jacques Lacan*. Bk. I, *Freud's Papers on Technique 1953–1954,* translated by J. Forrester. New York: Norton, 1988.

Lakoff, Robin Tolmach, and James C. Coyne. *Father Knows Best: The Use and Abuse of Power in Freud's Case of Dora*. New York: Teachers College Press, 1993.

Langan, Thomas. *The Meaning of Heidegger: A Critical Study of an Existentialist Phenomenology*. New York: Columbia University Press, 1959.

Langfur, Stephen J. "Death's Second Self: A Response to Heidegger's Question of Being through the Insights of Buber and the Findings of Freud." Unpublished dissertation. Ann Arbor, MI: University Microfilms International, 1977.

Laplanche, Jean. *Life and Death in Psychoanalysis*. Baltimore: Johns Hopkins University Press, 1976.

Law, David R. *Kierkegaard as Negative Theologian*. Oxford: Clarendon, 1993.

Lear, Jonathan. *Open Minded: Working Out the Logic of the Soul*. Cambridge, MA: Harvard University Press, 1998.

Levin, David M. *The Body's Recollection of Being: Phenomenological Psychology and the Deconstruction of Nihilism*. Boston: Routledge & Kegan Paul, 1985.

————. *The Listening Self: Personal Growth, Social Change, and the Closure of Metaphysics.* New York: Routledge, 1989.

————. *The Opening of Vision: Nihilism and the Postmodern Situation.* New York: Routledge, 1988.

Levinas, Emmanuel. *Totality and Infinity.* Pittsburgh: Duquesne University Press, 1969.

Lienhardt, Godfrey. *Divinity and Experience: The Religion of the Dinka.* Oxford: Clarendon, 1961.

Lipsey, Roger. *Coomaraswamy.* Vol. 3, *His Life and Work.* Bollingen Series 89. Princeton, NJ: Princeton University Press, 1977.

Loder, James E. *Religious Pathology and Christian Faith.* Philadelphia: Westminster, 1966.

Ludwig, Arnold M. *How Do We Know Who We Are? A Biography of the Self.* Oxford: Oxford University Press, 1977.

MacGregor, Geddes. *He Who Lets Us Be: A New Theology of Love.* New York: Paragon, 1987.

Mackey, Louis. *Kierkegaard: A Kind of Poet.* Philadelphia: University of Pennsylvania Press, 1971.

Macomber, William B. *The Anatomy of Disillusion: Martin Heidegger's Notion of Truth.* Evanston, IL: Northwestern University Press, 1967.

Macquarrie, John. *Jesus Christ in Modern Thought.* Philadelphia: Trinity, 1990.

Mageo, Jeannette M. "'Ferocious Is the Centipede': A Study of the Significance of Eating and Speaking in Samoa." *Ethos* 17 (1989): 387–427.

Magurshak, Dan. "The Concept of Anxiety: The Keystone of the Kierkegaard-Heidegger Relationship." In *International Kierkegaard Commentary,* vol. 8, *The Concept of Anxiety,* edited by R. L. Perkins, 167–95. Macon, GA: Mercer University Press, 1985.

————. "Despair and Everydayness: Kierkegaard's Corrective Contribution to Heidegger's Notion of Falling Everydayness." In *International Kierkegaard Commentary,* vol. 19, *The Sickness unto Death,* edited by R. L. Perkins, 209–37. Macon, GA: Mercer University Press, 1987.

Mahler, Margaret, Fred Pine, and Anni Bergman. *The Psychological Birth of the Human Infant: Symbiosis and Individuation.* New York: Basic Books, 1975.

Malantschuk, Gregor. *Kierkegaard's Concept of Existence.* Translated by H. V. Hong and E. H. Hong. Milwaukee, WI: Marquette University Press, 2003.

————. *Kierkegaard's Thought.* Translated by H. V. Hong and E. H. Hong. Princeton, NJ: Princeton University Press, 1971.

Martin, Ralph. *Carmen Christi: Philippians ii. 5–11 in Recent Interpretation and in the Setting of Early Christian Worship.* Cambridge: Cambridge University Press, 1967.

——. *Carmen Christi.* Reprint with new preface. Grand Rapids, MI: Eerdmans, 1983.

Marx, Werner. *Heidegger and the Tradition.* Translated by T. J. Kisiel and M. Greene. Evanston, IL: Northwestern University Press, 1971.

Masson, Jeffrey M. *The Assault on Truth: Freud's Suppression of the Seduction Theory.* New York: Farrar, Straus and Giroux, 1984.

Mehta, J. L. *Martin Heidegger: The Way and the Vision.* Honolulu: University Press of Hawaii, 1976.

Meissner, William W. *Freud and Psychoanalysis.* Notre Dame, IN: University of Notre Dame Press, 2000.

Merton, Thomas. *The Asian Journal of Thomas Merton.* Edited by N. Burton, P. Hart, and J. Laughlin. New York: New Directions, 1973.

Moltman, Jurgen. *God in Creation: A New Theology of Creation and the Spirit of God, The 1984–1985 Gifford Lectures.* San Francisco: Harper & Row, 1985.

——. *The Trinity and the Kingdom.* New York: Harper & Row, 1981.

Moseley, Romney M. *Becoming a Self before God: Critical Transformations.* Nashville: Abingdon, 1991.

Mugerauer, Robert. *Heidegger's Language and Thinking.* Atlantic Highlands, NJ: Humanities Press International, 1988.

Mumford, Lewis. *The Transformations of Man.* Gloucester, MA: Peter Smith, 1978.

Murti, T. R. V. *The Central Philosophy of Buddhism.* 2d ed. London: George Allen and Unwin, 1960.

Nagera, Humberto, et al. *Basic Psychoanalytic Concepts of the Theory of Instincts.* Hampstead Clinic Psychoanalytic Library 3. London: Maresfield Reprints, 1970.

Napier, Augustus Y., and Carl A. Whitaker. *The Family Crucible.* New York: Harper & Row, 1978.

Nicholson, Graeme. *Illustrations of Being: Drawing upon Heidegger and upon Metaphysics.* Atlantic Highlands, NJ: Humanities, 1992.

Nishida, Kitaro. *Last Writings: Nothingness and the Religious Worldview.* Translated by D. A. Dilworth. Honolulu: University of Hawaii Press, 1987.

Nishitani, Keiji. "Ontology and Utterance." *Philosophy East and West* 31 (1981): 29–43.

―――. *Religion and Nothingness.* Translated by J. Van Bragt. Berkeley: University of California Press, 1982.

Nordentoft, Kresten. *Kierkegaard's Psychology.* Translated by B. Kirmmse. Pittsburgh: Duquesne University Press, 1978.

Nussbaum, Martha C. *The Fragility of Goodness: Luck and Ethics in Greek Tragedy and Philosophy.* Cambridge: Cambridge University Press, 1986.

O'Brien, Peter G. *The Epistle to the Philippians: A Commentary on the Greek Text.* Grand Rapides, MI: Eerdmans, 1991.

Oden, Thomas C. *The Word of Life.* Vol. 2 of *Systematic Theology.* San Francisco: Harper & Row, 1989.

Olafson, Frederick. *Heidegger and the Philosophy of Mind.* New Haven, CT: Yale University Press, 1987.

Oliver, Harold H. "The Relational Self." In *Selves, People, and Persons: What Does It Mean to Be a Self?* edited by L. S. Rouner, 37–51. Notre Dame, IN: University of Notre Dame Press, 1992.

Ott, Hugo. *Martin Heidegger: A Political Life.* Translated by A. Blunden. London: Harper Collins, 1993.

Pannenberg, Wolfhart. *Jesus, God and Man.* 2d ed. Philadelphia: Westminster, 1977.

Paul, Robert A. "Did the Primal Crime Take Place?" *Ethos* 4 (1976): 311–52.

―――. 1980. "Symbolic Interpretation in Psychoanalysis and Anthropology." *Ethos* 8 (1980): 286–94.

―――. *The Tibetan Symbolic World: Psychoanalytic Explorations.* Chicago: University of Chicago Press, 1982.

Pelkon, Michael. "Kierkegaard the Theologian: The Roots of His Theology in *Works of Love.*" In *Foundations of Kierkegaard's Vision of Community,* edited by G. B. Connell and C. S. Evans, 2–17. Atlantic Highlands, NJ: Humanities, 1992.

Perkins, Robert L. "Kierkegaard's Teleological Humanism." In *The Question of Humanism: Challenges and Possibilities,* edited by D. Goicoechea, J. Luik, and T. Madigan, 138–49. Buffalo, NY: Prometheus, 1991.

Perkins, Robert L., ed. *International Kierkegaard Commentary.* Vol. 14, *Two Ages.* Macon, GA: Mercer University Press, 1984.

Perse, St–John. *Collected Poems.* Translated by W. H. Auden et al. Bollingen Series 87. Princeton, NJ: Princeton University Press, 1971.

Philipse, Herman. *Heidegger's Philosophy of Being: A Critical Interpretation.* Princeton, NJ: Princeton University Press, 1998.

Plato. *Symposium*. Translated by A. Nehamas and P. Woodruff. Indianapolis: Hackett, 1989.

Pöggeler, Otto. "Being as Appropriation." In *Heidegger and Modern Philosophy,* edited by M. Murray, 84–115. New Haven, CT: Yale University Press, 1978.

———. *Martin Heidegger's Path of Thinking*. Translated by D. Magurshak and S. Barber. Atlantic Highlands, NJ: Humanities Press International, 1987.

Polt, Richard. *Heidegger: An Introduction*. Ithaca, NY: Cornell University Press, 1999.

Pomedli, Michael M. "Heidegger and Freud: The Power of Death." Unpublished dissertation. Ann Arbor, MI: University Microfilms International, 1972.

Pritchard, James B. *Ancient Near Eastern Texts Relating to the Old Testament*. 3d ed. Princeton, NJ: Princeton University Press, 1969.

Rae, Murray A. *Kierkegaard's Vision of the Incarnation: By Faith Transformed*. Oxford: Clarendon, 1997.

Rapaport, David, and Merton Gill. "The Points of View and Assumptions of Metapsychology." In *The Collected Papers of David Rapaport,* edited by M. Gill. New York: Basic Books, 1977.

Richard, Lucien. *A Kenotic Christology: In the Humanity of Jesus the Christ, the Compassion of Our God*. Washington, DC: University Press of America, 1982.

Richardson, John. *Existential Epistemology: A Heideggerian Critique of the Cartesian Project*. Oxford: Clarendon, 1986.

Richardson, William J. *Heidegger: Through Phenomenology to Thought*. The Hague: Martinus Nijhoff, 1963.

———. "The Place of the Unconscious in Heidegger." In *Heidegger and Psychology,* edited by K. Hoeller, 176–98. Atlantic Highlands, NJ: Humanities, 1992.

Ricoeur, Paul. *Freud and Philosophy*. Translated by D. Savage. New Haven, CT: Yale University Press, 1970.

Rieff, Philip. *Freud: The Mind of the Moralist*. 3d ed. Chicago: University of Chicago Press, 1979.

Rilke, Rainer M. *Letters of Rainer Maria Rilke, 1910–1926*. Translated by J. B. Greene and M. D. H. Norton. New York: Norton, 1969.

Rorty, Richard. *Contingency, Irony, and Solidarity*. Cambridge: Cambridge University Press, 1989.

———. "Taking Philosophy Seriously: Heidegger et le Nazisme by Victor Farias." *The New Republic* (April 11, 1988): 31–34.

Rosen, Stanley. *Plato's Symposium*. 2d ed. New Haven, CT: Yale University Press, 1987.

———. *The Question of Being: A Reversal of Heidegger*. New Haven, CT: Yale University Press, 1993.

Roth, Sheldon, M.D. *Psychotherapy: The Art of Wooing Nature*. New York: Aronson, 1987.

Rudd, Anthony. *Kierkegaard and the Limits of the Ethical*. Oxford: Clarendon, 1993.

Safranski, Rüdiger. *Martin Heidegger: Between Good and Evil*. Translated by E. Osers. Cambridge, MA: Harvard University Press, 1998.

Sanders, Jack T. *The New Testament Christological Hymns: Their Historical Religious Background*. Cambridge: Cambridge University Press, 1971.

Santas, Gerasimos X. *Plato and Freud: Two Theories of Love*. New York: Basil Blackwell, 1988.

Sartre, Jean-Paul. *Being and Nothingness*. Translated by Hazel E. Barnes. New York: Philosophical Library, 1956.

Schafer, Roy. *Language and Insight: The Sigmund Freud Memorial Lectures 1975–1976*. New Haven, CT: Yale University Press, 1978.

Schalow, Frank. *The Renewal of the Heidegger-Kant Dialogue: Action, Thought, and Responsibility*. Albany: State University of New York Press, 1992.

Schillebeeckx, Edward. *Jesus: An Experiment in Christology*. Translated by H. Hoskins. New York: Crossroads, 1979.

Schmidt, Dennis J. *The Ubiquity of the Finite: Hegel, Heidegger, and the Entitlements of Philosophy*. Cambridge, MA: MIT Press, 1988.

Scholem, Gershom. *Kabbalah*. New York: Quadrangle, 1974.

———. *Major Trends in Jewish Mysticism*. 3d rev. ed. New York: Schocken, 1954.

Schrag, Calvin. *Existence and Freedom: Towards an Ontology of Human Finitude*. Evanston, IL: Northwestern University Press, 1961.

Schur, Max. *Freud: Living and Dying*. New York: International Universities Press, 1972.

Schürmann, Reiner. *Heidegger on Being and Acting: From Principles to Anarchy*. Translated by C- M. Gros. Bloomington: Indiana University Press, 1987.

———. *Meister Eckhart, Mystic and Philosopher*. Bloomington: Indiana University Press, 1978.

Scott, Charles E. *The Language of Difference*. Atlantic Highlands, NJ: Humanities, 1987.

————. *The Question of Ethics: Nietzsche, Foucault, Heidegger*. Bloomington: Indiana University Press, 1990.

Searles, Harold F. *Countertransference and Related Subjects: Selected Papers*. New York: International Universities Press, 1979.

————. *The Nonhuman Environment in Normal Development and in Schizophrenia*. New York: International Universities Press, 1960.

Sherover, Charles M. *Heidegger, Kant, and Time*. Bloomington: Indiana University Press, 1971.

Shmuëli, Adi. *Kierkegaard and Consciousness*. Translated by H. Handelman. Princeton, NJ: Princeton University Press, 1971.

Shore, Bradd. *Culture in Mind: Cognition, Culture, and the Problem of Meaning*. New York: Oxford University Press, 1996.

Smith, Joseph H., ed. *Kierkegaard's Truth: The Disclosure of the Self*. Psychiatry and the Humanities 5. New Haven, CT: Yale University Press, 1981.

Spanos, William V. *Heidegger and Criticism: Retrieving the Cultural Politics of Destruction*. Minneapolis: University of Minnesota Press, 1993.

Spence, Donald P. *The Freudian Metaphor: Toward Paradigm Change in Psychoanalysis*. New York: Norton, 1987.

————. *Narrative Truth and Historical Truth*. New York: Norton, 1982.

Sponheim, Paul. *Kierkegaard on Christ and Christian Coherence*. New York: Harper & Row, 1968.

Stack, George J. *Kierkegaard's Existential Ethics*. University: University of Alabama Press, 1977.

Stambaugh, Joan. *The Finitude of Being*. Albany: State University of New York Press, 1992.

Stepansky, Paul E. *A History of Aggression in Freud*. Psychological Issues Monograph no. 39. New York: International Universities Press, 1977.

Stern, Daniel. *The Interpersonal World of the Infant: A View from Psychoanalysis and Developmental Psychology*. New York: Basic Books, 1985.

Sulloway, Frank J. *Freud, Biologist of the Mind*. New York: Basic Books, 1979.

Sykes, S. W. "The Strange Persistence of Kenotic Christology." In *Being and Truth: Essays in Honour of John Macquarrie*, edited by A. Kee and E. T. Long, 349–75. London: SCM Press, 1986.

Taminiaux, Jacques. *Dialectic and Difference: Finitude in Modern Thought*. Translated by J. Decker and R. Crease. Atlantic Highlands, NJ: Humanities Press, 1985.

————. *Heidegger and the Project of Fundamental Ontology.* Translated by M. Gendre. Albany: State University of New York Press, 1991.

Taylor, Mark C. *Kierkegaard's Pseudonymous Authorship: A Study of Time and the Self.* Princeton, NJ: Princeton University Press, 1975.

Taylor, Vincent. *The Person of Christ.* London: Macmillan, 1958.

Theunissen, Michael. *The Other: Studies in the Social Ontology of Husserl, Heidegger, Sartre and Buber.* Translated by C. Macann. Cambridge, MA: MIT Press, 1984.

Thiele, Leslie P. *Timely Meditations: Martin Heidegger and Postmodern Politics.* Princeton, NJ: Princeton University Press, 1995.

Thulstrup, Marie M. "Kierkegaard's Dialectic of Imitation." Translated by H. R. Harcourt, in *A Kierkegaard Critique,* edited by H.A. Johnson and N. Thulstrup, 266–85. New York: Harper, 1962.

Thulstrup, Niels. *Kierkegaard's Relation to Hegel.* Translated by G. L. Stengren. Princeton, NJ: Princeton University Press, 1980.

Tugendhat, Ernst. *Self-Consciousness and Self-Determination.* Translated by P. Stern. Cambridge, MA: MIT Press, 1986.

Turner, Victor. *Dramas, Fields, and Metaphors: Symbolic Action in Human Society.* Ithaca, NY: Cornell University Press, 1974.

————. *The Forest of Symbols: Aspects of Ndembu Ritual.* Ithaca, NY: Cornell University Press, 1967.

————. *From Ritual to Theatre: The Human Seriousness of Play.* New York: PAJ Publications, 1982.

————. *The Ritual Process: Structure and Anti-Structure.* Ithaca, NY: Cornell University Press, 1969.

Ueda, Shizuteru. "Emptiness and Fullness: Sunyata in Mahayana Buddhism." Translated by J. W. Hesig and F. Greiner. *The Eastern Buddhist* 15 (1982): 9–27.

Vail, Loy M. *Heidegger and Ontological Difference.* University Park: Pennsylvania State University Press, 1972.

Veith, Ilza. *Hysteria: The History of a Disease.* Chicago: University of Chicago Press, 1965.

Voegelin, Eric. *Order and History.* Vol. 1, *Israel and Revelation.* Baton Rouge: Louisiana State University Press, 1956.

Walker, Jeremy D. B. *Kierkegaard: The Descent into God.* Montreal: McGill-Queen's University Press, 1985.

Wallace, Edwin R. *Freud and Anthropology: A History and Reappraisal.* Psychological Issues Monograph no. 55. New York: International Universities Press, 1984.

Walsh, Sylvia I. "Forming the Heart: The Role of Love in Kierkegaard's Thought." In *The Grammar of the Heart,* edited by R. H. Bell, 234–56. San Francisco: Harper & Row, 1988.

Wanamaker, C. A. "Philippians 2.6–11: Son of God or Adamic Christology?" *New Testament Studies* 33 (1987): 179–93.

Webb, Eugene. *Philosophers of Consciousness.* Seattle: University of Washington Press, 1988.

———. *The Self Between: From Freud to the New Social Psychology of France.* Seattle: University of Washington Press, 1993.

Welch, Claude. *Protestant Thought in the Nineteenth Century.* Vol. 1, *1799–1870.* New Haven, CT: Yale University Press, 1972.

Weston, Michael. *Kierkegaard and Modern Continental Philosophy.* New York: Routledge, 1994.

Westphal, Merold. *Becoming a Self: A Reading of Kierkegaard's* Concluding Unscientific Postscript. West Lafayette, IN: Purdue University Press, 1996.

———. *Kierkegaard's Critique of Reason and Society.* Macon, GA: Mercer University Press, 1987.

Winnicott, D. W. *The Maturational Processes and the Facilitating Environment.* New York: International Universities Press, 1965.

———. *Playing and Reality.* London: Tavistock, 1971.

Wolin, Richard. *Heidegger's Children: Hannah Arendt, Karl Löwith, Hans Jonas, and Herbert Marcuse.* Princeton, NJ: Princeton University Press, 2001.

Wolin, Richard, ed. *The Heidegger Controversy: A Critical Reader.* New York: Columbia University Press, 1991.

Wolkstein, Diane, and Samuel N. Kramer. *Inanna: Queen of Heaven and Earth.* New York: Harper & Row, 1983.

Wollheim, Richard. *Sigmund Freud.* New York: Cambridge University Press, 1971.

Wolz, Henry G. *Plato and Heidegger: In Search of Selfhood.* Lewisburg, PA: Bucknell University Press, 1981.

Wong, T. Yai-Chow. "The Problem of Pre-Existence in Philippians 2, 6–11." *Ephemerides Theologicae Lovanienses* 62 (1986): 267–82.

Wright, N. T. 1986. "harpagmos and the Meaning of Philippians 2:5–11." *Journal of Theological Studies,* n.s.37 (1986): 321–52.

Wyschogrod, Edith. *Spirit in Ashes: Hegel, Heidegger, and Man-Made Mass Death.* New Haven, CT: Yale University Press, 1985.

Wyschogrod, Michael. *The Body of Faith: Judaism as Corporeal Election.* New York: Seabury, 1983.

———. *Kierkegaard and Heidegger: The Ontology of Existence.* New York: International Universities Press, 1954.

Yalom, Irvin D. *Existential Psychotherapy.* New York: Basic Books, 1980.

Zimmerman, Michael E. *Eclipse of the Self: The Development of Heidegger's Concept of Authenticity.* Athens: Ohio University Press, 1981.

Index